Praise for *Coping with Toxic Managers, Subordinates ...and Other Difficult People:*

"In any organization, recognizing and understanding the nature and impact of toxic behaviors can provide for the ability to manage the adverse environment and mitigate the potential risks that we often face in the workplace. In *Coping with Toxic Managers,* Roy Lubit skillfully tackles this senting the psychological aspects of toxic behaviors standable and embraceable. This is not one of th pop-psychology books—it's truly about the science o think, act, and react. Read this book and you may start l organization quite differently."

—MICHAEL CHUCHMUCH,
V.P. Business Transformation and Change Management, UNISYS Corporation

"I found this book to be right on the mark and learned a lot from it. Lubit understands the problems people in business face from difficult people above and below them and comes up with very insightful and practical ways to deal effectively with the situations. If all of my managers read this book they would do their jobs better."

—JEFF SCHINDLER,
President and CEO, Etronics

"Executives, and the senior HR officers who counsel them, struggle every day with how to deal with toxic leaders, the ones who try to achieve high performance by abusing, intimidating, mistreating, and demeaning their subordinates. Finally someone has written a book on how to handle the various types of corporate ax murderers, how to help them develop, and when to let them go."

—MICHAEL FEINER,
Professor, Columbia Business School;
formerly Sr. VP and Chief People Officer for Pepsi-Cola worldwide

"Roy Lubit's new book is an exciting breakthrough for anyone who has ever had a boss! It's hard to remember that bosses are only people. This book helps you understand what makes them tick, how to understand their different styles, how you can manage them effectively from below, and how to get everyone working on the same team. Lubit's secret ingredient is his incisive knowledge of how people and organizations work. A must read!"

—JEFFREY P. KAHN, M.D.,
President, WorkPsych Associates, Inc.;
Clinical Associate Professor of Psychiatry, Cornell University;
and former President, Academy of Occupational and Organizational Psychiatry

manage effectively, we need to understand the people with whom we ... *oping with Toxic Managers, Subordinates...and Other Difficult People* is ...n excellent and thorough book containing crucial insights into why managers behave as they do, and how to cope with different types of people. It will not only help you to understand and better deal with toxic managers, but it will also help you work with yourself and with the normal vulnerabilities of managers with whom you work everyday."

—RONALD A. HEIFETZ,
Co-Founder, Center for Public Leadership,
John F. Kennedy School of Government, Harvard University

COPING WITH TOXIC MANAGERS, SUBORDINATES

...AND OTHER DIFFICULT PEOPLE

FT Prentice Hall
FINANCIAL TIMES

In an increasingly competitive world, it is quality
of thinking that gives an edge—an idea that opens new
doors, a technique that solves a problem, or an insight
that simply helps make sense of it all.

We work with leading authors in the various arenas
of business and finance to bring cutting-edge thinking
and best learning practice to a global market.

It is our goal to create world-class print publications
and electronic products that give readers
knowledge and understanding which can then be
applied, whether studying or at work.

To find out more about our business
products, you can visit us at www.ft-ph.com

Pearson
Education

COPING WITH TOXIC MANAGERS, SUBORDINATES

...AND OTHER DIFFICULT PEOPLE

ROY H. LUBIT

An Imprint of PEARSON EDUCATION
Upper Saddle River, NJ • New York • London • San Francisco • Toronto • Sydney
Tokyo • Singapore • Hong Kong • Cape Town • Madrid
Paris • Milan • Munich • Amsterdam

www.ft-ph.com

Library of Congress Catalogine-in-Publication Data

Lubit, Roy.
    Coping with toxic managers, subordinates...and other difficult people./Roy Lubit
       p. cm.—(Financial Times Prentice Hall books)
    Includes bibliographical references and index.
    ISBN 0-13-140995-6
    1. Managing your boss. 2. Emotional intelligence. 3. Executives—Psychology.
    I. Title. II. Series

HF5548.83.L83 2004
650.1'3—dc21   2003062416

Editorial/production supervision: *Kerry Reardon*
Cover design director: *Jerry Votta*
Cover design: *Mary Jo DeFranco*
Art director: *Gail Cocker-Bogusz*
Manufacturing manager: *Alexis Heydt-Long*
Manufacturing buyer: *Maura Zaldivar*
Executive editor: *Jim Boyd*
Editorial assistant: *Richard Winkler*
Marketing director: *John Pierce*
Marketing manager: *Laura Bulcher*
Development editor: *Russ Hall*
Full-service production manager: *Anne R. Garcia*

© 2004 Pearson Education, Inc.
Publishing as Financial Times Prentice Hall
Upper Saddle River, NJ 07458

Financial Times Prentice Hall offers excellent discounts on this book when ordered in
quantity for bulk purchases or special sales. For more information, please contact: U.S.
Corporate and Government Sales, 1-800-382-3419, corpsales@pearsontechgroup.com. For
sales outside of the U.S., please contact: International Sales, 1-317-581-3793,
international@pearsontechgroup.com

Printed in the United States of America

First printing

ISBN 0-13-140995-6

Pearson Education LTD.
Pearson Education Australia PTY, Limited
Pearson Education Singapore, Pte. Ltd.
Pearson Education North Asia Ltd.
Pearson Education Canada, Ltd.
Pearson Educación de Mexico, S.A. de C.V.
Pearson Education–Japan
Pearson Education Malaysia, Pte. Ltd.

FINANCIAL TIMES PRENTICE HALL BOOKS

For more information, please go to www.ft-ph.com

Business and Technology

Sarv Devaraj and Rajiv Kohli
> *The IT Payoff: Measuring the Business Value of Information Technology Investments*

Nicholas D. Evans
> *Business Innovation and Disruptive Technology: Harnessing the Power of Breakthrough Technology…for Competitive Advantage*

Nicholas D. Evans
> *Consumer Gadgets: 50 Ways to Have Fun and Simplify Your Life with Today's Technology…and Tomorrow's*

Faisal Hoque
> *The Alignment Effect: How to Get Real Business Value Out of Technology*

Economics

David Dranove
> *What's Your Life Worth? Health Care Rationing…Who Lives? Who Dies? Who Decides?*

John C. Edmunds
> *Brave New Wealthy World: Winning the Struggle for World Prosperity*

Jonathan Wight
> *Saving Adam Smith: A Tale of Wealth, Transformation, and Virtue*

Entrepreneurship

Oren Fuerst and Uri Geiger
> *From Concept to Wall Street: A Complete Guide to Entrepreneurship and Venture Capital*

David Gladstone and Laura Gladstone
> *Venture Capital Handbook: An Entrepreneur's Guide to Raising Venture Capital, Revised and Updated*

Thomas K. McKnight
> *Will It Fly? How to Know if Your New Business Idea Has Wings… Before You Take the Leap*

Erica Orloff and Kathy Levinson, Ph.D.
> *The 60-Second Commute: A Guide to Your 24/7 Home Office Life*

Jeff Saperstein and Daniel Rouach
> *Creating Regional Wealth in the Innovation Economy: Models, Perspectives, and Best Practices*

Stephen Spinelli, Jr., Robert M. Rosenberg, and Sue Birley
> *Franchising: Pathway to Wealth Creation*

Marshall Goldsmith, Cathy Greenberg, Alastair Robertson, and Maya Hu-Chan
Global Leadership: The Next Generation

Management

Rob Austin and Lee Devin
Artful Making: What Managers Need to Know About How Artists Work

J. Stewart Black and Hal B. Gregersen
Leading Strategic Change: Breaking Through the Brain Barrier

William C. Byham, Audrey B. Smith, and Matthew J. Paese
Grow Your Own Leaders: How to Identify, Develop, and Retain Leadership Talent

David M. Carter and Darren Rovell
On the Ball: What You Can Learn About Business from Sports Leaders

Subir Chowdhury
Organization 21C: Someday All Organizations Will Lead this Way

Ross Dawson
Living Networks: Leading Your Company, Customers, and Partners in the Hyper-connected Economy

Charles J. Fombrun and Cees B.M. Van Riel
Fame and Fortune: How Successful Companies Build Winning Reputations

Amir Hartman
Ruthless Execution: What Business Leaders Do When Their Companies Hit the Wall

Harvey A. Hornstein
The Haves and the Have Nots: The Abuse of Power and Privilege in the Workplace… and How to Control It

Kevin Kennedy and Mary Moore
Going the Distance: Why Some Companies Dominate and Others Fail

Roy H. Lubit
Coping with Toxic Managers, Subordinates…and Other Difficult People

Robin Miller
The Online Rules of Successful Companies: The Fool-Proof Guide to Building Profits

Fergus O'Connell
The Competitive Advantage of Common Sense: Using the Power You Already Have

W. Alan Randolph and Barry Z. Posner
Checkered Flag Projects: 10 Rules for Creating and Managing Projects that Win, Second Edition

Stephen P. Robbins
Decide & Conquer: Make Winning Decisions to Take Control of Your Life

Stephen P. Robbins
The Truth About Managing People…And Nothing but the Truth

I dedicate this book to my children

Rina, Talya, and Lia,

and to my wife

Elana

Their support, patience, and love made this book possible. I hope that my children's generation will inherit a gentler and more productive world.

I learned early in my career that it was easier and better to prevent people from being hurt than to wait until the damage was done and then try to heal their injuries. Dealing with the problem of toxic managers will decrease the emotional distress most people periodically suffer at work, decrease the resulting waste of energy, and increase productivity and well-being.

Contents

V   IMPAIRED MANAGERS

Introduction

This book is written for

- ◆ People who must deal with narcissistic, unethical, aggressive, rigid, depressed, or anxious individuals and want to know how to more effectively manage the situation.
- ◆ Senior managers and human resource professionals who are concerned about toxic managerial behavior in their organization.
- ◆ Those who want to enhance their interpersonal skills and advance their career.

Toxic managers dot the landscape in most organizations making them feel, at times, like war zones. These managers can complicate your work, drain your energy, compromise your sanity and destroy your career. You may not yet have been subjected to aggressive, manipulative, unethical, rigid, or narcissistic behavior by bosses or subordinates. If so, count yourself lucky. In time, however, you will almost certainly experience such behavior.

Your ability to deal with difficult managers will have a significant impact on your career. The knowledge you gain from reading this book will help you to deal with them and to avoid letting them derail your projects and your career. This book will help you learn how to recognize toxic managers sooner so that you will be better able to protect yourself. You will develop your understanding of what makes them tick so that you can more effectively design a course of action to deal with their destructive behavior. Some managers are toxic because they are clueless about their effect on others; some are toxic because they do not care if they hurt others; some are toxic because they enjoy hurting others; and some are toxic because they are simply overwhelmed with stress. You will learn how to avoid becoming a scapegoat, how to survive aggressive managers' assaults, and how to give narcissistic and rigid managers the things they need to be satisfied with you. This book can also help you to recognize toxic behavior in yourself, to realize its impact on others, and to contain it.

First and foremost, this book is designed to increase the emotional intelligence of the reader. By helping the reader to understand different types of difficult personalities and suggesting ways to more effectively deal with them, it will improve the reader's social competence. For those who are brave enough to recognize difficult behavior in themselves, it will increase their personal competence as well.

The last chapter provides a toolkit for developing your emotional intelligence, shielding yourself from some of the pain toxic managers generally cause, and for senior management and human resources to better protect their organization from the destructive impact of toxic managers.

This book is designed to be easy to understand. No prior knowledge of psychology is needed. It provides concrete, easy-to-follow solutions to ameliorate the impact of toxic behavior. It also provides a sophisticated understanding of why people behave in destructive ways. Understanding the motivations for toxic behavior is not a sidelight. The basic premise of the book is that understanding the different types of toxic managers and the different motivations that can drive a certain type of toxic behavior is crucial to selecting an effective way to cope.

The stories in this book are, unfortunately, true. The names and identifying details have been changed to protect the guilty as well as the innocent. These are events I witnessed or was told about by those who experienced them. I did not use examples from my work as a therapist and executive coach.

For Senior Managers, HR, and Professionals

This book will be of interest to senior management and human resources as well as to those with a difficult superior. It is built on an understanding of organizational dynamics and the business environment. It discusses how rigid, unethical, and aggressive behaviors affect productivity and retention and explores what HR and senior management can do to contain this behavior in their organization. In addition, by helping the reader to understand different personality types it enables managers to more effectively motivate, persuade, and develop all of the individuals they work with. The more you can tailor your management style to each individual, the more success both you and those who report to you will have.

Many researchers on organizational productivity and success have argued that the key to success lies not in having the perfect strategy, nor in being in the right industry, nor in having an ideal change management plan, nor in charismatic leadership. Rather, the key to success is growing your human resources. Jim Collins writes in *Good to Great*: "We expected to find that good-to-great leaders would begin by setting a new vision and strategy. We found instead that they *first* got the right people on the bus, the wrong people off the bus, and then the right people in the right seats—and then they figured out where to drive it." Charles O'Reilly and Jeffrey Pfeffer in *Hidden Value* discuss how companies have gotten extraordinary results out of ordinary people and how this is the key to success in today's economy.

These researchers focus attention on the crucial role of leadership concentrating on the organization's values and culture. These are very important. But, there is another crucial part of the equation that is less talked about: dealing with the toxic managers who damage the productivity of those under them and above them. Toxic managers interfere with the development of social capital and with the ability and desire of people to trust each other and to be willing to go out of their way for each other. Social capital is very important in improving productivity. In addition to motivating and guiding workers through a strong culture, companies need to remove the obstacles to their performance by decreasing the toxic behavior they face and improving their skills to deal with difficult bosses. Intensive efforts in this area are as yet an unexplored but potentially fruitful area for organizational improvement. It holds tremendous potential for unlocking blocked productivity and for improving the company's ability to hire and retain the best people. Working on the company's culture is an important lever in improving how people treat each other. It is not, however, the only lever. The book discusses many different levers to building organizations in which people can grow and give their best.

Outline of this Book

This book is divided into five parts:

- ◆ Part I—Narcissistic Managers
- ◆ Part II—Unethical Managers
- ◆ Part III—Aggressive Managers
- ◆ Part IV—Rigid Managers
- ◆ Part V—Impaired Managers
- ◆ Part VI—Developing and Harnessing Emotional Intelligence

Each part begins with an introduction to the general issues covered in the section: narcissism, unethical behavior, aggression, rigidity, and impairment. The introductions also begin the explanation of the differences between the types of managers discussed in that part so that you can quickly go to the type of manager you are having difficulty with and read that chapter in detail. Differentiating between different types of toxic managers is crucial, since interventions that work with one type of rigid or aggressive manager would backfire with another even though their behavior is similar on the surface.

Chapters on the different types of toxic managers begin with a discussion of how those managers behave and what drives their behavior. Detailed examples of such managers follow. The chapters then move on to discuss ways to cope with toxic managers above you and below you. The end of each chapter, and several of the special chapters, discuss how senior management and human resources can recognize potentially toxic managers early in their career, help toxic managers to contain their problematic behavior, place them so that they will not adversely affect the organization, and determine when to get rid of them.

- ◆ Chapter 1—Emotional Intelligence Approach to Coping with Toxic Managers and Subordinates: What Do I Do with These People?

Further Reading

Jim Collins. *Good to Great: Why Some Companies Make the Leap...and Others Don't.* HarperCollins, 2001.

Charles A. O'Reilly & Jeffrey Pfeffer. *Hidden Value: How Great Companies Achieve Extraordinary Results with Ordinary People.* Harvard Business School Publishing, 2000.

Jeffrey Kahn & Alan Langlieb (Eds.). *Mental Health and Productivity in the Workplace.* Jossey-Bass, 2003.

About the Author

The author has strong backgrounds in management consulting, psychiatry, and academia. Trained in psychiatry at Yale, Dr. Lubit earned a Ph.D. at Harvard writing a dissertation on organizational learning. After doing research at Columbia Business School, he joined a large consulting firm. This provided firsthand experience working with toxic managers. He is a member of the Consortium for Research on Emotional Intelligence in Organizations, a senior advisor to the Center on Social and Emotional Education (CSEE.net) and has taught on emotional intelligence and organizational behavior at the Zicklin School of Business of the City University of New York. Now an executive coach, business consultant, and psychiatrist on the faculty of Mt. Sinai School of Medicine in New York City, Dr. Lubit writes about what he has learned.

You may correspond by email: *roy.lubit@post.harvard.edu*. For information on the author's consulting firm, Roy Lubit and Associates, visit *www.roylubit.com*.

Acknowledgments

I wish to thank the many friends and colleagues who read multiple versions of this work and made numerous valuable suggestions. Don Haack, a management consultant, is first among equals. His numerous excellent ideas and endless generosity in helping have made this book much stronger than it would have been without his input. Michael Bendit, management consultant and developer of new ventures, gave fundamental assistance in structuring the book. Jim Cawood, an expert in threat assessment, has deepened my knowledge of dealing with dangerous managers and provided crucial advice to the chapters on homicidal managers and paranoid managers. Diana Adams, a law student at Cornell spending the summer working in a law firm with particular expertise on workplace harassment, helped me to better address the key issues that people face concerning sexual harassment and chauvinism. Isabel Rathbone, M.D., provided guidance on the treatment of alcoholism. Jim Boyd, publisher at Prentice Hall, suggested I write this book after reading an article I wrote on Narcissistic Managers in *Academy of Management Executive*. I also need to thank all of the difficult and sometimes toxic managers I've worked with who were so generous in providing examples of what not to do. Finally, let me thank Lynn Gonsor Anvari—the finest manager I have ever known. She showed me that even within large corporations managers can use a coaching style, tact, and respect with subordinates, and that doing so is far more effective than what usually occurs.

CHAPTER 1

Emotional Intelligence Approach to Coping with Toxic Managers and Subordinates

What Do I Do with These People?

Informed Consent for Those Who Read This Book

Politics and personalities present tremendous obstacles to your ability to do the work for which you were hired. To succeed in your job, you need to know how to navigate through these obstacles without crashing on the rocks or having someone drop a rock on your head. You need to be able to deal with different types of bosses and subordinates, some of whom are flexible and easy to work with, many of whom are abrasive or arbitrary.

As you progress up the ladder, you will encounter people with a wide range of personalities. Some are fair, considerate, and flexible, with styles that fit in nicely with your own personality and work style. Others are fair, considerate, and flexible, but have styles that do not fit in well with yours. Yet others are unfair, inconsiderate, and rigid—and you curse the day the company hired them. Some of these managers think that they are heaven's gift to your company, even though working with them makes you wonder why the heavens have decided to punish you so severely. Some behave as if they are in a war zone and you are the enemy.

Remarkable things occur in organizations. Otherwise nice people often behave in remarkably offensive ways under the pressure of organizational life. Moreover, there are many people in organizations who are not nice, and organizational stresses and politics bring out sides of them that are truly awful.

Toxic managers are a reality in organizational life. Your ability to deal with such managers will have a significant impact on your career. The difference between stars and average managers is often the ability to deal with the hardest situations, including the most difficult people. Some of these will be your bosses, some will be your subordinates, and some will be your customers and suppliers. The knowledge you gain from reading this book will help you deal with these people and avoid letting them derail your projects and your career. This book will help you learn how to avoid becoming a scapegoat, to survive aggressive managers' assaults, and to give narcissistic and rigid managers the things they need to be satisfied with you. This book will also help you manage toxic subordinates more effectively so that they will be an asset to your group rather than a time bomb. Toxic managers are a fact of life—how they affect your life depends upon the skills you develop to deal with them.

Senior management is also deeply affected by the presence of toxic managers because of their profound destructive impact on the organization. Grandiose, aggressive, and rigid managers damage morale. Faced with toxic superiors, people in your organization may withdraw, fail to share valuable information, no longer have the energy or incentive to go the extra mile, lose creativity, become irritable and oppositional, and leave. This book will help senior managers to recognize toxic managers early—hopefully before they are hired but certainly before they rise to positions of power within the organization.

The book will also help senior managers to manage toxic subordinates. A toxic manager can often function reasonably well in one position but create havoc in another. The Peter Principle—the tendency for people to rise to their level of incompetence—most commonly occurs when someone with troublesome personality traits (rigidity, narcissism, aggression) performs well in a position that shields him from the worst aspects of his personality. Senior management fails to pick up on the signs of the manager's toxic traits or fails to realize how the traits will sabotage the manager's ability to succeed in a new position. Recognizing toxic personality traits quickly and knowing in which positions the manager will perform poorly can spare the manager and the organization serious problems.

We all have abrasive edges, ways of behaving that inconvenience others. Managers differ in their ability to control and resolve their toxic traits and thereby become people you want to have in your company. Their ability to contain their rough edges depends to a great extent upon what lies below the surface: their underlying personality traits. If a manager is irritable and yells because of depression or attention deficit hyperactivity disorder (ADHD), appropriate medication can rapidly make an enormous difference in his or her behavior. A manager who yells because he or she came from a culture in which yelling is acceptable may be able to change relatively rapidly with education and practice. Managers with deeply ingrained personality disorders, such as marked narcissistic traits, will remain a problem for a very long time, probably until you fire them. Understanding the various types of toxic managers and what lies under their behavior will help senior management to know who to invest resources in trying to change, who to move to a new position requiring different skills, and who to encourage to leave.

Even when managers' personality traits are not severely impairing, the ability to quickly size up their personality style, along with knowledge of the impact of that style on work processes, will enable you to assign them to positions in which they are most likely to succeed. Sometimes, an outgoing, mildly grandiose, overly self-confident, and domineering manager is the most effective person to drive a project. On other occasions such managers can snatch defeat from the jaws of victory as they disrupt a team's functioning.

Attention to personality styles and problematic traits can also improve your ability to construct teams. Teams benefit from having people with a variety of styles for analyzing situations, dealing with data, and dealing with people. Teams need someone to focus attention on the work effort and make sure that problems are analyzed dispassionately. Teams also need someone to see to the human needs of team members and thereby maintain morale. Teams need people who are creative and who see the overall picture as well as members who pay attention to details and make sure that they are taken care of. Teams benefit from having some people who can keep their eyes on the main objective and others who keep their eyes open to new opportunities.

It is often difficult to create a team in which no member has toxic traits, since a high percentage of people do. How many team members can have such traits and what type of toxic behaviors can be mixed without crippling the team's function is therefore important to consider in building a team. A team may be able to tolerate one grandiose individual but is likely to run into marked turmoil if it has multiple grandiose members. Depending upon the type of rigidity, a team may function well with several rigid people on it, or it may become totally deadlocked. Aggressive managers are also a problem, but can often be adequately contained if people are aware of their problematic personality traits early and act to constrain them before too much damage is done. The more you know about managers' styles and how flexible they are, the better you will be able to assign people to positions in which they will succeed, avoid placing them where disaster could strike, and construct teams that are highly productive.

Emotional Intelligence Approach

This book aims to develop your emotional intelligence in the critical areas of dealing with difficult people. Emotional intelligence entails both being able to understand and having the skills to cope with your own feelings and the feelings of others. Considerable research during the past decade has shown how critical emotional intelligence is to business success.

Components of emotional intelligence include personal and social competence. Personal competence refers to the ability to understand your own feelings, strengths, and weaknesses, and the ability to deal with the feelings in appropriate ways rather than having them adversely affect your performance. For example, being able to contain your anger and anxiety and thereby think clearly in upsetting situations is crucial to making good decisions and effectively influencing others.

Social competence is the ability to understand what others are feeling and having the skills to effectively work with others. The ability to understand what is going on in a group or organization, to influence people, and to foster cooperation is the most important work of leadership and management.

Components of Emotional Intelligence ▬▬▬▬▬▬

Personal Competence

Self-Awareness

- ◆ Aware of your emotions and their impact
- ◆ Aware of your strengths and weaknesses

Self-Management

- ◆ Emotional self-control
- ◆ Adaptability: flexibility in adapting to changing situations and obstacles
- ◆ Integrity, honesty, trustworthiness
- ◆ Drive to grow and achieve
  - • Achievement oriented
  - • Continuous learner
  - • Willing to take initiative
  - • Optimistic

Social Competence

Social Awareness

- ◆ Empathy and insight
  - • Understanding others' perspectives and feelings
  - • Appreciation of others' strengths and weaknesses
- ◆ Political awareness

Relationship Management

- ◆ Respect for others
- ◆ Conflict management skills
- ◆ Collaborative approach
- ◆ Sense of humor
- ◆ Persuasive: visionary, diplomatic
- ◆ Able to leverage diversity

There are several good books that discuss the importance of emotional intelligence and how to develop general emotional intelligence skills that work with reasonable people. Dan Goleman's *Working With Emotional Intelligence* and *Primal Leadership* are particularly noteworthy.

Much of the time, however, we are faced with people who are not reasonable. Emotional intelligence entails having the skills to deal with toxic individuals as well as with those who are not difficult. Dealing with toxic individuals requires specialized skills, including an understanding of toxic personality traits and emotional problems that can impair performance. By providing you with an understanding of why difficult people behave as they do, recommendations on how to deal with such people, and how not to be undone by them, this book will help you to develop your emotional intelligence.

This book can also be helpful to difficult managers who have some capacity for insight into themselves but have difficulty containing their emotions, understanding others' feelings, or skillfully dealing with others. It can help difficult managers spot problematic patterns in their relationships and work styles, and can point the way to the skills they need to develop. For those managers adversely affected by anxiety, depression, attention deficit disorder, or posttraumatic stress disorder, recognizing the impact of these problems and then seeking help can often lead to rapid, marked improvements in functioning.

Developing Your Emotional Intelligence

Despite the importance of learning how to deal with difficult people, there is relatively little formal education available on how to deal with office politics and personalities. Rather, you often learn as apprentices do—by observing those above you. Those above you, however, have also never had formal education. Moreover, many of those above you are difficult people from whom you should only learn what not to do.

For many people, simply reading this book and applying its recommendations will foster significant improvement in troubling work relationships. For others, the book will be a prelude to engaging an executive coach. Having read the book should help the coaching experience to move much farther and faster than would otherwise have occurred. You will get the most out of the book if you stop and think about people you have known who fit into the various categories discussed, what problems they caused, what it was like for you to deal with them, and how they reacted to different interventions. Questions at the end of each chapter are designed to facilitate this exercise.

It is puzzling that we seek expert advice on improving our golf game but avoid professional advice on how to deal with other people. We pay for fashion consultants, someone to help with presentation skills, and interior decorators. We pay personal trainers remarkable fees one or more times a week to encourage us to exercise harder. We avoid, however, engaging an expert to help us learn more about ourselves and others—someone who could help us learn to deal with different types of stressful people. Somehow, we are supposed to be experts on dealing with other people and with our own emotions even though these issues were never formally addressed in our education and training.

People can make changes themselves and can effect change in others. You are unlikely to bring about wholesale personality change, but you do not need to. Rounding off rough spots and bringing greater flexibility and responsiveness to situations that most seriously affect your colleagues is all that is needed to make a significant improvement in the quality of the work environment and work output. This is very doable if handled with skill and understanding of what is needed for change.

Roots of Toxic Behavior

Underneath toxic behaviors are either toxic personality traits or disorders of mood or impulsivity. By personality traits, we mean enduring patterns of perceiving, interpreting, and relating to the world and oneself. In other words, personality traits concern how someone has learned to understand the world and his or her place in it. The toxic behaviors discussed in this book include narcissism, aggression, rigidity, and unethical behavior.

There are a variety of belief systems that underlie aggression. Ruthless managers perceive the world as a dog-eat-dog competition in which people are out to get you, and if you are not a predator, you will become someone's prey. Bullies obtain a perverse pleasure by intimidating others. Other aggressive individuals chronically view themselves as victims, and what others view as aggression they see as self-defense or compensation for wrongs done to them. Frantic and volatile managers have enduring problems modulating the intensity of their feelings and are often flooded by them.

Similarly, there are a variety of views of the world that can drive rigid behavior. Dictatorial and authoritarian managers believe that strict hierarchical organization and control are the best way for the world to work. Compulsive managers fear chaos in the world and in themselves. Oppositional and passive-aggressive individuals feel that their autonomy is constantly being threatened, and they must push back in order to defend themselves.

Narcissistic personality traits (arrogance, devaluation of others, limited empathy and conscience) play an important role in several types of toxic managerial behavior. The self-preoccupation, devaluation of others, and limited empathy and conscience of narcissistic managers free them to behave in markedly aggressive, controlling and unethical ways. People without narcissistic traits may want to behave in these ways at times but constrain themselves out of respect for other people.

Problems of mood and attention are generally more readily treated than are personality traits. Mood and attention have large, biological components and can readily change with medication. In contrast, personality traits depend upon the models in your head concerning how the world works, what type of person you are, and what your place is in the world (your identity). These mental models cannot be directly affected by medication and generally change slowly in psychotherapy.

However, when people are stressed by anxiety, depression, trauma, ADHD, alcohol, drugs, or a toxic environment, any tendency they have for aggressive, rigid, or narcissistic behavior intensifies. They may appear to have a personality disorder even if they do not. Treating the underlying mood problem can lead to rapid improvement. In fact, a lifetime of difficult personality traits can almost vanish if the underlying chronic depression or ADHD is treated.

An organization's culture, role models, and performance measurement system are also important in determining managerial behavior. They can either inhibit or foster toxic behavior in an individual who would otherwise behave in problematic ways. Figure 1–1 shows the factors that drive or inhibit toxic behavior.

Why Understand Difficult People?

Why should you try to understand difficult people? Why not just heed recommendations on how to respond to difficult behavior?

The key to changing problematic behavior is understanding what factors drive it and then designing an intervention to affect these causal factors. Interventions that would lead to a positive change in a manager with one underlying personality type could lead to intensification of the behavior in someone with another type. For example, aggressive behavior may be driven by fear and insecurity, by cluelessness, or by a ruthless desire to dominate

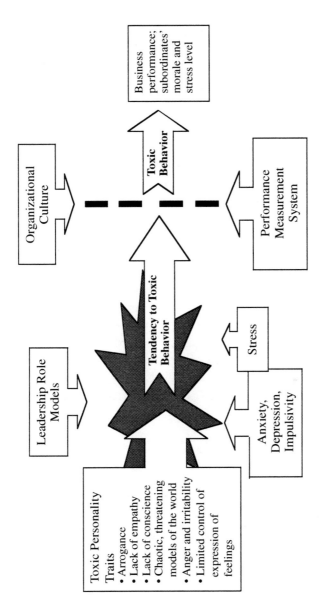

Figure 1-1 Factors driving and containing toxic behavior.

and control people. Managers whose aggression arises from fear and insecurity are likely to calm down if treated with tolerance and reassurance. Tolerance of aggression arising from ruthlessness, however, is likely to exacerbate the situation. Similarly, while a strong negative response to aggressive behavior may deter someone who is ruthless, it could increase the anxiety and tension of someone who is driven by fear and thereby worsen the problem.

The better you understand how other people view the world and what motivates them, the better you will be able to influence them to behave in ways that are helpful. The more you know about what motivates people with different styles, the better you will be able to defend yourself and encourage them to cooperate with you and provide the work products you need to do your own job.

Senior management and human resources need to understand why someone is doing poorly in order to know whether to try to help the individual or to let him or her go. You do not want to give too many chances to someone who rains chaos and problems on others. At the same time, you do not want to get rid of a potentially fine manager who is suffering from readily treatable anxiety, depression, stress, or abuse by a toxic manager. The more you understand about personality types, the impact of anxiety and depression, and the problematic behaviors that can be evoked by being placed in difficult situations (such as being scapegoated or bullied or placed in a job requiring the wrong set of skills), the better you will be able to determine whether to keep a manager who is currently having a problem or to have him or her find a new position.

Myths Rationalizing Destructive Behavior

People tend to accept rather than confront difficult behavior in others and in themselves. Effecting change is difficult. To avoid the stress of attempting to foster change, people often convince themselves that it is impossible to effect change or that the situation is not that destructive. Both of these beliefs are false (see Table 1–1).

Table 1–1 Myths Versus Reality About Destructive Behavior

Myth	Reality
I'm/he's too old to change or can't change.	The most effective managers are not the fast starters but the ones who learn throughout their careers. Old dogs can learn new tricks if they want to.
That's the culture.	The culture is often a reason why people do things as they do. Reasons, however, are not excuses. Those who can rise above a problematic culture and do things the best way are called leaders.
She's just blowing off steam.	Someone blowing off steam is harming others and needs to be contained.
This is the best way to motivate people and get things done.	A good manager understands the people she works with and designs her interactions to be most effective with each person. One size does not fit all.
There is one right way to do things.	This is the siren song of narcissistic and compulsive managers. It is rarely true.
That is just his style.	If someone's style seriously interferes with the effectiveness of other people and the overall team, he needs to modify his style.
It doesn't do any harm.	Closing our eyes to the harm being done may provide a temporary and uneasy sense of peace, but it doesn't last and isn't real.
She deserves it.	No one deserves to be screamed at, insulted, or treated badly. They may deserve to be taken aside and told the ways in which they need to change. They may deserve to miss out on a promotion or bonus. You may need to fire them. They do not, however, deserve abuse, particularly because we never know what is going on inside them, what pressures they are under, what good things they are doing, or what trauma they suffered earlier in life.

Further Reading

Daniel Goleman. *Working with Emotional Intelligence.* Bantam, 1998.

Daniel Goleman, Annie McKee, & Richard E. Boyatzis. *Primal Leadership: Realizing the Power of Emotional Intelligence.* Harvard Business School, 2002.

Linda A. Hill. *Becoming a Manager.* Harvard Business School, 1992.

Brittain Leslie & Ellen Van Velsor. *A Look at Derailment Today: North America and Europe.* Center for Creative Leadership, 1996.

Robert Sternberg. *Successful Intelligence.* Simon and Schuster, 1996.

PART I

NARCISSISTIC MANAGERS

Copernicus Was Wrong:
I'm the Center of the Universe

A central personality trait of many toxic managers is destructive narcissism. It is the core problem in grandiose managers, control freaks, paranoid managers, sociopaths, ruthless managers, bullies, and the most problematic, rigid managers. Destructive narcissism releases managers from normal moral constraints and concerns for fairness, and allows them to treat others as objects rather than as human beings with rights. It enables people to manipulate, bully, scapegoat, and exploit others without concern for the impact of their actions on the victim.

Definition of Narcissism

The term *narcissism* comes from the Greek myth of a beautiful youth, Narcissus, who callously spurned the affection of others and fell in love with his own reflection in a pool of water. He stayed by the water in a futile attempt to possess the reflection, and pined away.

Key characteristics of destructive narcissism include

1. Grandiosity and preoccupation with oneself
2. Arrogance and devaluation of others
3. A sense of entitlement to whatever one wishes

4. Sensitivity to slights, resulting in rage or desire for revenge

5. Lack of attachment to values

Narcissistic managers are grandiose and arrogant. They feel that they are qualitatively better than others and are destined for greatness. Devaluation of others helps to reinforce their sense of being better than those around them and therefore entitled to whatever they wish. Because they are so special, they do not need to be concerned about the rights and needs of others. This gives them permission to exploit people and to be callous toward the feelings and needs of those with whom they work and live. They are concerned only with how people serve their own needs. They expect high-level performance from subordinates, but often fail to provide the resources necessary to do their jobs.

Narcissistic managers have little attachment to values or normal conceptions of right and wrong, and break rules whenever it serves their purpose. Generally overly self-confident or even grandiose, they tend to believe that they can get away with misdeeds. In dealing with narcissistic managers, you cannot rely on the normal rules of decent behavior. They play by a different set of rules: All is fair in love, war, and business. They will exploit you and lie about you in ways that most people would not dream of.

Arrogant with peers and subordinates, they may suddenly become submissive in the presence of a superior. Once the superior has left, however, they may well disparage her. They may transiently idealize individuals with power who support them. However, they generally deprecate and exploit others, including former idols.

Adding to the danger they present, they are very sensitive to anything that challenges their self-esteem. Challenges and perceived slights can lead to narcissistic rage in which they lose all judgment and attack in ways that are destructive both to themselves and their victims.

Having negative thoughts about others helps to protect narcissistic managers from doubts about themselves, including an inner sense of shame. Negative images of others lead them to be suspicious, mistrustful, and prone to ascribe evil motives to others. They are preoccupied with the hidden motives of others and tend to exaggerate threats. They look for signs of shameful conduct in others in order to support the projection of their own shameful self-image onto others and to reinforce their sense of being better than others. Since almost anyone placed under a microscope can be found to have faults, destructively narcissistic people can generally find reasons with a grain of truth for devaluing someone they dislike. Viewing the world as hostile and forbidding, they trust only a few chosen subordinates, cater to them to keep their loyalty, and demand total devotion in return. Lacking real connections to people, they often use new allies to betray old ones.

Most of us have had the misfortune of working with managers who feel and act as if they were an inherently superior form of human being. They feel entitled to whatever they desire, exploit others without embarrassment, look down upon those they deal with, expect us to idolize them and to be interested in listening to their self-congratulatory stories, and perhaps even believe that rules and restrictions apply only to other, less important beings than they. When dealing with these managers, we wonder how long we can survive the abuse. When not acutely suffering, we wonder why and how they got as far as they did and when they will self-destruct.

Origins of Destructive Narcissism

Psychodynamic thinking holds that early childhood experiences have a great impact on our adult personality. Early experiences leave deep imprints on our identity, beliefs about right and wrong, tendency to become angry, reactions to events, and ways of dealing with people. According to this school of thought, narcissism arises when parents are out of touch with their children's wishes and feelings, and perhaps even express hostility to their children. This interferes with children's ability to learn to care for themselves and others, and undermines their development of a conscience—a sense of right and wrong. It also leaves a reservoir of anger. Some experts believe that the lack of empathy or conscience of narcissistic individuals is biologically based rather than based in experience.

Those who develop grandiose personality traits had parents who glorified some trait they had while ignoring their true feelings and wishes. They use grandiose fantasies to reinforce the fragile self-esteem that arose from their parents being out of touch with who they really were and what they actually wanted.

Case Study: Origins of Destructive Narcissism ▬▬▬▬

Tom was adored by his parents. The only male child and heir to the family dreams and business, everyone fawned over him. He had dominion over his parents and sisters. His parents frequently told him stories of how he would some day run the family business. He was proud that he was going to be an important person. Sometimes he had other fantasies: being a sports star, an astronaut, or a firefighter. When he tried to tell his parents about these dreams, they initially laughed. In time they responded by looking disapprovingly and telling him that he was better than that.

Tom had wanted a firetruck for his ninth birthday; instead he received a pen and desk set. People were upset when he wasn't happy with it. He learned to stop talking about what he wanted. Often, when he was sad or anxious or simply not feeling well, his parents would pay no attention. They were generally busy with more important things, such as entertaining business contacts.

Tom went through college, got his MBA, and joined the family business. He was confident, charismatic, and bright. He had what it took to succeed. He was somewhat arrogant, but people accepted it because he was the boss's son. His superiors knew they needed to treat him with deference, since he would someday run the business.

When the family business was bought by a larger company, Tom's immunity ceased. In the new company, many saw him as a tyrant. He disliked people who questioned him—he felt they were impertinent. On those occasions when they were right in questioning him, he became outraged, yelled, and pounded on his desk. Even those who liked him saw him as ruthless. He thought little of others' feelings.

In the new company was another fast-track manager whom Tom feared would eventually compete with him for promotion. Tom started spreading stories to destroy his competitor's reputation. Tom rationalized to himself that all is fair in love and war. Moreover, if the other person had thought of it, he would have done it first; if not, then he wasn't strong enough for the job. Besides, the ultimate good was served by whatever enabled Tom to advance.

Tom's friends and family were increasingly unhappy with his entitlement, self-centeredness, and temper. He was not concerned that they were unhappy. When his wife asked for marriage counseling, he told her she could have therapy if she wished, but he wasn't interested. He was quite happy with the marital arrangement. His wife kept the house going, and he spent a couple of evenings a week with a young, attractive junior manager who saw him as her way to jumpstart her career. When someone suggested that his wife might find out and have her own affair, he became outraged. He hired a private detective to follow her. He swore he would kill her if it were true. Fortunately for both of them, it was not.

Although progressively isolated from family and friends, Tom remained unconcerned. He wasn't drained by guilt or anxiety, as others might be if they exploited others. Tom's confidence allowed him to continue to rise in the company. He was the man for the job.

Healthy Self-Esteem Versus Destructive Narcissism

High levels of self-esteem are not the basis of narcissistic personality problems. Although on the surface, destructive narcissism may appear to be simply extremely high levels of self-esteem, this is not the case. Although both healthy self-esteem and destructive narcissism provide outward self-confidence, they are very different phenomena. Secure self-esteem facilitates an individual's ability to empathize with other people, care about others, and enjoy friendship and intimacy. It also supports commitment to values and ideals. The grandiosity of destructively narcissistic individuals, however, is not due to high levels of self-esteem. Rather, their grandiosity, arrogance, and devaluation of others is an attempt to seal over and protect their fragile self-esteem. Individuals with secure self-esteem have no reason to look down on and abuse others.

Stress intensifies the differences between those with healthy self-esteem and those with destructive narcissism (see Table I–1). Under stress, people with healthy self-esteem look to others for support and comfort. Valuing others, they can receive emotional support from others. When destructively narcissistic individuals are under stress, they reinforce their self-esteem by stepping on people more than usual.

Table I–1 Comparison of Healthy Self-Esteem and Destructive Narcissism

Characteristic	Healthy Self-Esteem	Destructive Narcissism
Self-confidence	High outward self-confidence in line with reality	Arrogant
Desire for power, wealth, and admiration	Desires power but also cares about morality, other people, and personal relationships	Seeks extraordinary levels of success; pursues them at all cost; lacks normal inhibitions in their pursuit
Response to frustration	Able to deal with frustration with some sadness and irritation	Frustration threatens self-esteem and leads to narcissistic rage in which judgment collapses and the person acts destructively to self and others
Relationships	Real concern for others and their ideas; does not exploit or devalue others	Concern limited to expressing socially appropriate response when convenient; devalues and exploits others without remorse
Attitude toward authority	Variable	Submits to authority transiently, either when temporarily idealizing a superior or believing that submitting will lead to concrete benefit; believes he or she should be in charge; sees self as exempt from standard rules
Ability to follow a consistent path	Has values; follows through on plans	Lacks values; easily bored; often changes course
Foundation	Healthy childhood with support for self-esteem and appropriate limits on behavior toward others	Traumatic childhood undercutting true sense of self-esteem, and/or learning that he or she doesn't need to be considerate of others

Types of Narcissistic Managers

Narcissistic managers can present in a number of ways (Table I–2). All narcissistic managers are arrogant, devalue others, and have limited conscience and empathic capacity. Important differences arise depending upon whether they have special abilities that can support grandiose fantasies; and whether they enjoy breaking the rules or hurting people. Grandiose managers, in addition to having fragile self-esteem, have some trait or ability that supports a grandiose self-image. They primarily seek to be admired and to live out their grandiose fantasies. Those with psychodynamically based narcissism have fragile self-esteem that they cover over by devaluing others. They become enraged and destructive when their self-esteem is threatened. Those with learned narcissism may behave poorly toward others out of cluelessness, but are neither vicious nor uncaring. They have not learned appropriate, considerate behavior because their power has interfered with their receiving negative feedback for inconsiderate behavior. Control freaks protect underlying fragile self-esteem by being arrogant and devaluing others. Compared to grandiose managers, they are more concerned with wielding power over people than with being admired. They often fear chaos and seek to micromanage events, since no one else is adequately capable. Paranoid managers see all events in terms of themselves and are preoccupied with fears that people want to hurt them. Unethical opportunists primarily have weak consciences and are willing to break the rules if it serves their needs. Ruthless managers have little respect for others' rights and feel entitled to exploit others if they need to. Antisocial individuals and bullies are aggressive narcissists. They have the important addition to their pathology that they not only have little conscience or capacity for empathy, but they intensely enjoy violating the rights of others and the rules of society even when there is no concrete objective that they seek by doing so. Antisocial individuals enjoy breaking rules; bullies enjoy intimidating people. These categories are not exclusive of each other. People often have the behavior problems of more than one of them.

Factors Worsening Narcissism

Narcissistic managers tend to become particularly toxic when under stress or depressed. Stress, anxiety, and depression generally make it harder for people to pay attention to others' needs and increase the need to reinforce one's self-esteem. Healthy people seek support from others when stressed. Narcissistic individuals seek to step on others when stressed. Narcissistic

Table I-2 Types of Narcissistic Managers

	Primary Traits	**Objective**
Grandiose: Psychodynamic	Outward grandiose self-image; exploits others; devalues others; enraged if self-esteem threatened; limited conscience and capacity for empathy; desperately protects underlying fragile self-esteem	Be admired
Grandiose: Learned	Grandiose self-image; exploits others out of carelessness; is inconsiderate in treatment of others due to not receiving negative feedback for behavior (see Chapter 2)	Be admired
Control Freak	Micromanages; seeks absolute control of everything; inflated self-image and devaluation of others' abilities; fear of chaos	Control others
Paranoid	Preoccupied with perceived threats; unable to trust others; may strike-out in self defense	Avoid danger
Unethical Opportunist	Moral inhibitions temporarily dissolve when a good offer presents itself	Things he needs
Ruthless	Calmly goes after what she wants without concern for others' rights; lacks both a conscience and capacity for empathy	Obtain desires
Antisocial	Takes what he wants, lies to get ahead, hurts others if they are in his way; lacks both a conscience and capacity for empathy	Excitement of violating rules and abusing others
Bully	Seeks to dominate and intimidate others; lacks conscience and capacity for empathy	Intimidating and hurting others provides excitement and a sense of power

managers are likely to become aggressive when depressed or stressed. Of great importance, some narcissistic managers become markedly less toxic when their problems with anxiety and depression are treated. In fact, some cease to be narcissistic.

Cultural factors also modulate the degree of toxic behavior a narcissistic manager engages in. In a culture that supports self-centered pursuit of objectives and mistreatment of others, a manager's tendency toward narcissistic behavior will come out. Place him in a different culture, and he will be in better control.

Attention deficit hyperactivity disorder (ADHD) can lead to behavior that resembles narcissism. The distractibility of ADHD interferes with being attuned to others' needs. The tendency of people with ADHD to talk a lot and interrupt others can appear to be lack of concern for the feelings and needs of others. Treat the ADHD with appropriate medication and the problematic traits will improve.

Part I Overview

Two types of toxic managers are discussed in Part I. Grandiose managers are the stereotypic narcissistic managers. Control freaks lack their flamboyance but replace it with a heightened need to control others. Paranoid managers, like grandiose managers and control freaks, feel that the world revolves around them. They are in touch with their vulnerability, however, and deal with it by seeing themselves as under attack from outside rather than weak inside. Grandiose managers, control freaks, and paranoid managers all have underlying fragile self-esteem (except for those with learned narcissism, discussed in Chapter 2), cover it over with arrogance, and are prone to severe anger when threatened. When grandiose managers and control freaks run into problems and become depressed, they often slide into paranoia.

- ◆ Chapter 2—Grandiose Managers: Legends in Their Own Minds

- ◆ Chapter 3—Control Freaks: You Will Do Absolutely Everything My Way

- ◆ Chapter 4—Paranoid Managers: They're Out to Get Me

Additional Material

War of the Roses provides an example of narcissistic rage.

CHAPTER 2

Grandiose Managers

Legends in Their Own Minds

Grandiose managers are legends in their own minds. Preoccupied with their exaggerated accomplishments and grandiose expectations for the future, they expect others to revere them—in fact, they insist upon it. They think a lot about themselves and talk a lot about themselves, since no other subject is as important or interesting. Constantly boasting, they resemble peacocks strutting around with their tail feathers unfurled.

The self-glorification of grandiose managers is part of a larger picture of dysfunction—the various aspects of a narcissistic personality. Like all varieties of narcissistic managers, grandiose managers lack empathy for others and have little if any conscience. They do not respect others' rights, are frequently arrogant, and devalue others. Feeling exempt from the normal rules of society, they exploit people without remorse.

Under the surface, grandiose managers struggle with fragile self-esteem. It is most apparent in the periodic geysers of anger that burst out when their self-esteem is challenged. They also have a sense of emptiness arising from their lack of true self-love and inability to care about other people or about abstract values such as honesty and integrity. Their grandiose fantasies are attempts to fill the emptiness and reinforce their fragile self-esteem.

Grandiose managers are often loose cannons who become furious when things do not go as they wish. They are particularly likely to fly into a rage when their grandiose self-images are threatened. The combination of arrogance, devaluation of others, anger, pursuit of their own needs without regard for the impact on other people or their company, and excessive risk taking makes them highly destructive to the organizations they work for and the family and friends that mistakenly trust them.

A milder variant of grandiose managers are those with learned narcissism. They are not desperately trying to hide and shield fragile self-esteem arising from a troubled childhood, as you generally find with narcissistic personalities. Rather, their success in some area has brought sufficient fame and fortune that they have been shielded from the normal consequences of behaving arrogantly and treating others poorly. Moreover, as people incessantly flatter them, they come to believe the glorifying compliments. These people have a conscience and feel some empathy for others; they simply do not realize the full impact of their behavior on others.

Organizational Impact of Grandiose Managers

The extreme confidence of grandiose personalities often makes them charismatic. This, along with the tendency of most people to equate confidence with competence, often fuels a rapid rise through the ranks of management. Their glibness enables them to sell themselves to senior management and further propels their advancement. More often than not, however, rather than being whiz kids who are the company's best hope for the future, they are masters only of smoke and mirrors who can foster their company's downfall. They not only damage the human capital of the company but can engage in disastrous risk taking, and even illegal activities, that can bring the company down.

The combination of a desire for excitement and a sense of invulnerability often leads to high-stakes risk taking. Focused on building their own power and glory, they tend to engage in empire building rather than in strengthening the core of the company. They may be addicted to the trappings of power and squander resources on extravagances.

They often squander the abilities and energy of those who work with them. They tend to disparage the good ideas of subordinates lest those ideas draw attention away from themselves. They do not want the real interchange of ideas needed for optimal decision making, and no one dares criticize the grandiose manager's ideas, so both creativity and critical assessment of

ideas are crippled. Grandiose managers are also weak at implementing programs and thereby waste the efforts of those who work for them. Their need
for excitement may lead them to change course rapidly and to neglect details, causing confusion and poor follow-through. In addition, their subordinates need to expend considerable energy feeding the manager's ego and
dealing with the complex political situation and frustrations inherent in
working under a grandiose manager. This massive drain on the energies of
the manager and subordinates can seriously compromise the department's
productivity.

Grandiose managers are neglectful of the needs of people who work for
them. They may do nice things for others or engage in social pleasantries
when it is convenient. But if they dislike a task, such as providing support,
responding to questions, dealing with organizational problems, seeing to it
that people have the tools they need to succeed, or writing performance
evaluations, they won't do it. As a result, the morale of their subordinates
diminishes, and people in the business unit begin to focus their energies on
political survival and dealing with their frustration with the narcissistic
manager rather than on doing their best work.

Grandiose managers are particularly destructive to the company's
human capital. Although they may support young colleagues for a while,
in time they are likely to undercut them, especially if the colleagues show
any signs of independence. Interested primarily in increasing their own
power, and tending toward authoritarian leadership styles, they do not adequately delegate authority. Capable junior managers will leave a grandiose
manager's unit, since they will not have the opportunities for decision making that they want and deserve. Grandiose managers promote those who
flatter them and are hostile to those who do not. Rather than supporting
the development of new talent, they undercut and get rid of the most talented people out of fear that such individuals will take away from their
own radiance. Many other good people flee to escape the toxic atmosphere
that grandiose managers create.

Origins of Grandiosity

Destructive narcissism can arise from early childhood experiences in which
a child's real self is neither valued nor responded to. At the same time, the
child is seen as incredibly special because of some special trait the child has.
The child is left with fragile self-esteem, which is covered over by a
grandiose self-image, a reservoir of anger, and little concern for others'

well-being. This psychodynamic path to destructive narcissism is not the only route by which grandiosity can develop.

Grandiosity can also develop in people with great power or glamour who receive only praise and reinforcement of their grandiose self-images. Perhaps most important, people don't give them negative feedback when they behave in a grandiose and arrogant manner. This "learned narcissism" can develop in those who are stunningly attractive or unusually bright or talented, such as star athletes and entertainers who are surrounded by people who treat them with great deference and fawn on them.

Case Study: Learned Narcissism

Alan was a relatively normal boy while growing up. He had friends and got along with people reasonably well. His parents doted on him and told him he was special. Unlike the parents of severely narcissistic people, they were able to respond to his feelings and needs, did not have a grandiose image of him, and loved him even when he was not perfect.

In time Alan excelled in sports. With his accomplishments, he became very popular, and friends and girls flocked to him. He no longer needed to be thoughtful or even nice in order to be invited to parties or to have friends to hang out with and girls to date. His sports prowess continued in college and was viewed positively when he went into the business world.

In business he was seen as a fair-haired boy on a fast track. His self-confidence was equated with competence; people liked it and trusted him. Because he was liked by upper management, when Alan made mistakes, people excused them and supported him when he blamed others. Clients' top-level executives liked him. He was personable and gregarious, talked about his days in football, and treated top executives very well. Client representatives not at the top were less impressed, since Alan did not give them much time or attention.

People who worked for Alan continually told him how bright he was. They had picked up on Alan's need for such compliments. Nevertheless, his subordinates were not that happy. He was often inconsiderate of their feelings, could be harsh when things did not go well, minimized his responsibility for problems, and tended to take most of the credit for successes. If people challenged him, he became angry and felt they were out of place. He was never outraged or cruel, however—simply arrogant and inconsiderate.

Much of any meeting with Alan consisted of his talking about himself and his accomplishments, and was punctuated by name dropping. Every story he told contained large quantities of self-congratulatory statements and a fair number of derogatory statements about others.

Alan disliked mundane activities and often neglected them. His failure to write performance evaluations for subordinates was legendary. No matter how many times he promised to do them, he would continue to delay until the person was literally in tears, knowing that Alan's failure would cost him or her a needed bonus. He once told a manager that the company did not really expect people at his level to spend time writing these evaluations. In fact, the company did expect it.

Good people tended to leave Alan's group or not be invited in. When someone in his group began receiving praise and attention from upper management, Alan became uncomfortable with him, withdrew, and found an excuse to transfer him. When a new, highly qualified person wanted to transfer in, Alan rejected her despite the strong, unanimous recommendation of the people who interviewed her. Alan offered little explanation for his actions, but people suspected that he was used to being the center of attention and felt uncomfortable with someone who might take some of the limelight. When someone left his group, Alan would reassure his coworkers—and himself—that the person had had a longstanding interest in her new activity and that she had not left because of dissatisfaction. He would then never speak of her again.

Interested in a new business concept, Alan hired Richard, who had an academic background. He spun out some ideas and then suggested that Richard develop a white paper. Although others in the group felt the white paper was good and used it to change the group's marketing strategy, Alan was ambivalent about it. For six months, Alan said he had pages of comments and new text he had written for the white paper, but he never sent them, although Richard repeatedly asked for them. In time,

Richard guessed that Alan had not been able to add anything to his work.

Alan's tendency to drive away the best people in his unit seriously interfered with the development of his division. The top leadership became increasingly disgruntled and rearranged the organizational structure, decreasing his autonomy and effectively demoting Alan. Unable to deal with this, he left the company.

Learned grandiose narcissism, albeit troubling and destructive to productivity, is much less of a problem than narcissism arising from early childhood deprivation and psychodynamic problems. Those with learned narcissism maintain an ability to be concerned with the well-being of others and respect for abstract values. They do not need to devalue others in order to protect fragile self-esteem and an underlying sense of shame and emptiness.

The psychodynamically based narcissism that arises from a childhood in which parents failed to respond to the child's feelings and wishes and to give the child a sense of being loved as an individual entails a far greater devaluation and inability to empathize with others. As a result, this narcissistic manager's willingness to devalue, manipulate, and exploit is far greater. The fragility of such a manager's self-esteem also leads to great anger at times and creates a far more destructive situation.

The higher narcissistic managers rise in a company and the more power they gather, the worse things become. Inhibitions melt away, and the power to act on grandiose desires increases.

Case Study: A Grandiose CEO

While we cannot credibly analyze someone's personality from a distance, we can say that actions described in published accounts illustrate a particular behavior. Therefore, the following paragraphs are not meant as an analysis of William Agee, former Morrison Knudsen CEO, but are simply a recounting of the newspapers' descriptions of managerial behavior that illustrates grandiosity.

Agee's career took off quickly. A Harvard MBA, he became CFO of Boise Cascade at age 31 and then CEO of Bendix (a $4 billion-per-year auto parts manufacturer) in 1976 at age 38. He ran into trouble at Bendix as a result of his rapidly promoting his assistant to vice president, allegedly having an affair with her, and later marrying her. Moreover, his attempt to buy out Martin Marietta backfired, leading to the sale of Bendix to Allied Corporation. Nevertheless, he became CEO of Morrison Knudsen (a dam, bridge, and factory builder) in 1988.[1]

Newspaper descriptions reported grandiose and entitled behavior. On first coming to Morrison Knudsen, Agee allegedly told the head of corporate communications to meet with both his own personal media consultant and an outside public relations firm. He converted the company's massive boardroom into his own office. In addition to arranging a high salary and oversized bonuses for himself and to living unusually lavishly, he reportedly misused company funds to such an extent that it was reported to the IRS by company employees. Agee was alleged to have used company money for personal legal fees, Waterford Crystal for himself, and petunia beds for his home. He ran the company from his home in Pebble Beach, California, rather than from corporate headquarters, flying executives back and forth to his house. In a particularly remarkable self-glorifying act, he removed portraits of the company's founders and commissioned a life-sized portrait of himself and his wife at company expense.[2]

Agee allegedly devalued others and got rid of people who threatened to detract from his prestige. He treated subordinates badly and undercut talented people who might take away some of the glory he sought. Agee was described as having a "high-and-mighty manner." He fired people—frequently high-ranking, talented managers—with little or no warning and even threatened to fire his pilot while they were still in the air. It is alleged that as soon as the board of directors began to like someone, Agee would state that the person was not a good performer, and then horror stories about that person would begin to circulate. A company executive reported that Agee's "inner circle was made up of sycophants and yes men. People at the next level down caught hell." "He was afraid to have talent around."[3]

Descriptions of Agee's behavior show both little attachment to values and a willingness to be unusually deceptive in order to give the impression that he was doing a good job. He treated the corporate board to lavish meetings away from company headquarters, making it hard for board members to have access to other company officials. Moreover, information provided to the board about the company's financial condition was reported to be markedly skewed, and accounting practices were deceptive to shareholders. For example, it is alleged that he reported money from the sale of businesses as operating income (rather than nonrecurring income), giving the false impression that his company's construction and rail businesses were going well. When the company filed claims to recover unexpected costs on construction projects, the money was often immediately booked as revenues even though the claim might never be paid.[4]

Accounts of his behavior illustrate the excessive risk taking that destructively narcissistic individuals often engage in. For example, he moved into areas where he and the company lacked expertise, such as large, risky construction contracts. Similarly, without commissioning research (as far as a company top executive knew), he moved the company into building a new locomotive and arranged to build new passenger railroad cars without building a prototype. The company's initial success with railroad cars came when the design and engineering for the cars was done by another firm. In time the contracts Agee entered into for locomotive manufacturing led to large losses. He was finally fired after Morrison Knudsen lost $310 million in 1994.[5]

Newspaper articles also describe paranoid behavior. Agee had a bodyguard on the firm's payroll, hid cameras in birdhouses, and allegedly wiretapped employees' phones. The bodyguard opened packages in search of bombs, fetched groceries and laundry, and escorted Agee's children to school and gymnastics practice. Agee posted an armed guard around his Pebble Beach estate. When the guard questioned whether a real threat existed, he was banished to Morrison Knudsen headquarters to do menial tasks. As ex-CEO of Morrison Knudsen, he employed multiple bodyguards to accompany himself and his wife when they went shopping.[6] There had been some triggers to his concerns. There was a reported break-in at his home, and he reported receiving a black rose in a box and threatening phone calls while at Morrison Knudsen.[7]

Agee's behavior so alienated people at Morrison Knudsen that when he was fired from his position as CEO, the employees of Morrison Knudsen gathered in the parking lot of company headquarters and cheered. A shareholder lawsuit cost him his severance pay and much of his pension.[8]

Emotional Intelligence Approach to Grandiose Managers

Coping with Grandiose Superiors

Working for a grandiose manager is very stressful. Nevertheless, your attitude and actions can significantly affect your stress level when dealing with such people. Attempts to change their behavior toward you by standard methods such as telling them how their behavior makes you feel will not work. In general, trying to change the behavior of narcissistic superiors primarily leads to frustration. It is best to accept that they were so damaged in their emotional development that they lack the ability to empathize and behave reasonably. Keeping this in mind will help you not to take their criticism personally and to avoid arguing with their criticism, since doing so will only enrage them.

There are other steps you can take to avoid problematic situations with grandiose managers. One is to identify those situations and factors that lead to problems and avoid them when possible. For example, avoid gossiping with narcissistic managers, and do not borrow from them or lend to them. If you borrow things they will later insist that you pay them back. If they borrow they are likely to not return your things.

Try to obtain written directions whenever possible, since it decreases the room for uncertainty and complaints about you. Document your work so you can defend yourself if they criticize you for failing to do your job properly. In addition, document interactions and the course of events so that if you need to defend yourself to someone higher up, you have the means to do so.

To survive working with a grandiose boss, you need to exercise an unusual level of tact. You need to protect the grandiose boss from threats to his fragile self-esteem. Therefore, don't try to show the boss the error of his ways. Don't criticize him. Don't point out mistakes or examples of unfairness. Avoid one-upmanship. All of these actions will lead to narcissistic rage and a blind desire to attack you. There is no chance that you will suddenly break through the manager's psychological defenses and lead him to see the error of his ways. Above all, do not challenge his authority, power, or greatness. Rather, support his self-esteem. Show respect and even admiration for his accomplishments. Do not show off. Do not even talk about your past accomplishments. If there are current accomplishments, give him the credit. Grandiose managers want to be not only the prima ballerina, but the only person on stage. When things do not go well, rather than noting that problems arose because of things outside of your control, accept responsibility and note what you will do to fix things and that you will handle things differently next time.

Moving to another position within the company to avoid the grandiose manager is generally the best long-term strategy. This is particularly important for very capable individuals, who a destructively narcissistic individual may see as a threat and therefore try to undercut. Once you are out of the grandiose manager's unit, it is helpful to report to superiors how he treats people. If possible, it is best to do this in conjunction with others so that your statements are validated. Informing superiors of the problem will help the company as a whole and improve the working environment for all.

Confrontation sometimes works with individuals with learned narcissism. This confrontation, however, needs to come from above or possibly from a peer—not from below. If a subordinate attempts to confront a superior about his behavior, whether the grandiose narcissism is mostly learned or mostly psychodynamic, the reaction will generally be anger and retaliation. It is safest for a subordinate to behave in an admiring manner, which tends to decrease tensions. You can, however, sometimes effectively confront a narcissistic individual in a group, much as you would confront a substance abuser who is in denial. Even then, avoid complaining about the negative impact of his actions on you; he will inevitably take it as an attack, become enraged, and retaliate. Frame your comments in terms of how they can further the narcissistic manager's interests.

Grandiose bosses do best if they have a "buffer"—someone to help them deal with the rest of the people in the organization. Buffers are able to tolerate the boss's anger by not taking it personally and are thereby able to maintain close contact. Buffers know how to present issues to the narcissistic boss to minimize explosions and maximize the chance that the boss will behave appropriately, or let the buffer handle the issue. Buffers know how to present ideas to a boss so that the boss can find a way to take credit for it and therefore be willing to accept it.

Dealing with Grandiose Peers

Working with grandiose peers is also difficult. They take credit for your work, disparage you to others, incessantly boast, and lie and mislead people often for no other reason than the desire to deceive others. They also act as if they know the best way to do everything, discount others' input, fail to respect boundaries (e.g., enter your office and borrow things without permission), expect favors but rarely do any in return, and give you instructions as if they were your boss. They borrow your things without returning them, but are very hesitant to let you borrow from them.

The key to survival is to watch your back; in all contacts remember what people are told when given their Miranda Rights: Whatever you say can and will be used against you. Above all else, do not tell them about your weaknesses and vulnerabilities. Do not expect them to behave fairly or to change. Do not count on them to do their share of work. Be careful to establish credit for your work and ideas before they claim them as their own.

There are no perfect solutions, only courses of action that do not make things worse and are better than doing nothing. If disparaging remarks are made about you, it is generally best simply to state that you do not agree with the criticism. Avoid getting into arguments or retaliatory attacks. They can make you look bad to others and provoke the destructively narcissistic person to launch further attacks. To avoid having credit for your work stolen, it is best to avoid sharing ideas with destructively narcissistic individuals until after you have told your supervisor and team of your ideas in writing. When asked for ideas, respond in writing with your name attached. Do not ask a destructively narcissistic individual for favors, and do not borrow or lend anything. If given orders by a destructively narcissistic colleague, either ignore it or write to your boss to ask for clarification on responsibilities. You and your boss should respond to boundary violations with clear, consistent statements about what you do not want this individual to do.

Dealing with Grandiose Subordinates

All of the rules of self-protection for dealing with a narcissistic peer apply to dealing with narcissistic subordinates. Grandiose subordinates will stab you in the back, use whatever you say about yourself to hurt you, and steal credit for your work. Their agenda is not the team's or company's success but their own. Don't get taken in by their flattery and admiration. It will not last.

In giving feedback, provide plenty of positive statements first, or they will totally disregard any criticism as a sign you are unfair and wish to hurt them because you are jealous. Take a coaching stance. Help them to see others as people who can help them rather than as competitors for promotion.

For HR and Senior Management

The first practical issue for dealing with the problem of grandiose/narcissistic managers is being able to identify them before they rise to positions of high power. On the way up in the organization, they are not likely to display their full potential for grandiosity and lack of respect for others to their superiors, since they have some internal inhibitions against acting in this manner, and they will have only limited power to do so. Nevertheless, there are often significant warning signs:

◆ Devaluing and exploiting others

◆ Lack of concern for the needs of subordinates unless convenient

◆ Trying to take all credit for success

◆ Not following rules

◆ Undermining competitors for promotion

◆ Excessively criticizing others

◆ Scapegoating (blaming some innocent person)

◆ Excessive self-promotion and attention-seeking behavior

◆ Seeing all events in terms of significance to their own careers

◆ Being highly defensive when criticized

◆ Harboring unfounded beliefs that others want to hurt them

◆ Currying favor with superiors while failing to support and develop subordinates

One of the best tools an organization has for recognizing narcissistic managers of all types is 360-degree feedback. By querying a manager's superiors, peers, and reports, the human resources department is likely to come across signs of narcissism in narcissistic managers. Although they may be able to contain their problematic tendencies with superiors, narcissistic managers are unlikely to contain them when dealing with subordinates and colleagues. A potential difficulty is that subordinates may fail to give accurate assessments out of fear that their negative comments about a manager will get back to the manager, be traced to them, and lead to retaliation. Therefore, 360-degree feedback needs to be part of the organization's routine, with all people expected to provide anonymous, confidential feedback on superiors. For problematic managers to change, however, someone must alert them to subordinates' concerns. To get around this conflict, organizations can make it clear to employees that negative comments about their manager will not be forwarded unless the concerns are widespread and unless the negative feedback can be shared in a way that protects the anonymity of the people who provided it. In addition to supporting 360-degree feedback, executives should foster communication across multiple levels of the hierarchy.

Another good tool for recognizing narcissistic individuals is to have them rate themselves before you show them their performance review. Narcissistic managers will go on at great length about exaggerated achievements and be unable to seriously discuss any weaknesses. Similarly, when superiors make critical comments, narcissistic managers will quickly make excuses or blame others rather than accept that there is need for growth.

How a company can best deal with a narcissistic manager depends upon how destructive the narcissistic behavior is to the organization, what redeeming talents the narcissistic manager has, and the likelihood that the person can change. Some self-aggrandizement and desire for attention can be a small price to pay for a dynamic, insightful, effective problem solver who knows the business.

If a narcissistic manager is replaceable then confronting the behavior in hopes of ameliorating it is a good place to begin. If the manager's narcissism is primarily learned behavior, confrontation and executive coaching are usually helpful. Confrontation can even ameliorate moderate psychodynamically based narcissism by strongly reminding narcissistic managers that they are subordinate to others. If the destructive narcissism is severe and based on psychodynamic problems and fragile self-esteem, however, confrontation may lead to rage and possibly to paranoia, making matters worse. Organizations may help these individuals function better by providing them with copious emotional support from consultants and people within the organization. In psychological terms, the consultant becomes a mirror. Skilled executive coaching that provides a combination of empathic support and recommendations on how to work with others can help a narcissistic manager contain some of the most damaging manifestations of destructive narcissism.

Stress leads to anxiety and depression, which decrease self-esteem and ultimately increase the rigidity of narcissistic managers' problematic personality traits. Treating their depression and anxiety with appropriate medication can help them to be less defensive, more responsive to others, and better able to look at their problematic behaviors and make progress in therapy or executive coaching.

The management of an executive with destructive narcissism can be very difficult. The situation becomes particularly complicated when the executive is difficult to replace in the near future, since confrontation of the behavior in the hope of ameliorating it can precipitate a crisis and be counterproductive. Calling in a consultant skilled in dealing with problems of narcissism and who can provide a complex mix of confrontation, coaching, and support can significantly ameliorate the situation.

Case Study: Dealing with a Narcissistic VP

Eric was vice president of a mid-sized company. His unit had grown rapidly and was profitable. He had special knowledge and skills that made him very valuable to the company. At the same time, the company's president was increasingly aware that the morale in Eric's unit was poor and that turnover was high. The president instructed Eric to obtain some coaching.

Ambivalent about meeting with the coach at first, Eric became much more interested when a battle began between key people in his unit. He did not have the people skills to fix it, and he turned to the coach, who was very helpful. At times, Eric asked for advice on how to deal with various issues; more often, however, he spent his coaching time complaining about people. His assessment of people often shifted suddenly. If a promising hire did not initially do as well as hoped, Eric would immediately turn very negative and say that he had always had reservations about the person. Problems were always blamed on others. He could generally not look at himself.

One day Eric simultaneously faced near-rebellion at home and at work with people making similar complaints. He went to the coach, desperate for help and with a promise to look at himself. He made some changes in his style and expressed an interest in learning more people skills. As things calmed down, however, he slipped into his historic ways of treating people. His coach suggested that he obtain 360-degree feedback to better understand how people saw him and reacted to his style. Eric objected, saying it was a waste of time and resources.

I was called in to consult on the situation.

It was a positive sign that Eric was sometimes willing to consider that he had a problem when he came under pressure. Some narcissistic individuals in this situation would have become more rigid and aggressive, and perhaps paranoid, rather than open to advice. Moreover, some narcissistic managers would not care that they treat others badly, since they devalue others and are concerned only with their own well-being.

Nevertheless, Eric's personality style was well ingrained, and his ability to look at himself was very limited. He found it painful to consider that he had problems, as narcissistic managers generally do. He had also shown that he was not able to simply learn about a new style of treating people and do it. He needed more than just suggestions on better ways to deal with situations; he needed help in dealing with the feelings and ways of perceiving the world that were driving his behavior and making it impossible to learn new ways of managing people.

It seemed very unlikely that he would engage in the deeper exploration of issues that he needed to in order to really improve his management style unless he was under real pressure to do so. I suggested that the president insist he engage in a more regular coaching schedule and pay attention to changing his way of dealing with people. His ability to improve his management style and increase retention in his unit should become a large part of his evaluation and bonus program. Three hundred sixty–degree feedback would highlight his issues. Moreover, repeated 360-degree feedback could serve as part of his performance evaluation.

In coaching and therapy, Eric needed to look at how his opinions of people rapidly changed. His tendency to switch from very positive to very negative opinions underlay his tendency to have favorites who he treated well and others who he devalued and treated so poorly that they left. He also needed to look at the situations that led him to become upset and to be harsh with subordinates. What pushed his buttons to such an extent that he blew up at people? Were there ways to avoid these situations? Were there ways to make the buttons less sensitive? What led him to become harsh, and what was he thinking and feeling when he became harsh? The task would then be to try to alter his experience at those times so that he could be in better control and choose a more effective way to behave. Given the cost of decreased efficiency of his unit and the high cost of rapid turnover of employees, providing therapy had a good cost benefit ratio for Eric's company.

Eric was skeptical about the work. When he felt threatened by what we were talking about, he would say he did not have time to meet, especially if things were going relatively well for him at work and home. When he experienced significant problems with several people in his group, or received poor feedback on a 360, or his family was angry with him, he became more amenable to meeting. He was never able to look deep inside himself, but he was able to decrease the frequency and intensity of his angry outbursts and his devaluation of people, and to be more responsive to the needs of his subordinates. He also learned to pause before speaking or making decisions rather than reacting in anger. The modest changes took the edge off of his abrasiveness and made a significant difference to his group.

Conclusion

Grandiose managers can turn a good job into a nightmare. Even if they are not actively exploiting or devaluing you, their demands for admiration, lack of concern for your well-being, and failure to give you what you need to do your job creates tremendous stress. You are unlikely to enjoy the ride, but you can take steps to make it more tolerable and decrease the chance that you will become a target for their anger. The basic recommendations are to act in an admiring way, give them credit for the good things you do, never challenge them, and try not to take their exaggerated criticism of you personally.

If you can tolerate their arrogance, act in an admiring manner, and avoid criticizing or challenging them, you may become invaluable to them by providing a buffer between them and those who are less tolerant. You will for a while be treated relatively well and have their support. However, good things rarely last forever with narcissistic managers. They do not feel much loyalty and will turn on you no matter how much you have done for them. If you have a period of low productivity, they will turn on you as soon as they find someone who might produce more. If you have done very well, they are likely to turn on you because you threaten to take away from their being in the limelight. Prepare yourself by documenting your work, building a relationship with a mentor who you keep informed about your work, and keeping your eyes open for other positions. If possible, jump ship before they turn on you.

If the grandiose manager reports to you, he can also give you nightmares, as he damages the company's human capital, diverts people's energies, fails to follow through on projects, wastes money on extravagances, undermines your position, and convinces your superiors that he is invaluable to the company and deserves the credit for your accomplishments. Although they may transiently idealize you, they will turn on you and attack you when they find that you are no longer useful to them.

Senior management has a difficult choice when faced with a charismatic, technically skilled, grandiose manager who knows the industry and has connections. Such managers can do tremendous damage to the organization by driving away and failing to develop new leadership, diverting people's energies away from the work of the company, and making disastrous business decisions. Problematic traits are likely to worsen as the grandiose manager rises within the company and grows older. When faced with a decision about a grandiose manager's future, it is often best to consult an expert. If the grandiosity is primarily of the learned variety, a result of people failing for many years to give him negative feedback and insist on appropriate behavior, the grandiose manager can change with gentle but clear confrontation from those above him. If the grandiosity is based in early developmental problems, confrontation will primarily lead to rage.

Your Turn

- ◆ What grandiose managers have you dealt with?
- ◆ Give examples of their
  - • Grandiosity and preoccupation with themselves
  - • Arrogance and devaluation of others
  - • Sense of entitlement to whatever they wish
  - • Sensitivity to slights resulting in rage or desire for revenge
  - • Lack of attachment to values
- ◆ How did their behavior affect you?

Table 2-1 Overview of Grandiose Managers

Symptoms	Underlying Factors	Impact	Ways for Subordinates to Cope	Ways for Senior Management to Cope
Believe they are qualitatively better than normal mortals	Fragile self-esteem	Damage morale	Don't criticize them	Watch your back
	Lack of empathy	Damage retention	Show admiration	Don't ignore signs of trouble
Sense of entitlement to whatever they wish		Divert attention from the real work of the organization	Don't outshine them; play down your accomplishments and ambition	Don't believe them over subordinates
Devaluation of others			Document your work	Assess if the narcissism is learned or from early development and if it can be modified with the help of a therapist/coach
No attachment to values			Build relationship with a mentor	
No loyalty				
Envious			Keep your eyes open for other positions	Get them coaching
Prone to severe anger if grandiosity threatened			Do not take their behavior personally	Get 360-degree feedback on them and use it as a major part of their assessment

- ◆ How did their behavior affect others?
- ◆ How did their behavior affect productivity?
- ◆ How did their behavior affect communication?
- ◆ What did you and others do to cope?
- ◆ What worked, and what did not? (What made things better, and what made things worse?)
- ◆ What did you learn?
- ◆ How would you do things differently in the future?
- ◆ What advice would you give to someone facing a grandiose manager?
- ◆ Do you at times act in similar ways?
  - • How does it affect people?
  - • How does it affect your team?
  - • How does it affect your career?

Further Reading

Roy Lubit. The Long-Term Organizational Effects of Narcissistic Managers and Executives. *Academy of Management Executive,* Spring 2002. (Much of the material in this chapter first appeared in this article.)

The careers of Julius Caesar and General Douglas MacArthur provide wonderful examples of brilliant but grandiose leaders whose arrogance and hubris eventually became their undoing.

Citizen Kane provides a depiction in film.

Endnotes

1. B. O'Reilly. 29 May 1995. "Agee in Exile." *Fortune, 131*(10), 50–61.

2. J. Hopkins. 13 February 1995. "Morrison Knudsen fires its extravagant CEO." *USA Today,* p. 2B; M. Groves. 3 February 1995. "The Corporate Hero Derailed." *Los Angeles Times,* p. D1; "Chief exec gets red carpet as his company bleeds red ink." 26 March 1995. *Denver Rocky Mountain News,* p. 102A; J. Rigdon & J. Lublin. 13 February 1995. "Management: Call to duty: Why Morrison board fired Agee." *Wall Street Journal,* p. B1; O'Reilly, B.

29 May 1995. "Agee in Exile." *Fortune, 131*(10), 50–61.

3. B. O'Reilly. 29 May 1995. "Agee in Exile." *Fortune, 131*(10), 50–61.

4. B. Feder. "Agee Leaving Morrison Knudsen." *New York Times,* p. D1, 2 February 1995; B. O'Reilly. 29 May 1995. "Agee in Exile." *Fortune, 131*(10), 50–61.

5. M. Groves & J. Sanchez. 11 February 1995. "Morrison Knudsen Chief Agee Forced to Step Down." *Los Angeles Times,* p. D1; B. O'Reilly. "Agee in Exile." *Fortune, 131*(10), 50–61.

6. J. Hopkins. 21 February 1995. "EX-CEO surrounded himself with security." *USA Today.*

7. B. O'Reilly. "Agee in Exile." *Fortune, 131*(10), 50–61.

8. J. Rigdon. 2 February 1995. "William Agee will leave Morrison Knudsen." *Wall Street Journal,* p. B1; D. Henriques. 10 February 1995. "A Celebrity Boss Faces Exile From 2nd Corporate Kingdom." *New York Times,* p. A1; "Morrison Knudsen agrees to settle shareholder suits." 21 September 1995. *New York Times,* p. D4; B. O'Reilly. 29 May 1995. "Agee in Exile." *Fortune, 131*(10), 50–61; "Chief exec gets red carpet as his company bleeds red ink." 26 March 1995. *Denver Rocky Mountain News,* p. 102A.

CHAPTER 3

Control Freaks

You Will Do Absolutely Everything My Way

Control freaks are a strange mix of kindergarten teacher and drill sergeant. Working for a control freak is as close an experience as civilians get to being in boot camp. Boot camp, however, is normally over after a few weeks.

Control freaks watch every step you take, tell you how to take each step, and expect absolute obedience. Their micromanagement of you can feel quite oppressive and infantilizing. In part, they feel they know better than you how things should be done. In addition, they often fear that their world is on the verge of going out of control and that they can prevent this by micromanaging those around them. They also get a sense of power and satisfaction from being able to control their environment. Some control freaks feel that you are being insubordinate if you make a suggestion. For you to think of something that they did not think of is a narcissistic blow and leads to rage.

Control freaks, like all narcissistic managers, are arrogant and devalue others. They have limited empathy for others and feel entitled to control others. Underneath their external confidence is vulnerable self-esteem and fear of the world descending into chaos. They need extraordinary levels of control over the people around them in order to deal with their fears of the world being out of control and their underlying sense of themselves as being very weak and vulnerable. Complicating matters, they see things in black and white terms. There is no sliding scale of control over their world or of people's obedience. The world is either in control or out of control. Devaluing others, they cannot rely on others to do the right thing. Any objection to letting them guide your every step is experienced as a threat to their basic sense of security and self-esteem, is seen as gross insubordination, and leads to narcissistic rage. In a narcissistic rage they are likely to strike out at you in vicious ways and attempt to destroy your career. Underestimating their willingness to hurt you can be a career-ending error.

In general, control freaks engage in less self-aggrandizement than do grandiose individuals and make up for it by intensified control of those around them. They micromanage family and peers as well as subordinates. On the surface they may appear simply to be compulsive. However, they have different personality structures, present different dangers, and need different interventions.

Working for a control freak is painful for almost anyone. How painful depends not only on how extreme the control freak is, but on whether it pushes your personal buttons. If you grew up in a home that gave you plenty of freedom to explore and to do things your own way, you will probably be able to tolerate most control freaks. You won't enjoy it, but it won't be intolerable. If you had parents or older siblings who were invasive and controlling, however, being assigned to a boss who is a control freak will stir up memories you wanted to forget and leave you filled with a mix of rage and fear whenever the manager comes around.

Working for a control freak not only causes those subject to them considerable stress, but damages productivity in various ways. Working for a control freak leads people to put less energy into work in general and to invest their time and energy elsewhere. Control freaks also cripple the exchange of ideas and innovation. They fail to develop the leadership and initiative skills of their people, and the best people often leave. Tolerance of control freaks, failure to appreciate the degree of damage they can do, can be very costly to organizations.

A Control Freak

Serena ran a boutique marketing firm. Both her talent and her firm were well respected. She was also considered to be a bit controlling. When clients did not fully agree with her recommendations, she smiled patronizingly and assured them of her expertise. Some clients were uncomfortable with the degree to which she dominated decision making, but since she was very good, and they did not want to go elsewhere, they accepted her style.

In time, however, serious problems arose. Specifically, as online marketing grew, Serena paid little attention to it. Several of her clients began talking among themselves about the need for an online component to their marketing campaigns. They decided to meet together with Serena to ask if her firm could provide this service for them. Serena was very upset at this challenge to her independence and authority. She felt that people were treating her as if she were simply their inhouse vice president of marketing rather than the owner of an independent business. Nevertheless, she agreed to provide online campaigns when appropriate.

After this confrontation, Serena's personality seemed to change. She became even more rigid. She sent out a notice stating that only one company had really been concerned about online marketing. She forbade the number two person in her firm, Wendy, from speaking with any of the companies that had voiced concerns about her firm's lack of online capabilities. Serena also became very irritable. Whenever Wendy had a new idea for a client, Serena became angry and reminded Wendy of who was in charge. When Wendy called in one day with a high fever and wanted to miss a client meeting, Serena insisted that she come in regardless of her illness, since Serena had a personal errand to run.

Wendy suggested it was time for her to move on to another firm. Serena strongly urged Wendy to stay; she said that Wendy would learn more by staying with her and that she had greater long-term security where she was. Wendy therefore turned down another job opportunity. Then, late in the hiring season, Serena told Wendy it was time for her to move on. Being highly capable, Wendy found a position at the last minute. Before the contract was signed, however, the new company called Wendy in to tell her that although all of her clients had said great things about her, Serena had given a very negative report, which put hiring Wendy in question. Her being hired was delayed for so long that she had to take a different job that paid less and had fewer benefits.

Character Assassination

Karen and Robert represented two divisions within a large corporation that were trying to collaborate on a high-profile project. Success of the project would propel both of their careers. There would be plenty of credit to go around.

Robert had an MBA from a top program and was placed in the position of subject matter expert on the project. He was to devote half of his time to the project and half to various activities within his division. Karen, who did not have an MBA, was placed in a coordination role that was technically above Robert's on the project. They were supposed to act as equals and represent their divisions.

Problems began early as Karen attempted to micromanage Robert's schedule. She wanted to know two weeks in advance what he planned to do each day and eventually obtain an hour-by-hour report of how he spent his time. Karen spent more time trying to convince Robert to do this than on the real work of the project. One day she handed him a template to use to write down what he did each hour. Robert took it and said that he would need to show it to his superior. Karen ripped it out of his hand and animatedly asserted, "You're so reactive!" When Robert discussed the event with his superior, Ed, Ed said that of course Karen was upset—she knew that he would not approve. He, not Karen, was Robert's superior, and he did not want Robert to give this detailed description of his activities to Karen.

Over the weeks Robert proposed several ideas for collaboration. Many people in Karen's department liked the ideas, but Karen vetoed each one. She proposed no alternatives. When Robert suggested to some people in Karen's division that they speak with people in his division, they became nervous and said that Karen would be upset if they spoke directly rather than going through her.

One very unpleasant day, Robert found out that Karen had told his superiors that people generally disliked him and that this was preventing crucial collaboration from developing between their departments. Robert asked his superior to investigate the allegations, but his boss said that Karen was the person he needed to work with and what she thought was all that mattered. Robert, having learned that discretion was the better part of valor, accepted an offer to join another project.

Meanwhile, Robert wanted to understand what had happened and to clear his name as best he could. He learned that Karen had tried to find complaints about him. When people would tell her that they thought Robert was fine, she responded that she was surprised they felt that way, since others reported disliking him. In fact, she was the only one who seemed to dislike him. In talking to a number of people who worked closely with Karen, Robert found out that she was not liked, was considered abrasive, and was doing a poor job of organizing her end of things.

In part, Karen was scapegoating Robert to cover her own poor performance. This didn't explain everything, however, since the project would probably have gone well if she had been able to cooperate with Robert. Her need to be in control and her fury at his refusal to knuckle under led her to block cooperation in which he would not be under her control. If she had not been a control freak, she would not have needed to scapegoat him. In time Karen's mentor left the company, and people increasingly realized that she had scapegoated Robert and sabotaged the project. She was advised to find another position.

Emotional Intelligence Approach to Control Freaks

Dealing with Controlling Superiors

Working for a control freak is very stressful. The natural reaction to someone invasively micromanaging you is to become angry and push back. With a reasonable manager who slides into being excessively controlling when under pressure, tactfully pushing can be helpful. Pushing back on a control freak, however, leads to disaster unless you have a better position waiting or a very large trust fund. Control freaks are extraordinarily sensitive to any challenge to their authority and may become enraged simply in response to someone having the audacity to make a suggestion. You need to be careful with narcissistic managers. Most of us would not knowingly rattle a lion's cage when the door is open and there is nothing preventing him from jumping out and having us as his next snack. In the same way, it is not a good idea to push back on a control freak or on any narcissistic manager unless you have a guaranteed escape route and some powerful allies.

To survive working with a controlling boss, you need to exercise an unusual level of tact. Don't try to show the boss the error of his ways. Don't criticize him or her. Don't try to point out mistakes or examples of unfairness. Avoid one upmanship. All of these will lead to narcissistic rage and a blind desire to attack you. There is no chance that you will suddenly break through the psychological defenses of such managers and lead them to see the error of their ways. Above all, do not challenge their authority, power, or greatness. Rather, support their self-esteem. Show respect and even admiration for their accomplishments. Do not show off. Do not talk about your past accomplishments. Give them the credit for new accomplishments. Avoid direct suggestions; let them think that new ideas are actually theirs. Meanwhile, document your work, build relationships with mentors, and keep your eyes open for other positions.

Dealing with Controlling Peers

Control freaks are painful to deal with whether they are your superiors or your peers. Most people have the self-control to avoid the momentarily satisfying, but ultimately destructive, act of telling off a controlling superior. Few people, however, have equal restraints when dealing with a peer. Nevertheless, it can be risky to tell off a controlling peer in a harsh manner. Control freaks are narcissistic. When their self-esteem is threatened, as it would be if a colleague told them off, they are likely to respond with narcissistic rage. Their anger is so intense that their judgment collapses, and they are so intent on destroying you that they will take risky and even self-destructive steps to do so. They may not be able to fire you or put a damaging assessment in your file, but they can hurt you in other ways, including lying about you or sabotaging your work.

For HR and Senior Management

It is important for human resources and senior management to be aware of the potential damage that control freaks can do and to take steps to prevent it. Senior management must be alert to signs of trouble, such as a unit with a high attrition rate or frequent absenteeism. Complaints by subordinates should not be automatically written off or explained away by the alleged control freak. Subordinates' compaints should be listened to and investigated. Three hundred sixty-degree feedback is very valuable. People usually do not complain about a superior unless they are specifically asked and can expect anonymity.

If you find a controlling manager in your organization, you must take action to prevent him or her from causing damage. You should insist that he or she obtain executive coaching, and you should make behavior, measured by 360-degree feedback, a large part of his or her performance measurement system. In many cases it will benefit the company to move the person to a job in which he or she can do less harm or to simply fire the person.

Conclusion

Control freaks turn work into a nightmare. While grandiose managers seek your admiration and paranoid managers want you to give them enough information so that they can reassure themselves that you do not intend to hurt them, control freaks want to invasively micromanage all that you do. They combine the most difficult traits of compulsive managers with narcissistic ones. While most rigid managers want important things done their way and compulsive managers want most things done their way, control freaks want to prevent you from having any autonomy of action. They attempt to reinforce their self-esteem by devaluing people and by taking charge of everything.

Like all narcissistic individuals, control freaks are unlikely to undergo a major transformation in the way they interact with others. Unless you are unusually thick-skinned or have your own way of dealing with the pain of working for someone who is constantly infantilizing you and ignoring your desires, it is best to get away from these managers. Meanwhile, HR and senior management should be alert to the presence of such managers and make it clear that the company does not tolerate such behavior.

Table 3–1 Overview of Control Freaks

Symptoms	Underlying Factors	Impact	Ways for Subordinates to Cope	Ways for Senior Management to Cope
Insist on things being done their way	Devaluation of others	Damage morale	Avoid direct suggestions; let them think new ideas are their own	Be aware of the potential damage and take steps to prevent it
Micromanage	Desperate need to be in charge to maintain their self-esteem	Damage creativity and innovation	Don't criticize them	Don't ignore signs of trouble
Prone to severe anger if control threatened	Limited conscience and empathy	Fail to develop new people	Show admiration and respect	Get 360-degree feedback on them and use it as a major part of their assessment
Sense of entitlement to whatever they wish		Damage retention	Don't outshine them; play down your accomplishments and ambition	Don't believe them over subordinates
Devaluation of others			Document your work	Arrange for coaching
No loyalty			Build relationship with a mentor	Seriously consider removing them
Envious			Look for other positions	
			Do not take their behavior personally	

Your Turn

- ◆ What control freaks have you observed?
- ◆ Give examples of their controlling behavior?
- ◆ What other maladaptive behavior did they engage in?
- ◆ How did their behavior affect you?
- ◆ How did their behavior affect others?
- ◆ How did their behavior affect productivity?
- ◆ What did you and others do to cope?
- ◆ What worked, and what did not? (What made things better, and what made things worse?)
- ◆ What did you learn?
- ◆ How would you do things differently in the future?
- ◆ What advice would you give to someone facing a control freak?
- ◆ Do you at times act controlling?
  - • In what ways?
  - • How does it affect people?
  - • How does it affect your team?
  - • How does it affect your career?

CHAPTER 4

Paranoid Managers

They're Out to Get Me

Paranoid individuals are frightening. When you inconvenience them, they believe that you were consciously trying to hurt them, rather than that you were not adequately attentive to their preferences. Some may even believe you are evil and that your actions need to be stopped. If you harbor an uneasy feeling that paranoid managers could be violent, you are right. Although few paranoid managers become violent, of those managers who do, a significant percentage engage in paranoid thinking. Learning about paranoia is like wearing a safety belt. In all likelihood, you will be fine without it. But should there be a problem, it is much better if you are prepared.

Paranoia comes in two forms: paranoid personality disorder and paranoid delusions. People with a paranoid personality disorder tend to interpret malevolent motives in your actions and to read any ambiguity of information as fitting into their preconceived belief not only that the world is dangerous, but that there are people intent on harming them. Seeing the world as dangerous, they maintain a state of constant tension and hyperalertness in order to avoid surprise. Feeling continuously threatened, paranoid individuals are at risk for striking out at someone. They tend to be hostile, sarcastic, secretive, argumentative, envious, and hypersensitive to slights. They may be shy and retiring or arrogant, aggressive and megalomaniacal. Very uncomfortable in dealing with people of higher status, they get along best with people who are compliant and dependent.

Paranoid Personality Traits ━━━━━━━━━━━━━━━━━━━

◆ Harbors unreasonable suspicions that people are exploiting, harming, or deceiving him.

◆ Preoccupied with unjustified doubts about people's loyalty, including spouse, friends, and colleagues.

◆ Reluctant to confide in others out of unjustified fear that the information will be used against him.

◆ Reads hidden demeaning or threatening meanings into benign remarks or events.

◆ Persistently bears grudges.

◆ Perceives attacks on his character or reputation that are not apparent to others and is quick to react angrily or to counterattack.

A paranoid delusion is a fixed false belief, not susceptible to logical arguments, that someone is trying to harm you or your interests. For example, if papers are missing, rather than believing they were misplaced, the paranoid individual will assume someone took them. Similarly, failure to give support is interpreted as an attempt to undermine and destroy the paranoid individual rather than as simply not having the time or energy to render help. The belief is a delusion if the individual is certain that it is true even though rational assessment supports other possibilities. Common paranoid delusions include being pursued by law enforcement agencies or by organized crime. There is often a grandiose component to paranoid individuals' thinking—they believe that they are special in some way, will have a great impact on the world, and will become famous. Paranoid delusions may be chronic or may come and go. An individual could be acting in a normal range and then, as a result of drugs, medical problems, bipolar disorder, or atypical psychosis, become paranoid.

Origins of Paranoia

Paranoid individuals externalize all blame for problems and failures. "It is their fault, not mine; I did not fail, they undermined me." As a result, instead of being upset with themselves for being weak and failing, they are angry with the world for trying to hurt them.

The underlying problem for some paranoid individuals is fragile self-esteem and an inner world filled with anger and negative self-images. Since they have such negative images of themselves, they assume others must as well. To protect their fragile self-esteem, they bury their self-doubts and negative self-images and replace them with arrogance. They are left with the belief that others are out to hurt them. This belief explains their failures, without damaging their self-esteem, and justifies their anger.

An abusive childhood provides fertile soil for a paranoid personality disorder. First, it provides a model for viewing the world. If your parents are abusive, can you really trust anyone in life? If the people who are nice and caring to you one minute abuse you the next, then you cannot trust anyone. Second, you need to constantly scan your environment for dangers. It is better to err on the side of reading danger when there is none, since there are many dangers, and if you miss one, you will be seriously hurt. Third, early abuse fills you with a sense of fragility. If your parents abused you, you must be pretty bad. Fourth, the abuse stirs great anger that you must hide. If the anger came out, it would place you in danger of attack by people more powerful than you.

Certain cultures and families are more likely than others to promote paranoid styles. Cultures in which blaming others (*externalization*) is common are likely to foster paranoia. Parents who teach their children that the outside world, rather than they themselves, is responsible for their failures are setting their children up to see the world as dangerous and destructive, and to blame others for their problems. If someone is not nice to you, and your parents say it is because they dislike you or are jealous of you, rather than simply acknowledging that people sometimes are not courteous, you are being taught to have a paranoid view of the world.

Defense Mechanisms ━━━━━━━━━━━━━━━━━━━━━━━━

Classical interpretations state that paranoia arises from a defense mechanism called *projection* in which people believe that feelings and impulses which they have are held by others, and deny that they themselves have those feelings.

Defense mechanisms are ways that we deal with painful feelings. For example, people who are very angry with their boss can do several things. Some people use the energy to work hard to impress the boss, or may vow to never treat people as their boss treats them (*sublimation*). Other people are uncomfortable with feeling angry; fearing that their anger will slip out and the boss will then really turn against them. They try to block the feeling from their mind. If they do this consciously it is called *suppression*. If it happens outside of the person's awareness it is called *repression*. Sometimes the anger is redirected (*displaced*) toward someone who cannot retaliate, such as a subordinate or family member.

In projection, people feel that others have the feelings, impulses, or desires that they themselves actually have (and are trying to deny having). Feeling angry and perhaps wanting to attack someone, they believe it is the other person who in fact wants to hurt them: "I am not angry with *him*; he wants to hurt *me*."

Depression can markedly exacerbate paranoid feelings. If we are depressed and have a negative self-image, we are likely to believe that others will feel the same way about us. It is important to know if a paranoid person is depressed, since if depression is present and treated, the person's condition may significantly improve. Moreover, depressed paranoid individuals can be dangerous.

Impact of Paranoid Managers

People with severe paranoid personality disorders have great difficulty in dealing with people and are unlikely to rise within an organization. A paranoid entrepreneur could, however, begin his own company and grow it. Moreover, an individual with mild paranoid traits could do reasonably well and then over time become increasingly paranoid, isolated, and potentially dangerous.

Paranoid managers interfere with the work of organizations in several ways. First, their attention and energy are focused on protecting themselves and asserting control, not on getting the job done. Second, they divert people's energies from the work they are supposed to be doing. Their anger and distortion of what they hear and see preoccupy others. Moreover, it is difficult to focus on productivity when dealing with an individual who threatens our psychological, emotional, and possibly physical well-being. Fear for your physical safety places you in a very different ball game than does dealing with difficult managers who may be upset with you but would never pose a threat to your personal safety. Third, they hamper communication by not sharing information which leads others to withhold information as well. Never knowing who is close to the paranoid manager and who is not, and never knowing how information may be used to hurt you, people in general cease sharing information. Moreover, no one wants to be the bearer of bad news to a paranoid individual. At the least, you will witness a tantrum. Very likely, you will be blamed. As a result, information ceases flowing.

Case Study: A Paranoid Manager ▬▬▬▬▬▬▬▬▬▬

Coworkers described Jake as a private person. Quiet and serious, he was always a bit distant, a bit isolated. He never spoke about friends or family. Marrying later in life, he had no children. Those who did not know him well sometimes thought that he was simply a tough businessperson who kept his cards close to his chest and focused overwhelmingly on work to the exclusion of friends and play. Those closer to him realized that work filled a gap in his life that was left by his inability to be comfortable with people.

Jake had initially worked in accounting, which provided a sheltered place with limited interaction with others. As he continued in the company and gained a combination of seniority and skill, he moved upward and was forced to have increasing managerial responsibilities within his department as well as interaction with other departments. With this, his paranoid traits began to come out. He was generally very uncomfortable in dealing with people. He had a tendency to question others' motives and loyalty. He often read between the lines of statements and found negative hidden meanings. He interpreted people as being critical or giving him a jab when no attack was meant. When superiors, or worse yet, subordinates, asked benign questions about projects, he often felt they were being critical of his work, and he responded defensively. He rarely confided in or trusted people, so there was no one he could bounce his fears off of or obtain reassurance from.

These traits placed a clear roadblock to any further significant promotion. When Jake was not promoted as quickly as he expected, and his evaluations noted his problems in dealing with people, his belief that there were people in the company who disliked him and were undermining his advancement solidified.

As Jake's paranoia grew, his wife became increasingly distant. He began to fear that she was having an affair. Her annoyance when defending herself and rejecting his assertions only made him more suspicious of her.

With the pace of his downhill slide escalating, the company asked Jake to have a psychiatric evaluation. He refused. He was now certain that they were trying to get rid of him. He believed that the psychiatric evaluation was requested only so that the company could gather ammunition to fire him. He made some veiled comments to a few people that he was going to see to it that the people who had sabotaged him were sorry.

Jake's skills and knowledge had become very valuable to the company. No one wanted to let him go, at least not yet. A forensic psychiatrist specializing in threat assessment was called in to evaluate the potential danger. He noted that whatever danger they now faced from Jake, firing him would only serve to exacerbate the danger. The company decided to monitor the situation and gently encourage treatment for stress. A man Jake trusted more than most was given the assignment of regularly checking in with him, reassuring him about his worries of being sabotaged and threatened, and keeping an eye on any development of symptoms that would indicate an increase in dangerousness. Meanwhile, Jake agreed to participate in a stress management program, including individual sessions with a psychologist who was aware of Jake's history and fears.

These interventions helped stabilize Jake's condition. The regular contact and reassurance from these people led his paranoia to decrease, and his relations with people improved. In time he was willing to try medication and was referred to a psychiatrist. Medication proved helpful in decreasing his paranoia and depression.

Not all paranoid-sounding fears are inaccurate. First, many people are out to get each other in organizations. Moreover, just because a manager is paranoid does not guarantee that someone is not out to get him. Paranoid individuals irritate others and lead many to think that the organization would benefit from the paranoid manager's retirement. It is important to evaluate if a paranoid-sounding fear might be true, particularly if it is the only significant indication of paranoia. The manager might need concrete assistance rather than observation. When I was in medical school, I was told of a patient on the psychiatric ward at Bellevue who claimed that he was of European noble stock and had been abducted, placed in a large suitcase, and flown across the Atlantic so that his relatives could steal his inheritance. The story turned out to be true.

Emotional Intelligence Approach to Paranoid Managers

Dealing with Paranoid Bosses

Being around someone who does not trust you, who regularly reads malicious intent into your actions, and who bears grudges is very stressful. Withdrawing or attacking, however, will fuel such a person's suspiciousness and make matters worse. Dealing with a paranoid boss requires considerable personal competence.

There are several key guidelines to keep in mind when dealing with paranoid people. First, you do not want to appear aggressive or threatening. It is not advisable to threaten to cut them down to size if they continue to behave in problematic ways. Doing so will increase their paranoia about you and could provoke an attack.

Second, you do not want to acquiesce to a paranoid individual's attacks lest it encourage him to keep coming after you. If you present yourself as a safe place to vent his aggression, he will use you as a target. Let him know that you hear his fears and that you are not against him and have no intention to hurt him. Avoid getting into arguments, since it will only heighten tensions. Moreover, if he thinks he has caught you in a contradiction, it will increase his paranoia.

Third, to decrease an individual's paranoia, it helps to overcommunicate. Transparency decreases paranoia. Give him ample information about what you are doing. In particular, you never want to surprise him. When communicating with him, send both voice and emails informing him of your activities and asking for input. Then, save your emails so that if he claims you did not inform him, you can show that you did.

Ultimately, unless there are strong reasons to stay, it is better to transfer to another position.

For HR and Senior Management

Your choices when dealing with a paranoid manager are to ignore the problem, monitor the problem, try to fix the problem, or get rid of the problematic person. The best choice depends upon how severe the paranoia is, the degree to which it interferes with work and retention of people, the likelihood of the person engaging in successful treatment, the risk of the problem worsening and violence occurring, whether firing the person would increase or decrease the risk of violence, and how valuable the person is to the company. A history of violence at any time in the person's life is cause for great concern and indicates a markedly increased risk of violence.

Paranoid individuals are among the potentially most dangerous people, since they view the world as hostile and threatening at the same time that they maintain the capacity for planned action. Deciding what to do is often difficult, and you will generally benefit from consulting a professional threat assessor or forensic psychiatrist/psychologist. The decision to remove someone in order to increase safety is particularly difficult, since the stress of being fired could push a paranoid manager over the edge and lead to violence that would not otherwise have occurred. Removing someone should be done very carefully. The more the person is treated with respect and the less they experience rejection and humiliation in the process of being transferred or fired, the better you will sleep at night.

Treating paranoid managers is always difficult and sometimes impossible. It is very hard for paranoid individuals to trust a therapist in more than a superficial way. In addition, their problems are deep-seated and slow to change at best. In addition to encouraging therapy, it is sometimes helpful to arrange for monitoring of their functioning, an early warning system to detect if they are becoming dangerous. For example, if there is someone in the company the paranoid person likes talking to, that person can establish regular contact with the paranoid manager and report on any significant deterioration in functioning such as increased isolation, fear, anger, and aggressive rumination and planning.

It is also important to consider if depression or drugs are contributing to the paranoia. If one of these is a large part of the problem, treating it could lead to rapid improvement.

Table 4-1 Dealing with Paranoid Managers

Symptoms	Underlying Factors	Impact	Ways for Subordinates to Cope	Ways for Senior Management to Cope
Unreasonably suspicious	Fragile self-esteem	Limited ability to cooperate with others	Avoid any actions that could raise suspicions	Keep an eye on the person's anger, depression, and increased paranoia, which signal a risk of violence
Questions loyalty of associates	Anger	Threat of assaults	Give plenty of information on activities	
Hesitant to confide in anyone lest it be used against him	Depression and negative self-image	Damages morale	Seriously consider a transfer	Consider encouraging them to leave
Sees hidden meanings in events and actions	Tendency to use externalization and projection to handle inner conflict			Avoid embarrassing or demeaning them
Perceives attacks on reputation that others do not see				Avoid letting this person become key to your functioning
Bears grudges				

Conclusion

Believing that the world is out to get them, paranoid individuals are potentially violent, especially if they become depressed. A high percentage of organizational violence is perpetrated by depressed paranoid individuals. Once a paranoid individual has significant symptoms that are impairing work or home life, professional assistance is necessary to deal with the risk of further deterioration of his condition as well as the risk of violence or other destructive behavior. Paranoid individuals do not ask for help. Someone needs to reach out to them and insist that they get help. After violence occurs, people often comment that they knew something was seriously wrong. Cultures in which people are willing to speak up and share information when someone is doing poorly are at less risk for violence than ones in which people leave each other alone.

Your Turn

- What paranoid managers have you observed?
- Give examples of their
  - Suspiciousness that others are hurting them
  - Preoccupation with doubts about others' loyalty
  - Reluctance to confide in others lest the information be used against them
  - Tendency to read hidden, demeaning, or threatening meanings into benign remarks or events
  - Tendency to bear grudges
  - Perceiving attacks on his or her character or reputation that are not apparent to others
  - Tendency to react with anger
- How did this behavior affect you and others?
- How did this behavior affect productivity?
- How did this behavior affect communication?
- What did you and others do to cope?
- What worked, and what did not? (What made things better, and what made things worse?)
- What did you learn?

- How would you do things differently in the future?
- What advice would you give to someone facing a paranoid manager?
- Do you at times act in similar ways?
  - How does it affect people?
  - How does it affect your team?
  - How does it affect your career?

Further Reading

David Shapiro. *Neurotic Styles*. Basic Books, 1972.

The captain in *The Caine Mutiny* provides a good depiction of a paranoid manager.

PART II

UNETHICAL MANAGERS

Rules Are Made to Be Broken

Unethical behavior is a serious problem in business as well as in most professions. It damages the company's reputation, damages morale, interferes with hiring the best people, and as we saw with Enron, Arthur Anderson, and Worldcom, can bring down a company.

There are a wide number of unethical behaviors that some managers engage in at work.

Pad expense accounts
Engage in creative accounting
Accept or give bribes/kickbacks
Cut corners on safety
Cut corners on quality control
Lie to customers
Price fix
Sell or steal trade secrets
Call in sick when well
Destroy incriminating documents
Engage in character assassination
Discriminate
Steal

Falsify accounting reports
Have sex to make a sale
Ignore violation of environmental
regulations
Cover up incidents
Make promises they cannot keep
Overbill
Engage in insider trading
Forge signatures
Lie on resumes
Steal credit
Bully, intimidate, sexually harass

Some of these are common practices. Others are eschewed by the great majority of people. All of those mentioned here create a cost to the companies that tolerate them or fail to find them. Enron and Arthur Anderson have been devastated by major improprieties. *The New York Times* suffered significant loss in prestige and trust because of the actions of one reporter and the failure of the company to adequately monitor and intervene.

Profits are a necessary part of economic life in a market economy. They are not, however, the heart and soul of all companies. Many companies, like people, seek to do something socially useful at the same time that they need to be economically solvent. The vision statements of great companies and the dreams of those who run them are usually not to make as much money as possible. Walt Disney seeks to "bring joy to millions." Sony sought to elevate the Japanese culture and national spirit, and experience the joy that comes from the advancement, application, and innovation of technology that benefits the general public. Hewlett-Packard seeks to make a contribution to fields in which it participates. Johnson and Johnson's vision is "to alleviate pain and disease."

Despite the visions that great companies espouse, those who work for them often slide into unethical behavior. It is not because the visions were publicity stunts. It is because under the pressures and stresses of organizational life, the things that need to be done to implement the visions are often not adequately attended to. Companies often do not pay enough attention to ethical issues when hiring, promoting, training, culture building, and measuring and rewarding behavior. Moreover, under the pressure of organizational life, seeing others break rules, and having the desire to move up and to take care of one's family's financial needs, otherwise ethical people may engage in significant improprieties. Moreover, those who lack ethical scruples, and whose conscience reminds you of a piece of Swiss cheese, can have a field day in organizations. Understanding what is driving unethical behavior is very important. With a better understanding of what motivates different kinds of unethical managers, companies can more effectively screen for them and train people to avoid such behavior.

There is a spectrum of people who engage in serious rule breaking or antisocial action. At one extreme are people who frequently lie, deceive, misappropriate funds, and commit larceny. At the other extreme are people who obey and almost always follow the rule of law and ethical standards. In between are people who go along with the culture of the organization they are in: If others are cheating on their expense accounts, they will. If others are not cheating, they will not. If others are sexually coercing women, they will join in.

Part II Overview

The chapters in Part II discuss the factors underlying unethical behavior, describe how these managers see the world and what guides their behavior, and provide information on how to most effectively deal with them and protect yourself. While antisocial managers lack a conscience and break rules both whenever convenient and simply for the thrill of ignoring societal edicts, opportunists primarily ignore ethical rules when they are under great pressure to achieve a goal and the rule is in the way.

- ◆ Chapter 5—Antisocial Managers: Breaking Rules Is Fun
- ◆ Chapter 6—Unethical Opportunists: I Have to Break This Rule

CHAPTER 5

Antisocial Managers

Breaking Rules Is Fun

Antisocial managers manipulate others and break rules because it provides a thrill, and not simply to attain concrete goals. Some find a sense of satisfaction in getting away with something. Some enjoy the act of hurting others. They all lack respect for the rights of others and have no empathy for the distress of others.

Antisocial individuals lack a conscience—what psychiatrists call a superego—and are therefore not constrained by normal inhibitions on acceptable behavior. They are relatively immune to guilt, remorse, and anxiety, although they may become anxious if they are about to be caught. Once caught, they blame others, make excuses, and feel no true remorse, although they may be sufficiently aware of normal social expectations that they will claim to be remorseful.

It is very hard for most of us to understand antisocial individuals. They relate in very different ways than most of us do. They lack real connections to people and empathy for other people. A particularly striking part of their emotional experience and presentation is their relative immunity to guilt, remorse, depression, and anxiety. They do not feel others' pain. They avoid responsibility for problems they cause and externalize all blame. They will explain why their girlfriend or wife deserves to be beaten or a company deserves to be robbed. They are glib, insincere, and unreliable. They are willing to exploit others and are very successful at convincing others that they are far more capable than they are and infinitely more truthful than they are.

Antisocial managers have remarkable talent for convincing others of their abilities, stealing credit from others, and being hired or promoted into positions they do not have the skills to perform. Part of the reason is the tremendous value businesses place on the presentation that aggressively narcissistic (antisocial) managers are able to provide. Their high levels of confidence, glibness, and even their ruthlessness are seen as unadulterated positives rather than as signs of potentially serious problems lying under the surface.

There are several reasons why someone may have a weak conscience or a conscience filled with holes that allows them to do things most people feel are wrong. Antisocial managers fail to internalize basic moral values concerning honesty and respect for the rights of others. Several things can get in the way. First, feeling that they are so special that the rules do not apply to them, antisocial individuals may never internalize their parents' rules for appropriate moral behavior. Alternatively, their parents or peers may not have valued honesty, so they never did. Another possibility is that they felt the world treated them unfairly, so they did not need to follow its rules and could take whatever they wanted, since they deserved it as compensation for having been wronged. Many children who were abused or who witnessed domestic violence later engage in antisocial behavior. It is also likely that antisocial individuals are born with different predispositions to form true attachments to others and to empathize with others. Those at the extreme end of the spectrum have little ability to empathize and therefore lack inhibitions on hurting and using others.

Some of the most puzzling examples of antisocial behavior involve highly successful, wealthy people who risk—and lose—their reputation, freedom, and considerable money for the sake of a few dollars that could never have made a difference in their lives. It is as if they do it for the sport, or because they feel that they are better than others and want to prove that the rules do not apply to them. In part, their grandiosity leads them to think that they can get away with disregarding societal rules. In addition, many of these people get high on the challenge of beating the system and winning money. Some people gamble at the race track, some in casinos, and some in their offices.

Manipulation is a game and a challenge to antisocial managers as well as a way to increase their power. They say negative things about those they work with and turn managers against each other. They use deceit to separate people, prevent them from working together, and thereby make themselves that much more crucial to the organization's functioning, since only they can forge the links necessary for communication and cooperative work. Antisocial managers also wish to separate people so that they do not come together and find out about their manipulations.

How these managers survive and flourish may seem puzzling. Their willingness to lie and their facility at confabulation allows them to play whatever role appeals to superiors. Their skill at manipulating, and co-opting, people enables them to gain the information needed to know just what to say. It also enables them to separate people who could pool their knowledge and realize that they are dishonest and a chronic cause of problems.

A crucial factor that contributes to the rise of an antisocial manager is that companies are often looking for managers who have external characteristics similar to those of antisocial managers. Their extreme confidence can be confused with competence. Their superficial charm and glibness are often seen as valuable skills for dealing with customers. Their aggression can be seen as ambition. Particularly important, once we have a favorable view of someone, we are willing to reinterpret or excuse negative characteristics and to overlook the need for substance and honesty. As a result, antisocial managers dot the organizational landscape and are landmines waiting to explode.

Aggressive Manipulation

George was just what the company was looking for to fill an open slot. He was not only personable, bright, high-energy, and well-spoken, but his resume seemed to have been designed for this position. (In fact, his resume *was* fabricated to fit the position.)

Once hired, he knew how to manipulate the system and play people against one another. He ingratiated himself to the CEO's assistant and his division director's assistant. Attention, flattery, promises to say wonderful things about them, and offers to eventually hire them into managerial positions were quite effective in forging bonds. In time they began telling others of George's wonderful accomplishments and told George of their bosses' interests, hobbies, and plans. He used this information to gain access to these executives and to then tell them of his ideas and interests (remarkably akin to theirs) and to steal credit for work his boss was doing.

George supported (or started) negative rumors about any managers he saw as a potential threat, particularly his current superior. To keep managers who might join forces against him from speaking to each other and joining forces, he passed along information leading each to be wary of the other.

His connections to the top made people hesitant to say anything negative about him and therefore blocked sharing and corroboration of observations that he was deceitful and manipulative. Initially amenable and ingratiating with his boss, as his connections grew with the level above, and he was successful in undermining his boss's reputation, George dropped the pretense of respect and ignored his superior's directives. His temper outbursts, always an issue, increased significantly. Whenever confronted with a problem in his work, he would strike back, blaming someone else or denying that there was any problem. By the time he had worked for the company for a few months, people on his level and under him were well aware of his grandiose self-image, bragging, taking credit for others' work, lying about his accomplishments, avoidance of any shred of responsibility when things did not go well, lack of fairness, misuse of company property, and tirades. By the time his boss realized that a disaster was unfolding, it was too late. He went to the division director, but George had already successfully undermined his boss's position. The director refused to fire George. George meanwhile asked for a transfer to a new position and received it. He came into the new spot with a reputation of being a favorite of the top brass and no one was willing to jeopardize their position by passing on the truth about him.

Emotional Intelligence Approach to Antisocial Managers

Robert Hare, perhaps *the* expert on antisocial behavior, makes a number of suggestions for what to do when confronted with a psychopath.

1. Know with whom you are dealing and respect their power. Appreciating that such people exist and are remarkably able to manipulate others is your first line of defense.

2. Try not to be overly impressed or blinded by people with a captivating presence. Try not to let yourself be taken in by their superficial warmth, charm, fascinating stories, intoxicating self-confidence, and promises. Moreover, avoid the overly intense, emotionless eye contact that can intimidate and transfix. People who seem too good to be true probably are.

3. Push for more detailed information and check the information they give you. If they are evasive and vague in response to attempts to find out about them, your radar should sound increasingly loudly.

4. Share information with people. Don't keep information to yourself out of embarrassment.

5. When you start worrying, keep worrying, and gather more information. If you walk out of a confrontation feeling that the other person is the victim, you are likely dealing with a skilled psychopath.

6. Avoid power struggles, since ruthless people unencumbered by normal inhibitions and empathy can be very dangerous. Just get away. Don't expect them to change.

7. If at all unsure, obtain professional consultation from someone skilled in dealing with antisocial managers. This does not mean that you should get them a therapist. Antisocial managers are very unlikely to improve in a positive way in therapy. They are more likely to use the experience to develop even better tools for manipulating people.

Dealing with Antisocial Superiors

Antisocial superiors are particularly dangerous. They will want you to engage in ethical and perhaps legal violations. If you refuse to go along, they may well turn on you and set you up. Even if they do not, they are unlikely to be fair to you. They are likely to resent your having ethical standards and to hold it against you.

They are also likely to self-destruct at some point, and when they do, they are likely to drag you down either through simple association or by implicating or blaming you for things they did. The bottom line is simple: Get away from them. If not, you will soon be confronted with a situation in which you are under pressure to do something unethical. Saying that your superior told you to do something is no excuse. At the least, do not become drawn into illegal activities or violation of company policy. You do not want to go to jail along with your manager. He or she won't be good company. As always, document what you know and talk to a mentor. You will need support.

Dealing with Antisocial Peers

In dealing with antisocial peers, as with antisocial superiors, the first rule is to not be dragged into their spider's web and become an accomplice. Also as with superiors, you should avoid provoking them or giving them ammunition against you until you are ready to go to war by exposing them. If they realize you are potentially threatening to them, they may launch a preemptive attack. You need to maintain your distance. If you cannot, you should leave the group or expose them. It is generally good to keep a record of what they did and what you did in preparation for this.

When they try to drag you into something unethical, the responsible move is to ask your boss if this is the way he or she wants things done. If the boss does, it is clearly time to leave this group. If not, you will now be a target for the antisocial peer's anger. Be very careful.

Dealing with Antisocial Subordinates

If you find an antisocial subordinate, it is best to help him or her find another job in another industry. This is obviously easier said than done. You don't want to send the person to a competitor if he has gathered proprietary information. You also do not want to keep the person and have him gather more and more proprietary information. He can bring you, your group, and your company down through serious ethical, and perhaps legal, violations.

Trying to reform someone with an antisocial personality disorder will be an exercise in futility. Antisocial individuals are very unlikely to cease their unethical behavior and turn over a new leaf. They may constrain themselves for a while, but it is not likely to last. Therapy is more likely to teach them how to be even more effective at fooling people than to convince them to reform.

For HR and Senior Management: Keeping the Barbarians Outside the Gates

There is a great deal that companies can do to avoid hiring and promoting antisocial managers. There are three key elements: be aware of the warning signs, pay attention to them, and diligently look into situations that present warning signs.

We often ignore or make excuses when we see warning signs. For example, we often ignore complaints by subordinates about superiors. It is subordinates who are likely to see the first signs of antisocial behavior. We often ignore a manager's willingness to bend rules until they break. Sometimes we ignore it because it is easier, and sometimes because we do not want to be in trouble ourselves for having let the rules be broken. We also often ignore the signs of antisocial behavior because they remind us of some of our own behavior or because we equate high confidence with capability rather than grandiosity.

The easiest place to guard the walls from grandiose and antisocial managers is by screening for them before they are hired. Behavioral Event Interviewing is a good way to begin the screening process. Ask applicants to talk about a time when things went well and a time when things did not go well. As they answer these questions, pay attention to what they thought the key factors for success and failure were. Do they keep all credit for themselves, or share it with others? Do they go on and on about how extraordinary they were? Do they pride themselves on having manipulated or used others, or on having beaten the rules? You can also ask applicants to describe situations in which they demonstrated various values that are crucial to the job you are considering them for. For example, ask them to describe situations in which they demonstrated leadership and teamwork or in which they developed others and dealt with problems in subordinates' behavior. Note whether they attempt to blame others for problems or take responsibility themselves. Do they show respect or disrespect for others?

You can also ask about managers/leaders whom they admired and why; managers whom they did disliked and why. Ask about examples of tough and of abusive managers they observed. How did they react, and why? Ask about managers who pushed the boundaries of the rules. What did they think about it? What did they do?

You can also ask about their weaknesses, worst mistakes, what people have complained about in them, things they feel guilty about having done, and what they want to change about themselves. Present ethical dilemmas and ask what they would do.

As they talk about life both at work and outside of work, look for signs of impulsivity, recklessness, and deceitful behavior. Pay attention to whether they value or devalue others, if they value or devalue honesty, whether they show concern and respect for others or if they focus on their own needs and desire for glory, and if they are able to feel remorse and guilt. Often, people are more willing to talk about reckless, impulsive, or bullying behavior during their childhood years, thinking that it is acceptable.

When you see warning signs, it is time to look further. You should do background checks, including speaking with people they worked with and people they noted in their discussions of their work to see if they described situations accurately and took only the credit that belonged to them. You can also check military, legal, work, and school records. The extent of the investigation should be governed by the importance of the position they are applying for and by the degree of suspicion of a problem raised by interviews.

The Hare Psychopathy Checklist Screening Version (Table 5–1) is a useful tool for beginning the process of weeding out antisocial managers before they wreak havoc with your business. The checklist consists of 12 items divided into two categories: psychopathic personality characteristics and social deviant behavior. These are things to look for as you review their history and behavior.

Table 5–1 Hare Psycholopathy Checklist Screening Version

Psychopathic Personality Characteristics	Social Deviant Behavior
Superficial	Impulsive
Grandiose	Poor behavior controls (inappropriate, angry outbursts; sexual inappropriateness)
Manipulative	Lacks goals
Lacks remorse	Irresponsible
Lacks empathy	Adolescent antisocial behavior (violations of others' rights, such as robbery, assault, property destruction)
Does not accept responsibility	Adult antisocial behavior (violations of others' rights, such as robbery, assault, property destruction)

Conclusion

Antisocial managers are not only the most dangerous people you will confront at work, but they are likely to win your confidence and esteem prior to putting a knife into your back. Their charisma and ability to be chameleons, promising you just what you want prior to turning on you makes them remarkably dangerous. Like all narcissistic individuals they lack a conscience and empathy for others. Making them even more dangerous is that many get high on abusing other people and the system. They are often primarily driven by the challenge of beating the system and not simply by attaining a particular goal, such as promotion. They push the limits for the sake of pushing the limits, and go beyond the limits simply to prove they can get away with it. In the process, they not only hurt individuals but can bring the company down.

The best way to protect yourself from antisocial managers is to avoid hiring them. You want bright, eloquent, personable people in your company. You do not want glib, manipulative ones. It is important to not confuse the two and to be wary when potential hires look too good to be true. They may well be antisocial managers.

The boundary lines separating grandiose managers from antisocial managers from bullies are not exact. There is tremendous overlap between the categories. Trying to fit a given manager into the exact best category is not crucial. What is crucial is seeing the signs of antisocial traits (see Table 5–2) as early as possible and protecting yourself and others before great damage is done. If you find one in your work group, get rid of him if he is your subordinate, leave if he is your superior, and avoid him if he is your peer.

Your Turn

- ◆ What antisocial managers have you dealt with?
- ◆ Give examples of their
  - • Unethical behavior
  - • Illegal behavior
  - • Manipulation
  - • Deceitfulness
  - • Exploitation
  - • Glibness
  - • Impulsiveness
  - • Irresponsibility
  - • Aggression

Table 5–2 Overview of Antisocial Managers

Symptoms	Underlying Factors	Impact	Ways for Subordinates to Cope	Ways for Senior Management to Cope
Glib	Likes to break rules	Puts organization at risk	Avoid provoking them	Get rid of them
Manipulative	Lacks normal inhibitions	Destroys morale	Transfer out before they destroy you	Damage control— review their actions and make amends to staff, customers, and legal authorities
Deceitful	Devalues people		Do not get dragged into their unethical/illegal activities	
Impulsive	Lacks empathy			
Irresponsible			Seek allies in coworkers and mentors	Be careful in hiring and promoting, and support a culture valuing ethical behavior
Inappropriate, angry outbursts			Seek executive coach to help you cope	Check on accuracy of resumes
Sexual inappropriateness				
Does not accept responsibility				
Exploits people without hesitancy or remorse				

- ◆ How were they able to fool people?
- ◆ What warnings signs were ignored and why?
- ◆ How did their behavior affect you?
- ◆ How did their behavior affect others?
- ◆ How did their behavior affect the company?
- ◆ What did you and others try to do to cope? What worked, and what did not?
- ◆ What did you learn? How would you do things differently in the future?
- ◆ What advice would you give to someone facing an antisocial manager?
- ◆ What advice would you give to someone facing an antisocial subordinate?
- ◆ Do you ever act in similar ways?
  - • How does it affect people?
  - • How does it affect your team?
  - • How does it affect your career?

Further Reading

Robert Hare. *Without Conscience*. Simon and Schuster, 1993.

Robert Hare. *The Hare Psychopathy Checklist: Screening Version (PCL:SV)*. Multi-Health Systems Press.

Brian Rosner. *Swindle*. Business One Irwin, 1990.

D. Cooke and C. Mechie. "Refining the Construct of Psychopathy: Towards a Hierarchical Model." *Psychological Assessment,* 13: 171–188, 2001.

The movie *Body Heat* provides an example of antisocial personality disorder.

CHAPTER 6

Unethical Opportunists

I Have to Break This Rule

Many managers who engage in unethical activities would be shocked to hear that you think they are unethical. (Actually, perhaps you don't think they are. Hopefully, this chapter will encourage you to reconsider.) Most people who periodically engage in unethical behavior consider themselves relatively ethical people who are only doing what others are doing. They see themselves as upstanding members of the community who generally obey the rules, and they see their stepping over the line as either trivial or expected and sanctioned by those in authority. A devoted family man might condone creative accountancy at work, or a famous woman might evade taxes.

So what happens? Why do generally honest people who condemn law-breaking by others do things that many consider unethical? Part of the issue is the power of group pressure. People are very affected by their culture. People take their cues about what is right and wrong from those around them as well as from what they learned over the course of their lives. Our conscience is soluble in groups, just as it is in alcohol. If everyone else is doing it, or if a boss orders it, people feel that the responsibility is not theirs and they are not culpable.

A second group of unethical opportunists has been taught from child-hood that it is acceptable to cheat on taxes or pad expense accounts by a few dollars. This is just the way things are done. Their parents did it, their parents' friends did it, and they assumed everyone does it. Moreover, they hear about the corruption in Washington and among the most powerful in corporate America. This is the way the world works, and only a fool or a chump would choose to follow rules no one else follows.

A third group of people are those who generally obey all the rules but can be pulled into unethical behavior bit by bit if under enough pressure. Crisis in their business or their personal finances places extra pressure on them, and they do things they would not otherwise do. They slide down a slippery slope, not realizing how close they are to sliding into icy water at the bottom and spending a few years in jail.

For all three groups, the more they bend the rules, the easier it becomes. The first time, people often feel distress and anxiety. The second time, it is easier. After a few more times, they don't even think about it. Expanding into new realms, if done slowly, also does not cause great distress. In time, they are doing things they once never dreamed of doing.

Many managers face tremendous pressures to violate ethical norms, and many succumb. One factor is preoccupation with the bottom line. People are expected, above all else, to make the numbers. If they make the numbers, all else is usually forgiven. If they fail to make the numbers, nothing else matters. Another factor that undermines concern for ethical issues is the tendency of many companies to focus on short-term expediency. A culture that exclusively values power and financial success, and pays no attention to decency and ethical behavior, encourages ruthless behavior. Companies generally do value their good name. This is different, however, from valuing being an ethical company. Often, companies care about their image rather than their substance. This encourages cover-ups and some of the worst unethical behavior.

Some people do not go along with rule breaking. They know that the rules are the rules, and their integrity is more important to them than a few extra dollars. They know that taking money that does not belong to them or making false statements is wrong, and they do not do it. These people are more common than you think. Some managers with whom I have spoken wish to justify their actions by saying that everyone breaks the rules, and they joke that the society of ethical managers had their national conference in a hotel room. In fact, many people are ethical.

There is a great deal that companies can do to foster ethical behavior. Companies can screen for ethical behavior prior to hiring and promoting managers. Companies can also offer workshops in which people think through the ethical dimensions of a problem. Top leadership by word and deed needs to send a message that unethical behavior will be neither condoned nor tolerated. Companies also need to decrease pressures that foster unethical behavior such as insistence on making the numbers at all costs, and willingness to forgive all else if the numbers are made.

Sliding Down A Slippery Slope

Walter considered himself an honest person. He paid his taxes and gave money to his church and to various charities. When it came to his expense account, however, he sometimes slipped in a few things. He began doing this when he saw a superior asking for extra cab receipts and heard him tell another manager that he needed to pad his account to cover uncovered expenses he incurred from being on the road, such as extra babysitting for his kids. Walter followed suit.

He was uncomfortable at first, but then it became easier. In time he stopped thinking about it. Each receipt seemed so trivial, and he justified his actions by saying that he deserved more money when he was on the road. He couldn't imagine taking money from an open cash register if no one was around. Nor could he imagine falsifying reports or records in order to steal a thousand dollars at one time. Over the course of the year, however, his false padded expense reports added up to more than this.

Feeling Desperate

Brent was vice president of marketing for a rapidly growing company. His salary went up each year; he was making more money than his friends. He became used to spending more than his friends. His children were in private schools, and his house pushed the limits of his income.

One day, he heard the news that a major account was lost and a major brokerage house was planning on downgrading the company's stock. The price would crash. All of his retirement money was invested in the company's stock. He would have to choose between paying his mortgage and keeping his kids in private schools. His wife had warned him about leveraging their finances so heavily. He felt desperate. He decided to sell off much of his stock in the company before the stock tanked.

Not Giving In to Pressure

Selling the company's product was becoming more difficult. Competition had grown. Kurt was used to making promises he could not keep and then blaming production. He was sufficiently glib that customers always believed him.

A new salesperson came to the department and showed concern about making promises that she knew could not be kept. Kurt argued that people knew the promises were bogus and that other companies did the same. If they started speaking truthfully, the company would make no sales and people would wind up being just as inconvenienced, but this time by other companies.

The new salesperson seemed uneasy. Kurt couldn't deal with this holier-than-thou attitude, gave her a poor performance rating after 3 months, and encouraged her to transfer out.

Selling Oneself Under Pressure

Ellen was trying to conclude the biggest sale of her career. If Steve agreed to buy her company's equipment, she was sure to get a promotion. Her performance would be assessed not simply by making the sale but by the price. Steve was leaning toward the competitor's product and thought that he would finalize his decision very soon. Ellen was going through the various advantages of her product. She wasn't impressing him. She needed to pull out a wildcard.

Company policy was not to sleep with clients, since it gets in the way of business. This time, however, it might be the only way to get the business. Besides, she was attracted to him. She wasn't seeing anyone, and if they had met under different circumstances, they might well be dating and on the verge of sleeping together. She asked Steve about her competitor's representative. Steve replied that her competition was 50 years old and had a baritone voice. Ellen smiled, said she hoped she was more fun to be with, and touched Steve's hand. She noted that they would have a lot of contact over the next couple of years if Steve went with her company. She promised that she would see to that Steve was delighted with the services provided and that this was as important as the exact specifications of the product, since both met Steve's needs. He noted she made a good point. She started playing with his fingers.

She said it would be great if they could come to an agreement that evening. He said she would have to drop the price, and he wrote a number down on their scratch pad. It was within the acceptable range, but it would not thrill her superiors. She wanted a home run so she could get the bonus she hoped for. She wrote down a higher number. Steve looked a bit uneasy. Ellen noted that if they could come to an agreement, perhaps they could go back to his place and celebrate that night. She could have the new price put into the contract, have it faxed to Steve's home, and the two could sign it over breakfast. They agreed.

Organizational Impact

Unethical behavior destroys the reputation of the individual and of the company. Sometimes clients feel that they can no longer trust the company to deal fairly with them. Sometimes they do not want to be associated with a company that has a poor reputation.

Even if the company and individual are not financially hurt, unethical behavior eats away at their purpose. Consider the blow *The New York Times* took in admitting one of its reporters filed bogus stories. The paper came clean and fired the reporter, but over 100 years of integrity in reporting was damaged.

Emotional Intelligence Approach to Unethical Managers

Dealing with Unethical Managers

Dealing with an unethical superior is tricky. She can drag you into unethical behavior that can compromise your future business career as well as your inner sense of decency. She can place tremendous pressure on you to support her unethical agendas. To protect yourself from the consequences of not cooperating with an unethical manager (from perhaps being fired), try to get her orders in writing so you can show that you failed to do what your boss asked because it violated ethical standards.

Avoid getting into mutual recriminations in which you tell a manager that she is unethical. She will not want to hear it and will likely retaliate. Instead, when discussing your reluctance or refusal to follow instructions, focus on your own discomfort with such actions. If you handle the situation tactfully and avoid criticizing your superior's actions, the unethical manager will often help you find another position (she would, after all, prefer someone on her team who has no qualms about her questionable practices).

Dealing with Unethical Peers

Opportunistic peers can sometimes be dangerous. They will try to drag you into their own wrongdoings, if for no other reason than to convince themselves that what they are doing is not so serious, since you also do it. Don't let them.

Dealing with Unethical Subordinates

The first step in an emotional intelligence approach is figuring out if the unethical behavior is opportunistic or antisocial. Opportunistic, unethical managers can generally learn to live by the rules. Moreover, the scope of their violations will generally be limited. They may benefit from ethics training, periodic discussions of ethical considerations in the context of business decision making, discussions of why ethical violations are inevitably harmful, and reminders that you will not tolerate ethical lapses. Antisocial managers will neither be limited in their violation of the rules nor subject to turning over a new leaf. If the opportunistic subordinate's actions can threaten you or the company, you must report him to higher-ups. You don't want him to take you down. Don't cover up for him; you will only be engaging in your own unethical behavior by doing so.

HR and Senior Management

There are a number of things that HR and senior management can do to decrease unethical behavior. The standard methods of fostering a culture all apply:

◆ Be a role model for what you want others to do (be ethical).

◆ Preach the importance of ethics.

◆ Tell stories that support taking an ethical stance and not succumbing to temptations.

◆ Create a measurement/reward system that supports ethical behavior.

◆ Hire and promote only those people whom you believe to have high ethical standards.

Additional important steps include decreasing pressures to violate ethical principles. Intense pressure to make the numbers and a culture focused on short-term expediency undercuts ethical behavior. Rather than encourage people to make the numbers, urge them to do their best within the context of ethical behavior and the basic values of the firm. Training is also important. People need to be taught to see ethical problems in different types of behavior. Talks and CD trainings are a start but are not sufficient. The questions upper-level managers ask and what they talk about sets a tone for those below. Subordinates should continually be encouraged to think about ethical issues and to discuss them with their groups. If 360-degree feedback (having superiors, subordinates, and peers all give feedback about a manager) is obtained, managers should ask if others behave in ethical ways and should openly address the issues so that everyone is reminded of their importance. It is crucial to protect whistleblowers. Historically, they have not done well after their revelations. Peer reporting should also be encouraged. This is not tattling. It is protecting the company. To not report ethical violations is essentially to cover them up.

Maintaining Integrity I ══════════════════════════════

Jenny entered a new sales group. At the end of the month, she was told that everyone padded their expense reports and then shared in the profits. She was not sure what to do. She did not want to alienate people. Nevertheless, she felt very uncomfortable about cheating the company. Jenny decided to hand in her true expenses and told her boss that she did not want to receive any of the overflow. She was never again asked to lie. She kept her job.

We often pay a price for maintaining our integrity: The post-disclosure histories of whistleblowers are usually poor. People may be wary of hiring them. Fortunately, there are tactful ways to back out of an ethical dilemma. If most people did, those who are unethical would eventually get the message. Even if you know someone else will do the thing you refused to do, there is still value in refusing—you keep your hands clean. There are probably many managers and accountants who refused to become involved in the problems at Enron and Arthur Anderson, and are now elated that their careers are not buried under the debris caused by the collapse of these companies.

Maintaining Integrity II

Donald was asked to review an internal investigation of another manager. He did, and wrote a report clearing him, which inevitably placed questions on the behavior of others who were more powerful. He was ordered by his superior to write a report condemning the manager in question and to sign his own name to it. He refused, which cost him his job, but he kept his integrity. Perhaps with more political finesse, he could have avoided writing the report and kept his job.

Conclusion

Unethical behavior sometimes has short-run advantages and long-term costs. It damages a company's reputation both with customers and good managers who might otherwise have wanted to work there. It shows people that all is fair in love, war, and business, and it impedes a corporate culture of cooperation and honesty.

The paths to unethical behavior are varied (see Table 6–1 and Table 6–2). Some who engage in unethical behavior are severely narcissistic and believe that laws and rules were made for others, not for superior beings such as them. Others have a degree of narcissistic traits and a greater willingness to eschew the rules than most of us have. Others are average people who succumb to pressures—which becomes easier to do with time. The path back to integrity is harder than the slide into unethical behavior.

It is possible to maintain your integrity and eschew unethical behavior. The first step is valuing your integrity. The second is realizing that disaster can strike if you break the rules. Many close their eyes to the danger and believe they could never be caught. Third, it is important to avoid slippery slopes, group pressure, and "going along" with the crowd. One of the most brilliant lines I have heard in this regard was made by Sir Thomas Moore In *A Man for All Seasons*. Several bishops of the church asked him if he would go along with them for camaraderie's sake, and take the Oath of Supremacy making King Henry VIII supreme over the Church of England, rather than the Pope. Moore asked them whether when they went to heaven for following their conscience and he went to hell for not following his, would they join him out of camaraderie?

Companies can do a great deal to protect themselves by using caution in hiring and promoting people and by fostering a culture that supports ethical behavior.

Table 6–1 Types of Unethical Managers

Personality Type	Reason for Breaking Rules	When They Abuse Others	Dealing with Them
Antisocial (includes many bullies)	Exciting to break rules	Whenever possible	Generally need to be let go
Unethical opportunist	Pressure to obtain objective	If necessary	Educate on costs and set clear limits
Grandiose narcissist	Feels entitled to do whatever needed to obtain desires	If helpful	Set clear limits and educate on risks

Table 6–2 Overview of Unethical Opportunists

Symptoms/Ethical Violations	Underlying Factors	Impact	Ways for Subordinates to Cope	Ways for Senior Management to Cope
Mislead customers	Feels pressure to make the numbers or to advance at all costs	Damages organization's reputation	Do not get dragged into their unethical/illegal activities	Closely watch them; put them where they can't do damage, or get rid of them
Engage in bribery		Puts organization at legal risk	Tell a superior	
Accept kickbacks			Transfer out before they destroy you	Damage control—review their actions and make amends to staff, customers, and legal authorities
Cut corners on safety				
Turn their heads on violation of environmental regulations			Seek allies in coworkers and mentors	
Cut corners on quality control			Seek executive coach to help you cope	Be careful in hiring and promoting, and support a culture that values ethical behavior
Cover up incidents				
Have sex to make a sale				
Sell or steal trade secrets				Lessen pressure to make the numbers at all costs
Overbill, call in sick when well				
Steal, forge signatures				Provide training in ethical behavior
Falsify accounting reports				
Destroy incriminating documents				Encourage reporting of unethical behavior
Lie on their resumes				
Steal credit				
Destroy others' careers				

Your Turn

- ◆ What unethical opportunist managers have you dealt with?
- ◆ Give examples of their violations of the rules.
- ◆ How did they seem to feel about violating rules?
- ◆ How did they justify their behavior?
- ◆ Did they seem to consider the risks to themselves and the company?
- ◆ Why do you think that they are unethical rather than antisocial opportunists?
- ◆ What risk did they create for themselves?
- ◆ What risk did they create for the company?
- ◆ What risk did they create for you and others?
- ◆ How did their behavior affect you and others?
- ◆ What did you and others try to do to cope? What worked, and what did not? (What made things better, and what made things worse?)
- ◆ What did you learn?
- ◆ How would you do things differently in the future?
- ◆ What advice would you give to someone facing an unethical opportunist manager?
- ◆ Do you at times act in similar ways?
  - • How does it affect your company and team members?
  - • What are the benefits to your career?
  - • What are the risks to your career?
  - • How does it affect your purpose and identity in life?
  - • How do you justify it?

Further Reading

"Business Ethics: A View from the Trenches." *California Management Review,* 17(2), 8–28, Winter 1995.

Susan Squires, Cynthia Smith, Lorna McDougal, & William R. Yeak. *Inside Arthur Andersen: Shifting Values.* Financial Times/Prentice Hall, 2003.

Barbara Ley Toffler & Jennifer Reingold. *Final Accounting: Ambition, Greed and the Fall of Arthur Andersen.* Broadway Books, 2003.

Laura L. Nash. *Good Intentions Aside: A Manager's Guide to Resolving Ethical Problems.* Harvard Business School Press, 1993.

Linda Klebe Trevino & Katherine A. Nelson. *Managing Business Ethics: Straight Talk About How to Do It Right.* Wiley & Sons, 1998.

Barbara Toffler. "Managing Ethics and Legal Compliance, What Works and What Hurts." *California Management Review*, Winter 1999.

Part III

AGGRESSIVE MANAGERS

How Many Ways Are There to Hurt You?

Aggressive behavior is behavior that unjustifiably harms another. An aggressive manager either intends to do harm or is willing to do harm to obtain an objective. Types of harm may include damaging someone's reputation, career, goals, emotional state, or health. Harmful behavior includes unusual displays of anger; unwarranted attacks on someone's decency or ability, either to her face or behind her back; attempts to damage her career or reputation; and refusal to comply with reasonable requests that cause the person significant difficulty. An aggressive manager will attack your capabilities and reputation, ignore your prerogatives, take what he wants, and line your path with obstacles.

There is a lot of aggression in organizations. We cannot stop it, but we can decrease it and limit the extent to which we are the target. To do this, it is important to know what drives aggression, why certain people are chosen as targets, and what can deter an aggressor.

Aggression is driven both by frustrations that are inherent in working in organizations and by competition to advance one's personal and work agenda. Most people experience these feelings. Most of us are aggressive at times. Not everyone, however, acts on these feelings in ways that are markedly unfair and hurt others. Some people seem to have an unusual talent for stepping on those around them. An individual's personality traits, moral beliefs, and the culture in which she works and lives have a tremendous impact on how aggressively she acts at work.

Underneath aggression may be narcissistic or rigid personality traits. Narcissism brings a lack of empathy for others' positions and lack of respect for others' rights. These release the manager from the normal inhibitions people have on behaving aggressively. Narcissistic managers are also prone to rage when their sense of being better than others is challenged. Rigid personality traits lead to aggression by making it hard for an individual to compromise. Rigid managers push hard for what they want, and are willing to get into a battle if need be to have their way.

Problems with mood, stress, and attention can also foster aggressive behavior. Depression and anxiety foster irritability and can lead to angry outbursts. Part of the syndrome of attention deficit disorder is impulsivity and poor frustration tolerance, both of which can lead to angry outbursts. Traumatic experiences can markedly increase a manager's aggressive behavior by leading to increased fears of the world, hypervigilance, irritability, and a tendency to startle easily.

An emotional intelligence approach to dealing with aggression begins with understanding what lies underneath the behavior. The right strategy for one personality type is likely to backfire if used for a different personality type. Moreover, successful treatment of depression and anxiety (with either cognitive behavioral therapy or medication) or of ADHD can often significantly improve functioning. More often than not, these issues are not recognized or treated.

The Many Faces of Aggression

Some people divide aggression into two types: hot and cold. *Hot aggression* includes those who are upset when they hurt you. *Cold aggression* refers to those who are calm and calculating.

There are two types of hot aggression. The most commonly talked about situation is the irritable person who lashes out in frustration or revenge. Another type of hot aggression involves people who have no desire to hurt you but are frazzled and accidentally run over you. These are the stereotypical bulls in a china shop who do a great deal of damage unintentionally, often without even realizing it.

Cold aggression includes bullying and ruthless behavior. Ruthlessness (instrumental aggression) entails a willingness to treat others unfairly in order to have one's way. Calmly telling destructive stories about someone to discredit him and get him out of the way is instrumental aggression. Sometimes this is done covertly and sometimes overtly. People who do this are ruthless. Their ruthlessness may be the result of their personality and lack of scruples or the result of the cultures they have worked in. Predatory aggression is particularly dangerous. These individuals hurt others neither because they are angry nor because the victim is interfering with their goals. Rather, they enjoy the act of hurting people.

Passive-aggressive behavior involves passive resistance to demands that interfere with others' goals. Passive-aggressive people sabotage rather than directly attack what they do not like. Their motivation could be anger or jealousy (hot aggression), or it could be instrumental. Procrastination and negativity are classic passive-aggressive behaviors. People who are uncomfortable with being assertive are likely to engage in passive-aggressive activities both because they are restrained from direct acts of aggression and because their hesitancy in being assertive leads to frequent frustration that seeks an outlet. Passive-aggressive individuals are both rigid and aggressive. This personality type is discussed in greater detail in Chapter 20 in the section on rigid managers.

Part III Overview

The chapters in Part III cover a variety of types of aggression (see Table III–1 and Table III–2). Chapter 7 begins by discussing ruthless managers— cold and calculating cutthroats who will manipulate, scapegoat, and undermine others without remorse. They have significant narcissistic and antisocial personality traits. Rather than acting out of anger, they attack you to get you out of the way. They have no scruples about how they remove you. Chapter 8 discusses bullying managers. They are also very narcissistic and antisocial. They seek to attain a sense of power by intimidating you. Homicidal managers (Chapter 9) are more intense versions of ruthless and bullying managers. They are often driven by paranoia or narcissistic rage.

Chapters 10 and 11 discuss sexual harassment and chauvinists. There is usually a degree of narcissism in their personalities. In some cases lack of education and cluelessness (low emotional intelligence) play a large role. Both sexual harassment and chauvinism, when not due to cluelessness, are forms of bullying.

Chapters 12 and 13 are about volatile and frantic managers. They behave in problematic ways when they experience more stress than they can handle. Volatile managers become angry in response to a specific frustration. Once they have blown off some steam, they have no desire to hurt you. Frantic managers race around due to stress and anxiety, and violate your boundaries without malice, and often without realizing it.

The last two chapters in Part III provide more general information about anger. They cover the underpinnings of aggression and how to deal with aggressive people as well as with your own aggression.

The managers discussed in Part III are not the only aggressive managers discussed in the book. They are placed in this part because their aggression is the most prominent aspect of their presentation. Narcissistic, paranoid, and passive-aggressive managers, as well as all rigid managers, are at times aggressive.

- ◆ Chapter 7—Ruthless Managers: Cold, Calculating, Cutthroat
- ◆ Chapter 8—Bullying Managers: Haze Week Never Ends
- ◆ Chapter 9—Homicidal Managers: You Won't Get Away with That
- ◆ Chapter 10—Sexual Harassment: I Won't Take No for an Answer
- ◆ Chapter 11—Chauvinists Needing Diversity Training: I'm Better than You
- ◆ Chapter 12—Volatile Managers: Everything Upsets Me
- ◆ Chapter 13—Frantic Colleagues: I Can't Stop Racing Around
- ◆ Chapter 14—Underpinnings of Aggression: Why Am I So Angry?
- ◆ Chapter 15—Surviving Aggression: Strengthening Your Defenses

Table III–1 Overview of Aggressive Managers

Types of Aggression	Feeling When Aggressive	Situations Driving Aggressive Behavior	Perspective on Own Behavior	Predisposing Personality Traits
Ruthless	Calm	Desire for a goal	Remorseless or feels justified by greater good	Narcissistic, compulsive, authoritarian
Volatile	Angry	Frustrated or threatened	Sometimes feels justified, sometimes sorry	Borderline
Bullies	Enjoys it; outwardly angry	Desire to hurt and dominate or get revenge	Remorseless	Narcissistic, psychopathic; very limited conscience (superego)
Homicidal	Calm or angry	Desire to get rid of an obstacle or get revenge	Feels justified	Narcissistic or paranoid, may be psychotic
Frantic	Agitated	Pressure to get a lot done	Clueless, or feels it is necessary	Hypomanic: anxiety disorder
Passive-aggressive	Quietly angry, feels weak	Dislikes someone else deciding what to do	Feels justified	Discomfort with being assertive
Sexual harassment: Clueless	Calm	Problems in education and cultural background	Feels remorseful	Low emotional intelligence
Sexual harassment: Angry	Powerful, angry, threatened	Feels threatened and wants to dominate women	Feels justified	Sociopathic, narcissistic
Chauvinists	Retaliatory, strong	Feels threatened	Feels justified	Narcissistic

Table III-2 Types of Aggressive Managers

	Primary Traits	Objective	Surviving Them
Ruthless	Calmly goes after what he or she wants	Get what he wants	Watch your back
Volatile	Grandiose self image; exploitive	Be admired	Provide admiration and gently let them know their behavior is destructive
Bully	Seeks to intimidate for the pure excitement of it	Dominate and intimidate	Stay out of their way; don't let them see that you are intimidated
Homicidal	Often desperate, narcissistic, and depressed, paranoid, or antisocial	Rid herself of an obstacle or source of humiliation	Avoid them, contact police, call in a professional
Frantic	Generally agitated and pressured	Avoid being in trouble; accomplish a lot	Help them with their objectives; help them see that a frantic pace may be counterproductive
Sexual Harassment or Chauvinists: Clueless	Lack of appreciation of cultural values	Flirt and date	Educate them
Sexual Harassment: Angry	Narcissistic; angry	Demean	Strongly confront with risk of termination or lawsuit
Chauvinists	Narcissistic;, angry	Demean	Confront with risk of termination or lawsuit

CHAPTER 7

Ruthless Managers

Cold, Calculating, Cutthroat

Ruthless managers take what they need when they need it, without concern for fairness, ethics, decency, or you. Modern-day disciples of Machiavelli, they believe that all is fair in love, war, and business. Hurting others in the pursuit of a personal or corporate objective is seen as acceptable, albeit regrettable, collateral damage.

Ruthless managers have narcissistic personality structures: arrogant, devaluing of others, limited empathy for others, a limited conscience, and willingness to exploit others. They lack the flamboyant self-glorification of grandiose managers, the pleasure at hurting others that bullies experience, the complete absence of a conscience found in antisocial individuals, and the need for interpersonal control of the control freak. However, their willingness to violate the normal rules of society leaves them very dangerous if you get in their way. There are many ruthless people in business. Recognizing who is ruthless and watching your back when dealing with them will help your career to continue.

Certain ruthless behaviors are particularly common in organizations. Scapegoating—placing the blame for a problem on someone who does not deserve it—is a common tool of the ruthless manager. Someone may scapegoat you in order to protect herself from blame or as a political move to weaken your position. Stealing credit for your work is another common ruthless behavior. Pressuring you to work extraordinarily long hours or failing to give you reasonable time off for family emergencies because it would interfere with a project is also ruthless.

If a ruthless manager is ruthless in all aspects of her life, she is not simply a ruthless manager with a few holes in her conscience. Similarly, managers who engage in full-blown, unjustified character assassination are generally more than simply ruthless. They are likely to be antisocial or bullies or both. If the manager does not have an instrumental reason, something to concretely gain, then she is more sadistic than ruthless and fits better into the categories of antisocial manager or bully. Knowing which category a manager falls into is valuable, since the intervention to ameliorate the situation varies.

Case Study: An Overtly Ruthless Manager ▬▬▬▬

Some saw Arnold as ruthless, some saw him as compulsive. Unfortunately, both were right. Vice president for a mid-sized company, he liked to be in control. He wasn't mean; he didn't want to hurt people. He was very stressed working for a company president who was both younger than him and highly controlling. Angry with the president, but unable to take out his anger directly, he gave the president's protégé a hard time instead.

A rising manager named Terry reported directly to the president rather than to Arnold. Terry had proven herself as both capable and willing to go the extra mile in a series of problems that had arisen for the company. The president increasingly turned to her for special projects. Terry had more than her fair share of work to do. Nevertheless, when Arnold asked her to help with some tasks, Terry said yes. She wanted to be on good terms with him.

Going out of her way for Arnold did not build a good relationship, however. Part of the problem was that Terry was clearly on a fast track and was accomplishing things that Arnold was not. Arnold kept Terry from a working group that she was very interested in joining and that other people thought she should have been part of. At the same time that Arnold would not let Terry join the special group, he insisted that people who worked for him be included in a project that Terry was leading. Terry reluctantly acquiesced in order to maintain good relations. Arnold, however, never saw to it that his people did the promised work. In time, after the work was long overdue, Terry reassigned it to her own people.

When Terry volunteered to stay late to help Arnold and one of his managers deal with an emergency, Arnold was appreciative. Some follow-up was needed the next day. Terry assumed that Arnold's manager would take care of it, since it was for his department and within his set of responsibilities. It was clearly outside of Terry's responsibilities. Arnold, however, insisted that Terry take care of it, saying that no good deed goes unpunished.

In time, to her dismay, Terry was assigned to Arnold's department. With this, the situation became unbearable. Arnold told Terry that she needed special permission to work outside of her office, even though her primary assignment was to develop new materials and was often best done from other locations. Behind Arnold's demands was a desire to know all that Terry did so that he could take credit for Terry's work and limit her rise within the company. Moreover, Arnold placed burdensome work requirements on Terry and claimed that the rules were general policy and everyone followed them. A few questions to colleagues quickly showed that no one actually did these things.

Terry said that the job was not something she wanted. Arnold became furious. The company's president, not wanting to lose her, had Terry once again report directly to him. Arnold realized that if he wanted Terry's cooperation in the future, he would need to be nice—only then did he begin to treat Terry with reasonable respect. In time they got along well.

Snakes generally show little evidence of the threat they pose until they attack. Without warning, they can strike from behind.

A Covert Ruthless Manager

Lisa, an up-and-coming manager on the fast track, was a snake. She was accustomed to being the brightest person in the room, and she hated competition. The night before the kick-off for a new project, she met Howard. Howard was also very bright, better educated than Lisa, and was significantly more knowl-edgeable than Lisa about the substance of the new project. Being insecure, Howard wanted to make a good impression, so he showed off his knowledge when they first met. He also said he wanted to have as much responsibility as possible so that he could increase his chance of promotion. The next morn-ing, at the project kick-off with upper-level managers present, every time Howard said something, Lisa interrupted and said Howard was wrong. After the meeting, two managers sepa-rately took Howard aside and told him that he needed to be careful, that it seemed that Lisa had it in for him.

Over time, she became increasingly controlling. She de-cided most issues herself without discussing them in the team, as was the company's culture. Lisa had some understanding of her own behavior. One day the issue of birth order came up, and she laughingly noted that she assumed people could guess she was the eldest of several children.

Lisa made promises for deliverables that became hard to develop. Howard spoke to senior managers with whom he was friendly to ask for advice. They told him that Lisa should never have made the promises she did and that the tasks could not be done on budget. Although it was initially everyone's responsi-bility to see to it that the promised data was gathered, in time when it seemed increasingly likely that the material could not be obtained, Lisa changed the project plan and put only Howard's name by it. She also did not give him credit for cre-ative work he did when it was passed on to a superior.

Having gone way over budget, Lisa needed to take one of her two subordinates off of the project. Howard was cut. He asked Lisa for feedback and was told that he had done well but was not yet ready to run a project team himself. A few days later, he was shocked to read his project evaluation. It castigat-ed him for the project's going over budget and failing to produce the key deliverable he had been assigned. A few months later Howard was laid off.

The case described above was a brief attack on a manager by a more senior manager who needed someone to scapegoat. As we see in the following case, ruthless managers can also carry out long-term destructive campaigns when they need to.

Covert Ruthless Manager: A Protracted Campaign ▬

Seeking to become head of his department as soon as possible, Walter began a campaign to undermine the reputations of his department chief and the colleagues he saw as potential competition.

One week, having not yet done the work he needed to do for a weekly meeting, Walter asked the colleague who had organized the meeting to cancel. He then told the department chief that the colleague's canceling the meeting was an example of her failing to do her job. Similarly, knowing that the department head was going to a colleague's meeting, he called the colleague out of the meeting in order to make him look bad to the department head. He also went to colleagues' subordinates and convinced them to write negative letters about their bosses.

Walter got the position, quickly alienated innumerable people, and left to take another position.

Emotional Intelligence Approach to Ruthless Managers

There are many ruthless people in business. Limiting contact with them is your first line of defense. Often, however, that is not possible. At the least, you should be aware of who poses the greatest risk and avoid setting yourself up to be their victim when you work with them.

It is generally wise to avoid getting in the way of someone with a reputation for ruthless aggression until you have enough power and outside support to stand up to him. If you do not pose a threat to his wishes, he will have no reason to attack you. If you support him, he will want to help you. It may be annoying to go along with his agenda, but it is better than martyring yourself when there is little chance of victory.

When working with someone who poses a threat of ruthlessly undercutting your reputation and power (anyone you do not know well), it is important to check in frequently with superiors to get support for your actions and to heavily document what you do and why. Undermining you may include statements that your work was poor or that you failed to do important work, or attempts to usurp credit for your work. If you carefully document what you do and keep superiors informed in a timely fashion, it will be much harder for someone to either claim that you failed to do your work or that he deserves credit for it. If you keep superiors informed, it will also be harder for someone to attack your choices if things do not go well. You can also limit your vulnerability by getting ruthless managers to sign off on actions you expect to take. Then email them, and copy others, noting the understanding that the two of you came to.

Ruthless managers are unlikely to attack those they see as powerful. For example, if you have powerful supporters, and people know that you do, ruthless managers will be unlikely to attack you and risk reprisal from above. The wider and deeper your power base, and the stronger your reputation, the harder it will be for a ruthless manager to hurt you and the less tempting a target you will be. People will start questioning the honesty of someone who complains about you if you have a reputation for diligent, sound work. It takes considerable effort to build a stellar reputation, but it is generally worth it. Putting in extra work now is far better than having to pick up the pieces of your career after someone locks his radar on you and fires multiple weapon systems. Having a powerful mentor can also help you to deter attacks or to survive and recover from an attack. With a powerful mentor, you can rally support to counter the attacks. Ruthless managers will not want to go after someone who has a powerful protector who may turn on them. Finally, having a reputation for winning will inhibit people from trying to joust with you. You develop this reputation by engaging only in battles that you are pretty sure you will win.

In this chapter's case studies you learned about Terry and Arnold. We left off with Terry being assigned to Arnold's department and Arnold placing burdensome controls on Terry's work style. Terry first told Arnold that perhaps the position was not for her. Arnold became furious rather than realizing that Terry could easily take a walk and becoming more accommodating. At this point Arnold shifted from instrumental to angry aggression. Terry had another card to play. She had made herself very valuable to the head of the company, so she went to him. Terry was reassigned, did the same work, but did not directly report to Arnold. She then went out of her way to keep Arnold happy. Arnold quickly decided to make the best of the situation and began treating Terry well. Since his aggression had mostly been instrumental and not angry, he was easily able to make this shift.

We left Howard being subjected to Lisa's false assertions that he had failed to do his work. Howard had a powerful mentor, but Lisa's mentor was growing in power and was more of an activist than Howard's. Howard's reputation never recovered, and when the company downsized he was laid off. He was more careful next time around.

For HR and Senior Management

Senior management and HR should be wary of ruthless managers. They may appear to simply be playing the game or engaging in typical political maneuvering. They are, however, destructive to the organization. Their political maneuvering, undercutting of people, and bullying undermine decision-making processes. Instead of the best idea winning, the idea promoted by the most skillful political animal wins. Instead of the most creative, capable, and diligent managers rising within the organization, the most politically astute and ruthless people advance. The quality of management suffers seriously, and the culture suffers. Once you have a highly political culture and an organization populated by people who are predisposed to dirty politics, it will be very difficult to turn things around.

Senior managers and HR often do not know that a manager is engaging in dirty politics. The first thing to do is to keep your eyes, ears, and mind open. Complaints about subordinates and grabs for credit should be assessed and not immediately accepted. There is a tendency to automatically believe senior managers when they come into conflict with junior ones. Try to fight this tendency and be aware of other possibilities. Having 360-degree feedback as part of the evaluation process for all managers is helpful. Senior management can also make it clear by the example they set, the people they hire and promote, and the talks they give that dirty politics is not accepted in the company.

When you see ruthless managers who are willing to step on other members of your organization in order to get ahead, you should think twice before promoting them. You should also confront them with the behavior and let them know that it will not be tolerated, and that their careers are at stake.

Conclusion

Ruthless managers (see Table 7–1) believe that all is fair in love, war, and business, and that work entails a world war of all against all. Ruthless managers are unusually dangerous because they lack the moral inhibitions constraining most people and will therefore do things you would not expect.

Table 7–1 Overview of Ruthless Managers

Symptoms	Underlying Factors	Impact	Ways for Subordinates to Cope	Ways for Senior Management to Cope
Willing to do whatever is necessary to obtain an objective	Lack of normal inhibitions (conscience)	Interferes with optimal decision-making	Help them with their goals	If a hire appears to be too good to be true, he or she probably is
Lack of remorse for hurting people	Lack of empathy	Destroys people's confidence and fosters anxiety, depression, and burnout	Do not take it personally	Check on accuracy of resumes
Scapegoating		Damages organization's culture	Avoid provoking them	Close oversight of managers to continually assess their treatment of others
Glib			Document inappropriate behavior	
			Don't let them know they are hurting you	Do not automatically believe superiors over their subordinates
			Seek allies in coworkers and mentors	
			Seek executive coach to help you cope	360-degree feedback
			Transfer out	Place them where they cannot do serious harm
				Consider getting rid of them

Moreover, because they are cold and calculating, you may not know that they are acting against you until it is too late.

Sometimes they lack moral inhibitions in all aspects of their lives, and sometimes their Machiavellian attitude is limited to work. In either case, both those who work with them and the companies they work for need to beware, to not trust them, to not give them ammunition, and to stay alert. Whatever security one can develop when working with ruthless managers comes from making yourself useful to the ruthless manager and from developing relationships with people who will protect you. Superiors as well as subordinates of ruthless managers need to beware of the damage such managers can do to individuals and the organization. They will scapegoat others and steal credit for others' work. If you allow these things to occur, you will lose very good people, and your unit's culture will become one of self-protection rather than cooperation. As a result, productivity will suffer. Moreover, in time the ruthless manager may go after you.

Your Turn

- ◆ What ruthless managers have you observed?
- ◆ Give examples of their
  - • Machiavellian behavior
  - • Scapegoating
  - • Lack of remorse for behavior
- ◆ How do they justify their behavior?
- ◆ How did their behavior affect you and others?
- ◆ How did their behavior affect productivity?
- ◆ What did you and others try to do to cope?
- ◆ What worked, and what did not? (What made things better, and what made things worse?)
- ◆ What did you learn?
- ◆ How would you do things differently in the future?
- ◆ What advice would you give to someone facing a ruthless manager?
- ◆ Do you at times act in similar ways?
  - • How does it affect people?
  - • How does it affect your team?

- How does it affect your career?
- How do you justify it?
- How does it fit in with your life goals?

Further Reading

Richard III. Shakespeare presents a wonderful example of a ruthless, power-hungry individual. Act I, Scene YY.

Nicolo Machiavelli. *The Prince*. 1513.

CHAPTER 8

Bullying Managers

Haze Week Never Ends

A couple of weeks spent working with a bully will give you a year's worth of war stories with which to regale your friends. It won't, however, be worth it. The experience can shake the confidence and equilibrium of the most secure of us. Bullies exact a tremendous toll from both those they target and the organizations they work in.

The bully's objective is not a concrete one in which he wants to pressure you to do something. Rather, his agenda is to dominate and intimidate you because of the stimulation he gets from exercising power over people. At his core are narcissistic personality traits: arrogance, devaluation of others, little capacity for empathy, and a conscience with more holes than Swiss cheese.

There are a variety of weapons bullies can wield. They will humiliate you in front of others, berate you in private, and submit you to a constant stream of insulting emails. They can gratuitously subject you to unreasonable work demands and conditions, deny your abilities and accomplishments, and blame you for things that are not your fault. They can threaten to damage your career by making false statements about you or placing damaging notes in your file. They can even loom over you or block you from leaving your desk or your room and leave you fearing that they may be violent.

Bullies are very dangerous because their aggression is not limited by the moral inhibitions and empathy that restrain most of us from wantonly hurting others. Few people have the tools to deal effectively with them. The typical ways of dealing with someone who is being aggressive can backfire with bullies. While most people feel some compassion and limit their actions if you express pain and behave in a conciliatory manner, bullies are encouraged by this. Nevertheless, there is much you can do to detoxify the experience of working with a bully, although you cannot make it a benign experience.

Impact of Bullies

Bullies can decimate your self-esteem. After a sustained period of bullying, people cease to believe in themselves, their abilities, and even their right to be treated reasonably. Some develop what has become known as the *Stockholm Syndrome*. During a bank robbery in Stockholm, a number of people were taken hostage. After a day, many of the hostages began to feel connected to their captors and to protect them from the police. Patty Hearst reportedly fell prey to this phenomenon and went from kidnap victim to cooperating with her abductors in robberies. Battered women who stay with their abusers and refuse to press charges against them are a common example.

Even when the toll of bullying does not rise to this level, the impact can be very serious. Many victims suffer from anxiety or depression. They become preoccupied with the problem and have difficulty focusing on their work. Sleep and concentration deteriorate. Some develop physical complaints. As time goes on, the victims' self-confidence disintegrates, they are filled with a sense of shame and inadequacy, and they may begin to believe they do not deserve better treatment. Some victims become so desperate that they resort to violence or suicide

Origins of Bullies

The tendency to respond empathically to others' pain is inborn in most people. Very young children are sometimes seen giving toys to other children who are upset. While most people are distressed by other people's pain and want to soothe them, some are excited by it and enjoy it. Both genetic factors and early trauma probably play a role in this. Lacking an empathic connection to people, bullies feel no remorse after hurting someone.

They destroy another person's career with as little concern and inhibition as we throw away a piece of paper we no longer need.

A company's culture has a significant impact on the amount of bullying that occurs. Whatever inhibitions bullies have against hurting others are weakened when the work culture permits or encourages cutthroat competition. Moreover, bullying often requires the silent acceptance of coworkers. Some cultures preach everyone for themselves, while others preach mutual support. People stay silent when observing bullying for a variety of reasons. Some fear that speaking up will lead the predator to turn on them. Some blame the victim in order to attempt to deny that terrible things can happen to innocent people. If someone could be subjected to such treatment for no good reason, then it could happen to us.

When the CEO Is a Bully

Steve, president of a rapidly growing company, approached Ben about the position of VP of marketing. It was an interesting opportunity. The company had a good product and was gaining market share. Before accepting the position, Ben wanted to speak to the last two marketing directors, both of whom had lasted only six months. Steve told Ben that they had not been good performers and pushed aside the request to speak with them as inconvenient and unnecessary. Steve appeared to be congenial. The salary and bonus package were high for the industry. The chance to make the leap to VP for marketing was exciting, and Ben took the job.

The honeymoon period was short. After a month, Steve wanted an early morning meeting. Ben asked if they could make it a little later that day, since he had a doctor's appointment scheduled. Steve turned red and said that at what he was paying Ben, he expected him to be in the office during the workday and that the doctor was his servant and would see him in the evening. Ben was taken aback by Steve's anger. Later that day Steve walked into Ben's office and threw Ben's marketing report on his desk, using several four-letter words to describe the work. Several flaming emails followed.

Ben asked a couple of people if they had seen this before. They said that what was surprising was how long the honeymoon had lasted and how mild Steve's criticism was. In the past he had ripped up reports and thrown them in the VP's face.

Ben was actually far from alone in receiving this treatment. Secretaries, managers, and other VPs all received similar treatment. Steve would scream in people's faces, wag his finger or cigar at them, rip up their reports, and poke his finger in their chests. He left people trembling and in tears.

Meanwhile, one of Ben's crucial assistants quit. When Ben asked why, she said that her lawyer had told her to not talk about it. Through the grapevine Ben heard about the history of sexual harassment she had been subjected to. She had been promised Ben's job if she slept with Steve and was threatened with being blackballed in the industry if she did not. Ben gathered that Steve had come to a settlement, including a hush clause, for the sexual harassment.

After three months, Ben told Steve he wanted to resign. Steve called Ben a wimp (actually, what he said was worse, but the publisher wouldn't print it), threatened to destroy his reputation, told him he was doing a great job, and would not accept his resignation. Ben was stunned. He decided to continue.

A bully's behavior will be affected by the position he or she holds. In the CEO's seat a bully is likely to have very few inhibitions. In a mid-level position, however, a bully needs to be able to contain his or her assaults to a degree. These inhibitions will fade as the individual rises within the organization and when the person is under stress.

A Bully in a Suit

Mark was hired into an upper management position on the recommendation of a company executive who had been a childhood friend of his. Mark had had success elsewhere. He had also, unknown to the company, had problems elsewhere. Mark talked a lot about what he had done, who he knew, where he had been. He claimed to have worked with and written papers for well known people.

Although attentive to superiors and to peers who sometimes did his work for him, Mark was controlling and constantly critical of subordinates. For example, he frequently criticized one of his junior managers, Larry, falsely accusing him of failing to hand in deliverables. If Larry tried to explain what he had and had not done, Mark became enraged and stated that he did not want a response. On one occasion when Mark asked Larry to download files on various subjects, Larry said he thought that some of the work had already been done. Mark became furious, accusing Larry of suggesting that he was stupid.

While outwardly expressing the desire to help this new junior manager, Mark had no real concern for Larry's well-being. For example, without asking permission, Mark borrowed a key piece of Larry's computer equipment and then went out to lunch without telling Larry where he could find it. On several occasions, when asked to return borrowed equipment, Mark failed to do so. Particularly striking, after typing late one night for several hours while Mark dictated, Larry requested a two-minute break because his hands were cramping. Mark refused to allow it.

Mark was often envious. He complained that Larry got far more time with their mutual superior than junior people normally received. Mark also complained about how close Larry was to this superior and said he intended to wean Larry away from him. Angry about being given an office in the basement, Mark insisted that Larry work there as well, although there was no desk for him in that location. When Larry said he could work more efficiently at his own desk, Mark angrily accused Larry of feeling superior. When Larry needed to stop working with Mark for a day in order to work on an assignment for their mutual superior, Mark became infuriated, initially refused to talk to Larry, and threatened to put a damaging note in his personnel file.

After a couple of weeks, Larry told Mark that the current work arrangement was uncomfortable and requested another assignment. Mark defended his treatment of Larry by explaining that he treated Larry no differently than he treated others, and insisted that he, Mark, was behaving appropriately. Larry told their mutual superior the situation was intolerable. The superior expressed great surprise and eventually agreed to place Larry on another project.

A few months later, over drinks at a retreat, Larry found out that Mark had subjected others to almost identical abuse and that the superior, who had expressed shock at the story, had in fact heard about Mark's abusive behavior before. In time Mark crashed and burned, and was fired for alienating clients.

Emotional Intelligence Approach to Bullying Managers

Dealing with Superiors Who Bully

The first step in dealing with a bully is to be sure that you are in fact dealing with a bully—a person who is sadistic and enjoys intimidating and hurting people. Sometimes a manager who both lacks reasonable social skills and feels overwhelmed by work pressure can look like a bully. There is not much to lose in initially assuming that the manager is irritable and overwhelmed and seeing if he will respond to an intervention designed for this situation. You can start by telling the abusive boss that his raising his voice, calling your basic intelligence into question, ripping up your reports, and threatening you is not necessary to get your attention. In fact, it creates an atmosphere that interferes with rather than fosters motivation. You can then suggest alternative ways of getting your attention. If this fails and the evidence mounts that the primary motive for attacking you is the fun involved in pushing people around, it is time to move on to interventions for bullies.

Dealing with bullies calls for an integrated game plan. You need to decrease their desire to engage in bullying, decrease their interest in selecting you as the victim of choice when they do bully, and strengthen yourself against potential attacks. You can sometimes decrease their urge to hurt you by helping them to attain their goals. You can also make yourself less of a target by avoiding them during the times of day that they are most explosive and by putting in extra effort on those aspects of work that are a trigger for them to explode.

You do not want to threaten them or retaliate against a bully. This may feel good for a moment, but it will also provoke the bully and escalate the problem.

Since their primary motivation for attacking is the pleasure of seeing you squirm, not squirming decreases their interest in having you as the victim. In most situations we feel that if people see we are in pain, they will back off and apologize. This plan of action backfires with bullies. It is often impossible to take their attacks with equanimity, but you must do all you can to not let them see your distress. Sharks go after the wounded swimmer.

Fostering a relationship with a powerful mentor can provide needed political and emotional support. A mentor may be able to intercede with the bully, help you find a new position, or at least provide a recommendation if you leave. Having a powerful person on your side can also help you to maintain some of your self-esteem and sanity in the face of attacks by your boss. It is also helpful to keep records so that you can present a blow-by-blow account of the bully's behavior.

Talk about the problem with peers. Their emotional and perhaps political support is also crucial. The humiliation and destruction of self-esteem that being bullied causes can be lessened when others remind you that you are not the problem and that people like and support you. Many have a tendency to withdraw in shame and embarrassment after being bullied. It is crucial to fight this and avoid isolating yourself. Sometimes your colleagues can join with you in confronting the bully or meeting with senior management. Group action is far more likely to be effective than going at it alone. Bullies respond to power and senior management responds to group complaints.

Above all, do what is needed to maintain your sanity, self-esteem, and health. If you lose these, your job performance will collapse and you will be in more serious trouble.

Dealing with Peers Who Bully

Peers sometimes try to bully us. The best tactic is to let the person know that the behavior is unacceptable. Once again, don't let the person benefit from their bullying. You should also ask the person to communicate by email or in writing instead of verbally. This gives you an opportunity to pass it on to your superior for clarification. You also want to keep a close check to see if the bully slides into character assassination once he realizes you will not go along with his attempts to bully you.

For HR and Senior Managers

Bullies are a serious problem. They may produce for the company for a while, but they are not really loyal to the organization. They are loyal only to themselves. They are also very destructive of a company's human resources and social capital.

The first thing HR and senior management needs to do is assess if the problematic manager is a bully or is another type of aggressive manager. If the problem is really that the manager is depressed and irritable, severely stressed, lacking in social skills, or simply unaware of the company's culture, the problem can often be ameliorated relatively quickly through executive coaching and therapy.

Real bullying lies on a foundation of severe narcissistic and antisocial personality characteristics and is very difficult to change. It is best to get these people to leave and make them someone else's problem. If they do not have valuable proprietary information, you might want to encourage them to get a job with a competitor.

Conclusion

You probably thought that after leaving high school you would no longer need to deal with bullies. Unfortunately, some of them grow up and become managers. Tolerance for bullies is decreasing, but our society is still relatively slow to take action against bullies, whether it occurs in junior high school or at work. Meanwhile, the toll that bullying takes is substantial. There is much that we can do to protect ourselves and to decrease it within our organizations.

Perhaps the first thing to remember is that bullies are disturbed individuals. This is not simply another management style, it is abuse. These are not average people, they are sick puppies. Bullies (see Table 8–1) stand at the intersection of narcissism and aggression. The first trait you will see is their anger. You might initially think that their problem is irritability or ruthlessness. They are not, however, simply blowing off steam or willing to step on you as they pursue their objectives. Their central aim is to intimidate you and not simply to vent their frustration.

In addition to being very aggressive, they embody the key traits of narcissism: devaluation of others, entitlement to take whatever they want, and the belief that they are a breed apart from mere mortals like you. Combining marked aggression, devaluation of others, lack of moral inhibitions, lack of empathy, and pleasure in intimidating and dominating others makes bullies the most destructive and the most feared type of toxic managers.

The difference between bullies and antisocial individuals is hazy. Bullies want to dominate and see you squirm, while antisocial individuals seek to destroy or to obtain a concrete aim.

Table 8–1 Overview of Bullies

Symptoms	Underlying Factors	Impact	Ways for Subordinates to Cope	Ways for Senior Management to Cope
Demeans people	Power-hungry and enjoys hurting others	Destroys people's confidence and causes anxiety and depression	Avoid provoking them	Do background checks on new hires
Threatens career and even physical damage	Lacks normal inhibitions	Destroys morale	Help them with their goals	Have treatment of others be part of measurement and reward system
Goes after the weakest targets	Devalues people	Markedly impairs productivity	Seek allies and a mentor	Do 360 assessments on managers before promotion
Desires to intimidate	Lacks empathy	Impairs retention and hiring	Document treatment	Assess if treatable problems with alcohol, ADHD, anxiety, or depression are exacerbating their aggression
Lacks remorse for hurting people			Do not take it personally	
			Don't let them know they are hurting you	Focused coaching to modify abusiveness
			Seek an executive coach to help you cope	Get rid of managers who continue to bully people
			Transfer out before they destroy you emotionally	

Working for a bully is always a painful experience. The best you can do is be as calm and unperturbed as you can when under attack. Bullies seek to dominate. If they cannot dominate you, they will focus their attacks elsewhere. They may also engage in character assassination if they have gotten into a serious power struggle with you. Seeking emotional and political support is crucial to mitigate the emotional impact and protect your career. Getting away from them as soon as possible is generally a good idea.

Senior management should try to get rid of bullies as soon as possible. They destroy the organization's culture and will cost you your best workers as good people leave and other good people refuse to join.

Your Turn

- ◆ What bullying managers have you observed?
- ◆ Give examples of their
    - • Demeaning people
    - • Threatening people physically and politically
    - • Going after the weakest targets
    - • Enjoying intimidating people
    - • Lacking remorse for hurting people
- ◆ How did their behavior affect you?
    - • How did their behavior affect others?
    - • How did their behavior affect productivity?
    - • How did their behavior affect communication?
- ◆ What did you and others try to do to cope? What worked, and what did not? (What made things better and what made things worse?)
- ◆ What did you learn?
- ◆ How would you do things differently in the future?
- ◆ What advice would you give to someone facing a bullying manager?
- ◆ Do you act in similar ways at times?
    - • How does it affect people?
    - • How does it affect your team?
    - • How does it affect your career?

Further Reading

Harvey Hornstein. *Brutal Bosses: And Their Prey.* Riverhead Books, 1996.

Gary Namie & Ruth Namie. *The Bully at Work: What You Can Do to Stop the Hurt and Reclaim Your Dignity on the Job.* Sourcebooks, 2000.

CHAPTER 9

Homicidal Managers

You Won't Get Away with That

As difficult as dealing with compulsive, narcissistic, and even bullying managers can be, you are in an entirely different realm when someone presents a threat of murder. Such events unfortunately occur at times in corporate life.

In interviewing those who threaten to kill others, we often find a combination of aggressive narcissism, an antisocial perspective, and depression. Paranoia can also be a factor. Aggressive narcissism clears the path for the manager to seriously consider murder to meet a perceived need or goal. As we have discussed, for the severely narcissistic or antisocial manager, other people do not have rights. Rather, they are objects that are either useful or are obstacles. If they are obstacles, they can be dispensed with.

Depression raises the risk of murder by increasing the manager's sense of hopelessness and therefore desperation. It can also create a sense that many aspects of the world, possibly including yourself, are terrible and should be destroyed. The combination of desperation and seeing horrible things that should be destroyed leads some people to do things they normally would never consider. Some commit suicide. Some commit murder. Some do both—murder suicides.

Narcissistic individuals are particularly at risk for violence because of what psychiatrists call *narcissistic rage*. As discussed in Chapter 2, narcissistic individuals have fragile self-esteem. When their self-esteem is injured by criticism or failure, the narcissistic individual becomes enraged, and all judgment melts away. They try to heal themselves by destroying the cause of their pain and thereby reestablishing control. Meanwhile, they both lose all empathy for the hated person and lose all judgment and concern for harm they may do to themselves by taking revenge and attacking. All they can think about is the need to take revenge. The consequences for them do not carry any weight in their thinking.

Some people engage in violence because they deal with the world in a compartmentalized way. In seeking a solution for one problem, they often fail to look at the overall impact and fallout from their actions until it is too late. Simple examples include using a coercive management style, being inconsiderate to spouse and children, or having an affair. People often look at the short-term problem, such as dealing with their frustration, and fail to consider the long-term impact of their actions. They may be theoretically aware of the long-term risks, but fail to seriously consider them in their decision making, since all they can really feel is the pain of the immediate problem and the temptation of a particular solution.

There is a tendency to think that white-collar workers do not engage in physical violence. There is, however, considerable white-collar domestic violence ranging from child and spouse abuse to workplace murders.

Contemplating Murder

Lewis had gone to top schools, he had a nice family, and his career was going well. He was often generous with family and friends. In time he expected he would be running his own company. He also tended to think that he was special, different from others. He hoped he would soon be VP of sales. These thoughts were not that unusual at all for people in his position.

Things changed rapidly. The company hired a VP of sales who was younger than Lewis. Lewis realized he was now unlikely to obtain the position himself, and he began sliding into a deep depression. He began to feel that he had been betrayed, stabbed in the back, and that his dignity required correcting the miscarriage of justice. He began thinking about killing his superior. He bought a gun and told coworkers he was thinking about it.

A consultant was called in to assess whether Lewis was teasing or possibly serious. The issue of whether his leaving would make things more or less dangerous was carefully considered. The consultant said that the key issue was not to undercut Lewis's self-esteem and to give him as much of a sense of self-control as possible. The company convinced Lewis to resign and seek opportunities in other companies where there would be better opportunities to rise to the top position.

All acts become easier once you have become used to them. This includes giving a presentation before a large audience, cheating on taxes, and killing. People who grew up surrounded by violence in their home or on the streets may come to see it as a usable option. Psychiatrists use the phrase *identification with the aggressor* to explain how victims grow up to be perpetrators. In certain ways, it is less painful to identify with and model oneself after strong perpetrators than after weak and injured victims. In addition, the experience of using weapons in any socially acceptable context, including hunting, law enforcement, or the military, makes them less strange. On the one hand, experience in using weapons often inhibits inappropriate use by training people in safe use. On the other hand, when they are used by someone who has been trained, the weapons are more efficiently and destructively employed.

Used to Seeing Violence

Glen had done well but was now having problems. Born in a war-torn country, he had seen violence and served in combat. Now in the United States and educated, he landed a good job in accounting.

The demands of his job increased as the company rapidly grew. Feeling overwhelmed, Glen became increasingly depressed. He began talking about different ways of killing people.

People sensed no horror in him at the thought. In fact, he had been desensitized to killing from his childhood experiences. The company was so nervous, it hired people to monitor him. He was convinced to leave, went home, and committed suicide.

A particularly dangerous situation is the removal of a top executive. Seeing the end of his or her career and facing a future without the achievement, authority, and influence that had been the center of life, these managers become desperate and perhaps fall into a narcissistic rage. They not infrequently kill themselves or, at times, others.

Ousting the CEO

Sally had started her company from scratch and built it rapidly. A born entrepreneur, she did not have the skills to grow her company to the next level. She also did not get along with the new executives the investment bankers had her bring in, in order to obtain financing. Growth was stalling, and competitors were gaining market share. The board of directors asked her to step down.

Although rich beyond what most can imagine, she was beside herself with distress. Obsessed with growing the company, there was little else in her life. Her company was, needless to say, her child, her life. Paranoia and depression began to take over. She talked about having been sabotaged by people and about there having been a plot to oust her. She withdrew into herself. She had her office checked to see if it was bugged. When she wondered aloud if she could arrange to have the board of directors' meeting bombed, the police were called. Sally was taken to a mental hospital for observation.

In the hospital she was found to be depressed, narcissistic, and paranoid. Medication was begun for depression, and Sally began to pull herself together. She was also helped to make plans for a new startup with support from her original company. This gave her a focus and a mission and she did well.

Assessing the Danger

The most important step in dealing with a threat of violence is calling in someone skilled in dealing with these problems. Attempting to do it without professional assistance, waiting to gather more information, or hoping that the person is just joking may work the vast majority of the time, but such denial, rationalization, and minimization of the risk periodically leads to catastrophes that could have been averted. Prior to murder in an organization, there is almost always someone who notices that the future perpetrator is behaving in unusual ways that suggest a concerning risk of violence. Many lives could be saved if companies trained people in what to look for, and promoted a culture in which people informed the authorities when they perceived a risk of violence.

Professional threat assessors look at a number of factors that provide an indication of the likelihood of violence. If someone is diagnosed as being a psychopath by the Hare Psychopathy Checklist (see Chapter 5), his or her risk of violence is much greater than average. Among people released from prison, those with a history of psychopathy are four times more likely to engage in violence than those who do not meet the criteria for psychopathy.

The best predictor of future behavior is past behavior. Therefore, a history of violence increases the risk, particularly if it began very early in life (before age 10). This does not have to be violence at work. It could be violence toward one's spouse and children. It could be violence in one's youth.

A number of factors indicate or lead to high levels of anger (see Table 9–1). Preoccupation with weapons or violence is a sign of anger and danger. A recent humiliation is likely to leave the person enraged or feeling desperate. Depression, high stress, multiple losses, and manic episodes (see Chapter 27) often trigger high levels of anger and irritability. A person who hears voices telling her to commit violence is likely feeling overwhelmed by anger. Some drugs, such as amphetamines, can increase anger.

Various factors either indicate low levels of inhibitions or serve to lower inhibitions. Alcohol and some drugs decrease inhibitions. A history of head trauma leads to decreased inhibitions. A history of violence, drug abuse, promiscuity, running away, and engaging in dangerous activities show a potential for failing to consider the consequences of one's actions.

Paranoia—a tendency to interpret people as hostile, threatening, and out to get you—substantially increases the risk of violence (see Chapter 4). There are several key signs that the risk of violence has become very high.

- Preoccupation with violence or weapons
- Escalating aggression (angry outbursts, increased threats, increased weapons involvement—the potential perpetrator moves a gun from a locked storage compartment deep in the attic to under his pillow or in his office desk, and buys fresh ammunition)
- Approaching the target with increasing frequency

Table 9–1 Factors Increasing the Risk of Violence

Factors Driving Violence	Factors Decreasing Inhibitions	Factors Facilitating Violence
Anger due to frustration from multiple losses/stresses (financial, social, health, chronic pain)	Alcohol/drug use	Availability of weapons
	Antisocial personality/aggressive narcissism indicating limited empathy and conscience	Easy access to target
Paranoia-belief one is being persecuted		People ignoring the warning signs and threats
Perceived humiliation (possibly a result of the organization's response to the threat)	History of engaging in violence (especially childhood onset)	
	Increased risk of impulsivity as indicated by history of head trauma, exposure to violence as a child, or a history of impulsivity (drugs, promiscuity, high-risk activities)	
Auditory hallucinations telling the person to kill		
Psychosis, depression, bipolar disorder		
	Psychosis, depression, bipolar disorder	
	Isolation	

Initial Steps

There are initial steps you can take to limit the risk in these situations (see Table 8–2). First, avoid doing anything to humiliate or incite the person. This individual is probably already feeling desperate and is sending you a signal that he is on the verge of losing control. You want to avoid pushing him over the brink, and you want to do whatever possible to support his regaining judgment and self-control. If he has directly spoken to you about his thoughts of violence, listen to what he has to say. Respond empathetically to his feeling stressed and ask what would help him to feel less desperate. Aggressive confrontation or further humiliation will likely lead to provoking the person and increasing the risk of violence. Obtaining orders of protection tends to backfire, since it places the potential perpetrator's focus and anger even more intently on the person who took out the order.

A key part of any safety plan is keeping the target out of harm's way. Make sure that the person making the threat and the potential victims stay apart.

If you hear about a threat second-hand, bring it to appropriate channels. Do not take it lightly even if the person who heard it pushes it aside as frivolous. Do not count on someone else to bring the concern to appropriate channels. Usually, no one will. After shootings have occurred, people frequently come forward to acknowledge that they had heard the person talk about using violence or knew that the perpetrator had been preoccupied with violence and weapons. People fail to go to appropriate channels either because they do not believe the person is serious, they are uncomfortable in talking to people about their concern, or they assume someone else will do it. The assessment that the person is not serious often comes from what political scientists call *motivated bias*. When we are assessing a situation and the data is not clear, we have a tendency to believe whatever is most convenient to believe. To believe that someone is serious about possibly committing murder would make most of us very uncomfortable. In addition to being frightening, it would place us in the uncomfortable position of having to pass on the information and possibly be accused of being crazy ourselves. Therefore, people have a tendency to deny the risk and assume that the warning signs are not significant.

A general rule is to avoid humiliating people. Sometimes it can place you in danger. A man who came back from disability after a heart attack arrived to be insulted by his manager in the parking lot. The next day, he brought a gun to work and killed his manager. Most of the time, you can get away with humiliating people. Similarly, most of the time, you can get away with drinking and driving or standing in water while using electrical equipment. Every now and then, however, disaster can strike.

Winston Churchill wisely said that it costs you nothing to be polite to someone you are sending to the gallows. Keep this in mind when firing someone or telling her that her work needs massive improvement if she is to stay in the company—avoiding humiliation is useful. When someone threatens violence, it is tempting to go to court to obtain an order of protection telling the person to stay away from the potential target. Many experts, however, advise against doing this. An order of protection may be experienced as humiliating to the threatening individual and is generally felt to increase rather than decrease the risk of violence. One expert likened getting an order of protection to putting a bull's-eye on the potential target.

Basic Steps in Dealing with Threat of Violence

- ◆ Call in expert advice for assessment of risk potential and guidance on decreasing the risk
- ◆ Help gather data relevant to risk assessment: prior history
- ◆ Avoid provoking the person (for example, by getting an order of protection)
- ◆ Seriously listen to the potential perpetrator's complaints
- ◆ Offer to do what you can to help
- ◆ Remind the dangerous person that he can always act later, and that they should first try to find a nonviolent solution
- ◆ Keep the target out of harm's way

Conclusion

Unless you are in the military, police force or FBI you probably never expected that being shot at was in your job description. With 1200 murders and 2,000,000 assaults at work each year in the United States you will probably need to deal with the issue of workplace violence sooner or later. The most important thing to remember is that there are vulnerable people in any large organization who can be pushed over the edge by being demeaned. Assaulting someone's self-esteem is never necessary and always destructive. Even if you need to fire someone, there are ways to do it that can spare the individual's honor and minimize the chance of violence. It was not that long ago in our history that duels were a regular response to assaults on someone's honor. Many people continue to respond to assaults on their honor with deadly force.

If you are overwhelmed with frustration because someone has put in a terrible performance causing you massive amounts of extra work, or because they have been arrogant and obnoxious, or because you are having other frustrations in your life get some support and a way to deal with your anger before confronting the person. You'll sleep better at night.

If someone is showing signs of potential violence it is important to call in a professional. Risks of violence are not something for the nonprofessional. It is a specialized area within psychiatry/psychology. A rough rule of thumb is that threats in the context of aggressive narcissism and perceived humiliation, multiple recent losses or depression, paranoia, a history of violence or impulsivity, substance abuse, or access to guns are reason for serious concern. The presence of two or more of these or a pattern of escalating threats is cause for great concern and immediate action.

Your Turn

◆ What threats of violence or violence to yourself or others have you faced at work?
◆ What were the warning signs?
◆ How did people respond to the threats?
◆ What was the effect?
◆ What else could people have done?
◆ What got in the way of people responding more effectively?
◆ What did you learn?
◆ How would you do things differently in the future?
◆ People periodically make threatening innuendos or send threatening signals. Given what you know now what signals and innuendos would you ignore and what ones would lead you to take action? What would the action be?

Further Reading

Michael H. Corcoran & James S. Cawood. *Violence Assessment and Intervention: The Practitioner's Handbook.* CRC Press, 2003.

Threat Assessment Specialists: Factor One, (510)352-8660.

J. Reid Meloy. 2002 Violent Attachments. Jason Aronson.

CHAPTER 10

Sexual Harassment

I Won't Take No for an Answer

Sexual harassment is a serious problem that has only recently been addressed. The casting couch and its equivalents were tolerated for many decades. Close to half of women and 10 to 20 percent of men in the workforce experience sexual harassment. It is destructive not only to the individuals involved but to the company. Sexual harassment damages morale, increases absenteeism, damages the company's reputation and its ability to hire top people, increases turnover, and sometimes results in lawsuits.

Title VII of the 1964 Civil Rights Act forbids discrimination on the basis of gender. Both the creation of a hostile work environment as a result of sexual behavior and presentation of a quid pro quo for sexual activity are violations of the act. The legal system, however, is not a panacea—it is merely a measure for dealing with reported violations. Studies have shown that most women who are sexually harassed do not report it, and of those who do, most were unhappy with the outcome. Adequately containing sexual harassment requires solutions that are more readily applicable than lawsuits.

Complicating the situation, 70 percent of lasting relationships begin in the workplace. Therefore, forbidding workplace romance is unrealistic for any company that wants to hire single people.

There are several types of behavior that constitute sexual harassment:

◆ Offensive comments or jokes based on gender issues

◆ Persistent, unwanted sexual advances

◆ Sexual bribery or coercion—promises of career gain or threats of career sanctions related to acceptance of sexual activity

◆ Unwanted touching

A variety of factors can lead someone to engage in such behavior:

◆ Cluelessness

  • Different national culture

  • Dinosaur syndrome—beliefs come from growing up in a different era

  • Temporary loss of judgment from acute stress or alcohol

◆ Entitlement to the perks of position

◆ Misogyny

Judging If It Is Sexual Harassment

The current test for sexual harassment is whether a reasonable woman would consider an action to be sexual harassment. When judging your own behavior, it is generally effective to ask yourself if you would act this way in front of your spouse, your peers, or a television camera. Companies can not forbid all flirting at work. Seventy percent of permanent relationships begin at work. There is a gray zone in which reasonable people may disagree about whether requests for a date or flirtatious comments are somewhat harassing or are simply a demonstration of continued interest. The existence of this gray zone does not, however, mean that most problematic behavior could be debated. Unwanted touching, quid pro quos for sexual activity, refusing to take no for an answer, and sexually based jokes that offend someone clearly constitute sexual harassment.

Whether or not the behavior reaches the level of sexual harassment is not critical for our purposes. The issue is how to help everyone be comfortable and feel safe from harassment. Companies do not need to bar all flirting and requests for a date to avoid sexual harassment. Rather, people simply need to use discretion and err on the side of caution. In other words, you need to use emotional intelligence and caution when dealing with office dating.

Some managers believe that they own not only their company, but also the people within it. Like the feudal lords of the Middle Ages, they feel a right to obtain sexual favors from those they employ. They do not realize, or do not care, that they are unfairly using their power and placing their subordinates in a very unfair and likely destructive position. Often, they get away with it, but sometimes they do not, and the company suffers financial loss and damage to its reputation.

Droit de Seigneur

Todd had built the company. His father and his father's father had been high-powered executives. They had taught him about the business world and helped him with connections and investing in his new endeavor. Nevertheless, he had built the business. He saw it as his and his workers as part of his feudal kingdom. This is where problems began. He had grown up in a fairly paternalistic family where his father ruled the roost and his mother did what she was told, including putting up with his father's dalliances. Todd's father had also had a reputation for being a lady's man. In his younger years his affairs generally involved people he met in his travels.

As Todd grew older and his attention moved from growing his firm to harvesting its benefits, his inhibitions at pursuing young managers and administrative assistants declined. His caution and discretion also declined as he saw himself getting away with things year after year. His lunchtime alcohol consumption also contributed to his post-lunch appetite and lack of caution. Todd also often did not select suppliers who offered the best deal but the supplier whose sales rep was the most attractive and amenable to going more than an extra mile. Some suggested that his sexual behavior markedly increased after he saw a movie set in the Middle Ages about Droit de Seigneur, the right of the lord of the manor to sleep with any woman he wished.

Kayla had been with the firm for six months. She was clearly a star as well as very attractive. Todd invited her to lunch to discuss her career path in the company. He noted that since she did not play golf, they had not had the opportunity to get to know each other as he had with the new male managers, and this would pose a hindrance in her advancement. He suggested that she accompany him on a business trip. She agreed. When they arrived, she was more than a little surprised to find that Todd had booked only one room.

Cultures vary in terms of what is allowed and what is expected. Some cultures tolerate or encourage comments and touching that are not accepted in America. When people come from another culture, it is important to let them know what is appropriate and what is not.

Clueless in a New Culture

Dan and Jason (Americanized versions of their names) came to New York from overseas offices. They were young, spirited, bright, and eager. Neither had yet spent time in the United States, and both were unfamiliar with American culture and mores. Making matters worse, a practical joker had told them that single American women always play hard to get and are insulted if you do not pursue them. Pinching a female coworker's bottom was necessary, and to not do so would be the equivalent of calling her a dog. Moreover, American women always sleep with you on the first date unless they find you abhorrent.

When a female junior manager asked Jason to join her and her friends for drinks, he assumed she was very interested. After the drinks, when she agreed to come and see his place he was sure that he would be having company for the night. He was stunned when she announced she was going home shortly after arriving. The next day, he asked her out for dinner, but she said she was busy. He proceeded to drop by her desk a couple of times a day to talk and flirt and to ask her out. Her repeatedly telling him no had little effect. His comments about her lovely body and hair did not help to win her affection.

He was totally astonished when he received a call from HR that a sexual harassment claim had been made against him.

Some sexual harassment is driven by anger at women. The harassment is a means of devaluing them, by treating them as objects. The harassing manager may make insulting comments about women in general or inappropriate sexual comments, or may inappropriately touch someone.

Misogynist

Some thought that Charles was very fond of women, since he focused so much attention on them. Others realized that what he liked was conquering women and adding trophies to his collection. He would often hang out with the boys, making relatively raunchy jokes. But, where others would limit such joking to after-hours drinks in all-male crowds, Charles seemed to revel in making the comments when women were present.

When discussing potential hires, he would comment not only on their education, presentation, and technical skills, but on their legs and breasts; he made guesses as to whether they were likely to sleep with senior management and clients. Earlier in his career, Charles restricted these comments to the boys, but in time, as his power grew and his anger at women grew, he spoke freely in mixed crowds.

When Sara came to him to talk about her year-end review and ask about possibilities for a promotion, Charles said she would need to increase her value to him by sleeping with him. When Leah noted she was having trouble with a sale, Charles said she should sleep with the client. She responded that she was serious about trying to get some help. He said he was serious about his recommendation and that since she clearly couldn't make the sale any other way, he expected her to follow his advice.

He was less tactful with administrative assistants and rarely missed a chance to make a sexual comment. If a female admin looked tired or distracted, he would comment on how her boyfriend or someone she met at a bar must have kept her up and he hoped she had shown him a reasonable time. Sometimes he offered to help her develop her skills so that she could earn enough at her night job to not need to work during the day.

At times his behavior was even worse. He had slapped more than one female employee on the backside. On occasion he had literally backed women into a corner and pressed himself against them, saying that he had more to offer them than they had ever seen.

Some thought of suing for harassment; many thought of complaining to upper management. Those who did complain were asked if perhaps they had misheard; they were told that Charles was a crucial part of the business and that filing sexual harassment charges that they could not prove would not help their careers, whereas showing they were good sports and could handle common annoyances would help them advance. People relented under the pressure and did not file complaints. Charles' behavior continued and many good people left the company. In time a woman who could not be bullied by management decided to file charges. Charles' long history of sexual harassment came out and the company lost millions in the lawsuit.

Our understanding of the unfairness and harm resulting from the ways women have often been treated has grown. With it, the guidelines for acceptable behavior have changed. Some managers come from an earlier generation and have difficulty adhering to the new guidelines.

Dinosaurs

Peter knew that he was a bit of a dinosaur. He did not, however, realize that he stepped on people's toes as he walked around. His statements about the girls in the office and their being cute were not meant to be offensive. Comments about certain things not being appropriate for women did not come from a dislike of women but from having grown up in a different culture. His not being used to women in certain positions or on the golf course was also more out of habit than any lack of respect.

Growing older is difficult, especially in the absence of a satisfying family life. In an attempt to reclaim youthfulness or to gain some intimacy, people sometimes engage in inappropriate sexual behavior. Their judgment collapses under their emotional distress.

Growing Older and Lonelier ────────────────

There is a difference between not feeling your age and denying your age. Karl felt his age and wanted to deny it. He was not where he had hoped he would be by this stage of his life. His career had progressed well, but he had not reached—and would not reach—the top of his profession. He was well paid and respected, but he would not wow people at a high-school reunion of his preppy school. His home life was also mixed. He had three grown children who were all doing well and who even visited home. They did not come home that often, however, and when they did, it was more to see their mother. Even worse, his once adoring daughters now adored their boyfriends, and not him. His marriage was doing less well. He and his wife had grown disenchanted with each other and were considering separating. Karl was clearly depressed. His energy and concentration were suffering. He could get his work done, but not much more than that.

He mistook some of the smiles of administrative assistants and young managers as signs of romantic interest. He began hugging people too often, touching their arm or shoulder for too long, and standing too closely. His "touchy-feely" behavior was worse when he drank, and he drank more these days. It wasn't clear to either Karl or the women in the office whether his actions were meant as a come-on or if he was unaware of what he was doing. Nevertheless, some were very uncomfortable, especially those who had not known him over the years.

Men are also subject to sexual harassment. In general, men are even less likely than women to report it. Nevertheless, they can also be seriously hurt by sexual harassment.

Men Can Be Victims Too ────────────────

It is not clear whether Claire hated men in general or simply felt they were objects not worthy of respect. Her childhood had left her with the feeling that men were worthless and lazy—and dangerous. Regardless, it was hard to miss how uncomfortable she was around male managers. Her top people were always female. Men were given less responsibility and less interesting work. If a woman needed a few hours or a day off, she received it. Men were told to take a vacation day, but only with a month's notice. Men were also treated as women had stereotypically been treated. Male managers were expected to get her coffee, bring her lunch, and take her clothing to be dry-cleaned. Female managers, who in Claire's eyes had suffered doing such things over the decades, were never asked to do such things. Claire wanted to even the score.

Claire and some peers were a bit intoxicated at an offsite company gathering. Richard worked under her. He was on the quiet side, was small, and could be intimidated. Claire started treating him like a servant, wanting him to massage her feet. He started to leave, but Claire informed him that his biyearly review was coming up, and if he wanted to survive in the company, he had better massage all of the women's feet at the table. Richard felt sick to his stomach. He had a good job, good opportunities, and was with a name company. He began massaging his coworkers' feet, feeling quite sick. The women jostled him and patted his bottom, and one of them even tried to grab his zipper.

On Monday Richard was too embarrassed to go back in to work. Attempts to talk with friends were futile—they only laughed and said that it sounded like fun and he should have enjoyed the game. Richard rapidly slipped into a deep depression. His psychiatrist placed him on antidepressants. In a brief period when he was feeling better, his lawyer convinced him to sue for sexual harassment.

Emotional Intelligence Approach to Dealing with Sexual Harassment

Dealing with Sexual Harassment by a Superior

The first step in an EI approach to sexual harassment is assessing whether the offender is clueless, depressed and needy, a misogynist, a dinosaur, or someone who feels he has a right to the entire bounty of his company. Different steps are needed to deter sexually harassing behavior depending upon what is driving it.

If the offender is simply clueless, the path is relatively straightforward. A clueless person will generally curb offensive behavior when told that his or her actions are hurting you and seriously interfering with your ability to do your job. Be as specific about the offending behavior as possible. Allowing the person to save face maximizes the likelihood that the offender will respond to your complaint. Stating that you know that the person meant no offense, and perhaps even that you may unintentionally have sent the wrong signal, can help avert a polarized argument in which the person tries to defend his or her actions. If you back the person into a corner and attack, he or she is more likely to deny that the behavior was a problem or to assert that you encouraged the behavior.

If the person is remorseful, you usually need to do no more. If the person is dubious and does not think that his or her behavior is a problem, he or she may still agree to keep it under control. If, however, the person fails to keep it under control after this initial discussion or denies that there is a problem, ask if he or she would behave the same way in front of a spouse, or mother, or TV camera, or the boss. If the person is still unresponsive, explain that you will file a sexual harassment complaint if the behavior continues.

Misogynists and narcissistic managers, who feel that they have all rights to their company's property and employees, are more difficult to deal with. These managers are unlikely to respect your feelings but may respond to a direct confrontation and statement of consequences. Start with an informal, one-on-one discussion in which the unacceptable behavior is clearly described along with a statement that it creates a hostile work environment impeding your ability to do your work. Focus on the behavior. If the person indicates a willingness to change and actually does change, be satisfied. It is extremely tempting to attack the person's decency, to insist that he or she did awful things, and to want the person to take responsibility for being a jerk. You deserve to be able to do each of these, but doing so is not really in your interests, since it is likely to lead to a power struggle and interfere with your main objective, i.e., getting the person to cease the inappropriate behavior. It is generally best to accept lame excuses and let the person save face, as long as he or she promises that the behavior will end. You want to avoid getting into a power struggle in which the person feels belittled and feels a need to strike back. If you cause the person a narcissistic injury (a major embarrassment), he or she may become enraged, lose judgment, and strike out at you.

Carrying yourself with confidence is crucial. Misogynists and narcissistic managers are basically bullies they respect power and strength. If they see that they cannot intimidate you, they will be less interested in harassing you. If they see you as vulnerable and weak, they will attack; sharks go after the wounded swimmer. Knowing what the next steps are and being prepared to take them if your harasser is not responsive will increase your confidence. Therefore, it is important to have already developed your support system, spoken with people you can trust about the behavior, documented in detail all examples that you can, and to have done some probing around to see if others have been harassed and are willing to speak up. When possible, it can be helpful to confront the harasser in the presence of other people who have been harassed or witnessed the harassment. It is much harder to deny the behavior or to attack when facing two or more people who complain. There is great power in numbers.

Your inner confidence and the poise with which you carry yourself will be greater if you are prepared to take the next step in the event that the offender does not respond reasonably to your initial complaint. Therefore, before your initial encounter, you should know the company policies for making sexual harassment complaints. If the informal discussion fails, you can either go to HR or the chain of command or through formal complaint channels. Often, it is better to go to the offender's boss's boss than to his or her direct superior. By going up two levels, you will find someone who is less personally attached to the offending manager, less in need of his or her services, and therefore more likely to listen. Before choosing a path of action, it is important to learn as much as possible about how different channels are likely to handle your complaint. In some companies, certain channels are supportive while others are not. Some channels may automatically escalate the situation faster than you want to and faster than is helpful. Informal interventions by a third party can sometimes break through the harassing manager's resistance to listening without escalating the situation out of control.

It is usually best to delay making a formal complaint of sexual harassment until you have tried other options. Once you have made the complaint, the offender will need to defend himself by denying the behavior or claiming that you encouraged it. Given that the person has more power within the company than you have, your position may suffer whether or not you are in the right. Having the option of a formal complaint is a better deterrent than exercising it.

Lawsuits for sexual harassment are an option. They are costly to both victim and victimizer and should be used with caution. The decision to go this route is beyond the scope of this book.

Dealing with Sexual Harassment by a Peer

Sexual harassment by a peer can also be a significant problem. It can distract you from your work, preoccupy your thoughts, and cause significant distress.

It is not necessary to assess if the behavior you dislike is sexual harassment. All you need to assess is whether you dislike it. Then you need to tell the person. When first trying to stop the behavior, it is often better to not worry about whether it constitutes sexual harassment. Defining it as such is likely to increase your upset and make it harder to speak with the person. Moreover, if you decide it is not actually sexual harassment, you might hesitate in talking to the person. If someone's comments, touching, or staring cause discomfort, you should tell him or her how it affects you whether or not it crosses the line into sexual harassment.

When broaching the topic a simple statement that the behavior makes you uncomfortable and gets in the way of your work is usually sufficient. The person may make excuses. It is best to tolerate these attempts to save face and to focus on the issue of whether the behavior will end. It is often annoying to hear a silly excuse. Nevertheless, try to let it go and focus on making it clear that the behavior needs to end immediately. Sometimes, the person does not completely stop immediately. This could be due to testing you or to an honest mistake. Simply repeat the need for it to stop.

After you have twice stated clearly that the behavior needs to stop and it has not, it is time to do a more thorough assessment. A variety of things could be going on. People continue their behavior when told to stop for a variety of reasons:

- Not understanding what you want them to stop
- Not understanding why it is important and feeling you are being unreasonable
- Being preoccupied with other issues and accidentally falling into the old pattern (stressed managers, ADHD)
- Not appreciating that you are serious
- Disliking being told what to do (rigid managers)
- Not caring about your feelings (narcissistic managers)
- Wanting to provoke you (aggressive managers)

Someone who is preoccupied and forgets simply needs to be reminded. Some people will need further clarification of what you want stopped. Some will try and minimize the issue and not realize how important it is to you until you remind them. Some will need the extra push of having a colleague speak to them. It may need to come from HR or a superior. Narcissistic and aggressive managers are the hardest to deal with. They may relent once you have made it clear that you are serious and that you are willing to take the next step and make a formal complaint. If you do have to take this final step it is helpful to obtain backing from others who suffered from or witnessed the inappropriate behavior.

Dealing with Sexual Harassment by a Subordinate

If you see or hear about a subordinate who is behaving in ways that can make another worker uncomfortable, you should say something. The sooner you intervene, the less likely the situation will get out of hand. You do not need to launch a sexual harassment investigation unless a formal complaint has been filed. You need to speak to the person who is behaving in a questionable way and let him know that he is interfering with someone else's work and potentially placing himself and the company at risk. You may also want to speak to those who might be being made uncomfortable and see how they feel about the questionable behavior.

It is generally not a good idea for members of a team to date. There is great risk for uncomfortable feelings that can interfere with the work of the group. If a couple really wants to date, it is better if one of them moves to a different department. If someone is flirting with people within a group, you can gently discourage it. If people are going to date, they should be able to show enough discretion that no one else in the group knows about it.

For HR and Senior Management

The issue of sexual harassment and the multimillion dollar lawsuits that have arisen from it pose a serious problem for many firms. Many firms are tempted to bar dating. With 70 percent of people meeting their partners at work, however, companies that choose to do this could lose many desirable employees. It could also cut into people's willingness to work long hours, since it would require that single people spend more time outside of work in order to meet people. Some companies ask people to sign a contract that they will not sue the company as a result of their romantic involvement with someone, before having their first date. This has a somewhat stifling effect and invasive feel to it, and may well lose you people you would like to have work for you.

The best solution is generally to permit dating but to provide ample education on sexual harassment and an effective means by which people can seek redress within the company. A person's immediate superior should not be the person to whom you report sexual harassment problems, since this may well be the person who is behaving inappropriately. Moreover, an individual's immediate superior will also have other things on his or her mind than whether the harassment complaint is valid, such as the relative importance of each person to the team. It is also important to take steps against those who sexually harass others in order to clearly show that the company means business. A company can also bar managers from going out with people who report to them.

Companies can be held liable for sexual harassment committed by their employees. The risk of being held liable is less if there is an effective sexual harassment policy. An effective policy means, at a minimum, that

- ◆ The company has a sexual harassment policy overseen by a senior corporate official.
- ◆ It clearly informs people what sexual harassment is and that it will not be tolerated.
- ◆ All new employees are informed of the policy upon hiring, and all employees are periodically reminded of it.
- ◆ It establishes procedures for reporting abuse, including two routes for filing complaints (neither of which is through the person's manager).
- ◆ It trains managers to recognize and deal with harassment.
- ◆ Complaints are dealt with confidentially, protecting the rights of both the accused and accuser.
- ◆ Records are kept of the investigation.
- ◆ Accusations are quickly investigated, and violations are dealt with seriously.
- ◆ Accusers are protected unless a complaint can be proved malicious.

Dating and Flirting at Work

Flirting and dating at work are risky. It is understandable, given how much time we spend at work and the limited opportunities for meeting people outside, that if you meet someone interesting at work, you may want to pursue a relationship. Doing so has hazards. It is helpful to know what they are and to take some simple steps to minimize them.

First, conduct yourselves discreetly so that coworkers are unaware that you are dating. Don't flirt with each other at work, avoid touching while at work, and don't make plans for dates while there. Look outside the company for confidantes to discuss the relationship and its ups and downs with.

It is also best to go slowly in the relationship to lessen the likelihood of a sudden and messy breakup that will make it difficult to be in the same office. If flirting or signaling become at all complicated in a relationship with someone at work, it is best to back away. Work is not the place for confusing messages and the problems that occur when people are unclear about each others' romantic interests. Confusion at this stage is often a sign that things will be complicated down the road.

Even if things are going smoothly, it is good policy to discuss with the person you are interested in what it will be like to work in the same company if and when the dating relationship does not work out or you have different ideas of where you want it to go. Finally, be careful in the type of person you pick. An excitable, narcissistic individual may be attractive to you. You would not, however, want to be in the same work space with this person after a breakup.

If someone shows interest in you and you are not interested, you need to give a clear but gentle message. Think about how you would want to hear the message if your positions were reversed. At the same time that you are being tactful, it is important to avoid being unclear. If the person fails to hear your first message or wants to indefinitely discuss the issue with you, find new words to say the same thing. You may then need to state that continuing to discuss the issue would be harassment and destructive to your ability to work. It is also important to be able to take a quick no if you receive one from someone you are working with.

When ending a relationship, it is important, once again, to be tactful but clear. You need to avoid giving mixed messages about what you want. It will drive the other person crazy. This is not a situation in which you can tell someone the relationship is over and then act flirtatious or immediately turn them into a buddy you see often and confide in. If you hear that your partner does not want to continue the relationship, you need to be able to accept it. If you have difficulty with people ending relationships with you, you should not get into a relationship at work.

Conclusion

Sexual harassment is both a very destructive and a very common problem in organizational life. Complicating matters, victims are often afraid to report it, and for good reason. A boss who is willing to engage in sexual harassment will be willing to lie about it. Moreover, bosses' power within the organization often enables them to win, unless there is considerable collaboration of the complaints against them.

At the same time, the threat of sexual harassment claims can either deter or terrify those who might want to pursue a workplace romance using appropriate discretion and tact. It is impossible to know with certainty whether the person you are interested in might experience any show of interest as harassment, or in the midst of disappointment at the end of a relationship, might feel that he or she had been unfairly used and harassed. The best advice is to go very slowly, to err heavily on the side of caution, and never engage in an extended pursuit of someone who is not demonstrating clear interest. When a relationship goes slowly you will be better able to assess in time whether the person you are interested in has significant emotional issues that could lead to a post relationship vendetta. Murphy's Law is worth remembering, "Don't sleep with anyone crazier than yourself."

If someone is harassing you there are a number of ways to deal with the situation. The emotional intelligence approach holds that understanding what lies underneath a given behavior is crucial in dealing with it. A clueless individual simply needs education, while those who feel entitled to do as they will with subordinates need to be contained, or removed. Clear but nonattacking statements by the victim of what the harasser is doing that is discomforting is usually the best way to begin. The harasser's immediate response to the confrontation about their behavior, and the changes that do or do not occur over the ensuing weeks will tell you a great deal about their psychological makeup and what will ultimately be needed to ameliorate the situation. Finally, organizations need clear policies and ways for people to report abuse without fear of retaliation.

Your Turn

- ◆ What sexual harassment have you observed or experienced?
- ◆ What do you think lay underneath the behavior?
- ◆ How did the behavior affect you?
- ◆ How did the behavior affect others?
- ◆ How did the behavior affect productivity?
- ◆ What did you or others try to do to cope? What worked, and what did not?

- What did you learn?
- How would you do things differently in the future?
- What advice would you give to someone facing different types of sexual harassment?
- Have you ever been accused of sexual harassment?
  - Was the accusation fair?
  - What did you do?
  - How would you do things differently in the future
- Given the current climate and laws, would you date someone with whom you work?
- How, if at all, would you alter your normal dating behavior in order to avoid problems?
- What would you advise others regarding dating?
- What would you say to subordinates who wanted to date?
- What would you say to subordinates who were openly dating?

Further Reading

Shakespeare's *Romeo and Juliet* shows just how dangerous dating in a highly political environment can be.

CHAPTER 11

Chauvinists Needing Diversity Training

I'm Better than You

Nonsexual harassment and discrimination, like sexual harassment, are common and serious problems in organizations. They do considerable damage both to the individuals subjected to it and to the companies in which it occurs. Working to eliminate it is not simply a question of making a more pleasant workplace. Eliminating it can improve productivity, retention, information sharing, and gain clients.

Why Do People Harass and Discriminate Against Others?

People engage in harassment and discrimination for a wide variety of reasons. Some are uncomfortable dealing with anyone who is different from them—someone with a different ethnic, cultural, educational, or demographic background. Others have difficulty with one particular group as a result of a stereotype they hold. Rigid belief in stereotypes blinding people to what someone is really like can be driven by a desire to look down on others. Some people reinforce their self-esteem by looking down on others and then comparing themselves to this disparaged group. Similarly, some people want someone to blame for their own failures and weaknesses—a scapegoat. It feels better to blame someone else for your failures than to believe that you did not have what it takes to succeed. Other people are filled with anger and by having a group to focus their anger on, they can avoid having their anger spill out onto those they work and live without damaging those relationships. Stereotyping, exclusion, and harassment of an out-group also serves to support group solidarity. Social scientists have written of the "need to have enemies" in order to reinforce group solidarity and one's own identity. Other people think negatively about another group, or all other groups, because they were taught that they are superior or that another group is dangerous. Finally, some people take advantage of commonly held prejudices as a means of attacking someone they wish to attack for political reasons.

Understanding why someone is engaging in stereotyping and harassment will help you to intervene effectively.

The Cost of Harassment and Discrimination

Harassment and discrimination can be devastating to the person subjected to it. Being faced with anger and disparagement leads to fear and often anger that rob our energy, enthusiasm, and ability to think creatively and efficiently. It can lead to burnout, depression, destruction of self-esteem, and anxiety. Even at very low levels, it can damage work performance.

Harassment and discrimination also hurt the organization. They damage productivity and interfere with hiring and retention of good people. They also damage the organization's reputation and ability to attract and keep clients, and may place the organization in legal jeopardy. Female executives leave Fortune 500 companies at twice the rate of men. In a study of female executives earning over $150,000 a year, 39 percent said that the main reason they left was their firm's culture: closed management style, and denigration of their work.[1] Diversity increases an organization's ability to respond to clients of different backgrounds, to see new opportunities and perspectives, and to enlarge the potential pool of hires.

Chauvinism can occur in many forms. Sometimes, the main symptom is failure to give equal treatment in hiring, promotion, and work assignments to a particular group or to anyone not in your group.

Glass Ceilings

Greg was looking forward to lunch with the new hire. Chris had good credentials, went to the right schools, had good grades, was on the track team in school, and was recently married with a child. When Greg heard a knock at his door and opened it, he was startled to see that Chris was neither male nor white. Greg quickly regained his composure and invited Christine in, but a bit more formally than he had planned.

Greg felt that women did not belong in the workplace. Things became messy when women were at work. You had to watch your jokes. You couldn't relate to coworkers in the same way. You could not be yourself. Greg had never learned to treat women as equals who were able to do all that a man could do.

Greg avoided giving Chris an assignment on which they would be working together, even though he typically did so with new hires. Chris was puzzled, but accepted Greg's excuses for not needing her assistance until she found out that Greg sought the assistance of a young male manager. When Chris asked about it, Greg stumbled over his reply and said that he was actually about to give her an assignment. In doling out work to Chris and Eric, Greg showed a marked preference for giving the mundane work to Chris and the interesting tasks to Eric, even when Chris's background provided superior credentials. It was also much more common for Greg to ask Eric to get together after work or on the weekend. Chris could sense the difference and was very uncomfortable.

Sometime the core of chauvinism and harassment consists of caustic comments and teasing. The joking is not funny to the person on the receiving end.

Harassing Comments

Jim liked to tease and tell jokes. He thought he was funny; others thought he was demeaning. It is not clear whether he simply markedly lacked empathy and did not realize that many would find his statements offensive or whether he had a very good sense of what would push people's buttons. In any event, many were put off by his racial and religious comments. Every now and then, he threw in a joke about WASPs and presented that as proof that he was not a bigot.

He also liked to talk about sociology and history. His negative comments about crime statistics in the African American community were most likely to be mentioned when an African American was in the room. After 9/11, he made many negative comments about Muslims, their religion, their culture, and their history whenever a Muslim manager was present. He brought a friend to a company party, who proceeded to discuss similar issues, with even less tact that Jim, in front of a Muslim manager and an African American manager. Jim sat back and said nothing as his friend poured out venom.

The jokes and teasing upset many people. Good minority managers left the group and new ones refused to join. Productivity suffered. Nevertheless, Jim did not pick up on what was happening. He saw his group's failure to attract and retain good minority managers as evidence that they did not exist.

Emotional Intelligence Approach to Chauvinistic Behavior

When Your Boss Needs Diversity Training

You are in a particularly difficult situation when your boss is the one who needs diversity training. People in power are almost uniformly allergic to being criticized by subordinates. Nevertheless, there are things you can do.

As with all toxic people, the (emotional intelligence) EI approach begins by assessing what you are dealing with. Is your boss being a chauvinist from cluelessness, as a result of his cultural/family background, or from a need to deal with insecurities about himself? The more deeply seated the problem, the more difficult it will be to effect change. Perhaps even more important than what lies underneath the behavior is how narcissistic your boss is and therefore how open he or she will be to criticism, self-reflection, and possibly changing.

As with all toxic managers, the situation is generally easiest if your boss is simply clueless. It can still be hard if your boss is rigid or narcissistic and objects to someone educating him or her. For clueless superiors who simply do not understand the impact of their jokes and statements on the listener, it is generally good to begin by noting that someone might have been offended by the comments or jokes. If the manager attempts to push it away by saying that he doubts it, you can gently pursue the issue by saying that people were, in fact, ill at ease. You should then watch and wait. If your manager stops or significantly decreases his problematic behavior, it is generally helpful to note the positive change at some point and let him know you appreciate his sensitivity and response to your request. If change does not begin within a couple of weeks, you need to try harder to convince your boss by having additional people speak with him, either individually or in a group. Use your judgment of your boss's style in assessing whether a group or series of visits from people is best. Simultaneously, or if this approach fails, you can speak with HR about providing diversity training.

If the issue is a glass ceiling rather than caustic comments, you are likely to need a group, discussion from the start. It is in some ways easier to effect a change in policy than in speaking style, but it is often harder to convince someone of the need for this change.

If your boss grew up in a culture or home that taught negative beliefs about a specific group, or all who are not part of one's identity group, effecting change is more difficult. You are not likely to effect a sudden change in lifelong beliefs. You also do not have to. You only need to effect a change in behavior. The same interventions can be used with this group that you use with clueless individuals. Point out that there are good and bad people in every demographic group and that it is unfair to punish or reject good people because of their demographic or ethnic heritage. After all, we do not punish entire families because there is one black sheep in them or assume that everyone is like that one person. With a little luck, your boss has a relative he or she dislikes and will catch on to this idea. As always, group interventions have more power than individual ones. If they do not work, following up with HR is often useful.

Bosses who need to disparage others in order to feel good about themselves present a much more difficult problem. You can begin with the steps we just discussed, but you will almost certainly need to do more. You are not going to heal people's underlying psychological problems. You may, however, be able to encourage them to contain their behavior by pointing out the destructive impact of their statements on productivity. One person speaking to such bosses on one occasion will not be sufficient. You need the strength of numbers and repetition. Encouraging multiple people to speak to them will encourage them to take you seriously and to put energy into being more careful about their behavior. In these situations, it will generally be necessary to speak to HR or your boss's superior. It is generally best to go two levels up in speaking to superiors, since the boss's boss is likely to be loyal to him. The boss's boss picked him and would be inconvenienced if she had to replace him. In this interaction, do your best to not let your anger pour out, no matter how justified it is. People tend to listen better when you are calm. Someone who might have listened if you were calm may assume that you are an hysterical complainer and discount your complaints if you are very angry when speaking about the abuse you have suffered.

Dealing with Glass Ceilings

We left Chris and Greg in a standoff. Greg was being polite to Chris but was keeping her at arm's length, not giving her equal assignments to those Eric received, and not including her in activities. Chris's choices were to suffer in silence (not recommended), speak up calmly and logically, tell Greg off (satisfying but also not recommended), transfer within the company, or leave the company. She was prepared to leave but felt that there was no reason to start there. Besides, doing so would not fix the basic problem.

She began by telling Greg that it appeared that she was not being treated equally. It was very tempting to clearly say that she was being treated unfairly. She realized, however, that this would decrease her willingness to listen. She was more concerned with effecting change for the future than attaining an apology for the past or simply venting her annoyance. Her boss did, in fact, come up with excuses. She knew, however, that she had put him on notice. She left with his promise that in the future she would have the assignments she needed and that Eric would not be automatically getting better assignments. If she had not gotten this promise, she would have requested a transfer and discussed the issue with superiors.

Chris decided to also speak with HR to put them on notice. She did this only after being assured that the issue would be kept in confidence and would not go directly back to her boss or into the chain of command. She took the chance that HR would keep this private, and they did.

Her boss's behavior did change, and that was enough for now. Nevertheless, Chris was concerned about the future and rather than staying in this department indefinitely she took an opportunity to move on after a number of months.

Deciding when to stay and when to leave is frequently very difficult. If the behavior remains outrageous and causes you so much distress that your work, personal life, and health suffer, the answer is simple. If it changes markedly and you are able to forgive, the answer is also simple. Often, however, if offensive behavior improves rather than vanishes, and the chauvinist does not fully understand the problem. In these situations, the decision will depend upon your ability to look past it, how much distress it is causing you, and what alternatives you have for employment. There are no easy answers—just a list of factors that need to be carefully weighed and balanced.

Dealing with Racist Comments

Brad was ready to leave Jim's group and file a lawsuit for harassment because of Jim's constant racial jokes and slurs. A colleague said he sympathized, and in the end seeing might be necessary. He urged Brad to first try to mobilize support and have people confront Jim. They went to each person in the group who they thought would be sympathetic and discussed the problem in detail. They discussed how unfair and painful the comments were, and how they had cost the group good people.

The most influential group members set up an appointment with Jim to discuss the issue. They noted that they were speaking for a larger group. As much as some of them wanted to tell Jim off, they realized that painting him into a corner and saying what a jerk he was would only polarize the situation and make him more rigid. They cared more about changing the situation than about the pleasure they would have in telling him off. Therefore, they avoided direct attacks and focused on how the behavior was unfair and harmful to the group, as well as a potential legal problem. The group provided innumerable examples of painful comments. They did not argue with Jim's statements that he had not meant any harm and was simply joking. They realized that almost anyone, when criticized, initially responds with excuses. Moreover, if they insisted on an abject apology, they were likely to get nothing.

After going through the litany of problematic statements they focused on the need for a promise that things would be different. Jim agreed. He also realized he was on notice. In the weeks ahead, he made slips. People responded by noting them. He would then smile and apologize. The change was adequate.

A couple of years later, Jim called Brad in and apologized for his past behavior. This meant more to Brad than if Jim had made an immediate, but insincere apology under pressure.

When Your Peer Needs Diversity Training

If someone treats peers from certain groups unfairly or makes caustic comments, it is important to speak up. To be silent condones the behavior. The same interventions can be used that you employed for dealing with your boss. The primary differences are that the risk of retaliation is less and using high levels of tact, although always desirable, is not as crucial.

When Your Subordinate Needs Diversity Training

If a subordinate treats members of a racial or ethnic group unfairly or makes demeaning statements, it is crucial to step in and let them know, as well as those whom they are treating unfairly, that this will not be tolerated. Once again, avoiding unnecessary embarrassment is generally better unless you want the person to resign. Depending upon how deep seated the behavior is, you may simply need to speak to the person, send him to a diversity training program, or arrange for executive coaching/therapy. The central component is setting a clear limit and letting the offender know that the behavior is unacceptable and could lead to termination. If you fail to act you are essentially condoning the behavior and place yourself at risk.

For HR and Senior Management

Many diversity development programs have failed to bring about the desired changes. A common reason is failure to connect the program to the company's key success factors. As a result, senior management fails to appreciate the program's importance and therefore fails to supply adequate backing and resources. Moreover, resources are, at times, wasted because initiatives are carried out without an adequate understanding of the specific areas that need change or inadequate appreciation of what has already been accomplished through existing programs. Sometimes, people are not taught the skills they need to effect change. Another problem is failure to establish follow-through: monitoring of diversity issues in the months and years ahead.

A successful program sometimes needs a full scale change management initiative. This includes:

◆ Motivation for change

◆ Education on what needs change and how to accomplish it

◆ Skills development

◆ Modeling by leaders of the desired behavior

◆ Support of the new behavior by leaders' statements

◆ Support of change by hiring and promoting those supporting the new culture

◆ Performance measurement system taking the desired cultural attitudes and behavior into account

◆ Monitoring of change

Model Diversity Development Program

1. Do cultural audit (surveys, interviews, focus groups, people who left in the last year) to determine
   a. Experience of employees
   b. Impact of the culture on employees
   c. Professional development and sense of inclusion of groups
   d. Ways the firm's systems and culture support or inhibit diversity
2. Understanding of key success factors for the firm
3. Design diversity initiative to support firm's key success factors and current weaknesses
4. Propose options
   a. Seminars
      i. Diversity awareness
      ii. Benefits of diversity for the firm
      iii. Communicating across differences (case studies and role playing)
      iv. Sensitivity to others (case studies and role playing)
      v. Supporting diversity
   b. Coaching for change leaders
   c. Promote diversity in hiring and promotion
   d. Coaching for people needing one-on-one assistance

   e. Follow-up audits

   f. System for ongoing hearing of problems

   g. Exit interviews

   h. Support of diversity as part of measurement and reward system

Conclusion

The importance of diversity training to curb discrimination has gained increasing acceptance in recent years. Nevertheless, the potential positive value of diversity, along with the negative impact of chauvinism on companies, is often not appreciated. Companies that fail to support diversity will be handicapped in competing with companies that do. Chauvinistic companies will be handicapped in the pursuit of managerial talent and risk alienating potential customers. This handicap is likely to grow as groups learn how to wield their power and punish companies that treat them as second-class citizens.

Table 11–1 Overview of Chauvinism

Factors Promoting Chauvinism	Recommended Organizational Response to Chauvinism
Reinforce fragile self-esteem by looking down on others	Diversity training
	Zero tolerance for harassment
Avoid blame for failures by scapegoating	Having people work together for a common goal they cannot achieve alone
Displace anger to protect key relationships	
Reinforce group solidarity	Culture change initiative to promote a shared organizational identity
Endemic cultural attitude/early learning	Executive coaching and monitoring of behavior for the most serious offenders
Support a political agenda by manipulating people's prejudices	

The tendency of many to engage in stereotyping, harassment and discrimination can be contained by training and focused interventions with those who are most problematic. A modest investment in this area holds the potential for considerable rewards.

Your Turn

- ◆ What acts of chauvinism (nonsexual harassment and discrimination) by managers have you observed?
- ◆ Describe it.
- ◆ What do you think lay underneath the behavior
- ◆ How did the behavior affect you?
- ◆ How did the behavior affect others?
- ◆ How did the behavior affect productivity?
- ◆ How did the behavior affect hiring and retention?
- ◆ How did the behavior affect communication?
- ◆ What did you and others try to do to cope?
- ◆ What worked, and what did not? (What made things better, and what made things worse?)
- ◆ What did you learn?
- ◆ How would you do things differently in the future?
- ◆ What advice would you give to someone facing nonsexual harassment or discrimination?
- ◆ Do you at times act in similar ways?
  - • If so, where did your attitudes come from?
  - • How does it affect people?
  - • How does it affect your team?
  - • How does it affect your career?

Endnote

1. The Leader's Edge Research, 2002.

CHAPTER 12

Volatile Managers

Everything Upsets Me

Some managers are volatile and have a short fuse that burns with remarkable speed when they are under stress. If you catch them on the wrong day, you may face a deluge as their anger pours out in response to trivial issues. It can seem as if they were almost looking for someone to yell at, and you had the misfortune to be the one who walked into their office. Although caustic when upset they can also be very nice, leaving you confused about what to expect from one minute to the next. Since you do not know when they will be in one of their moods and you may inadvertently step on a hidden landmine, you are likely to be constantly on guard and ill at ease.

Origins of Volatile Behavior

Underneath the tendency of some managers to have explosive outbursts of anger, one generally finds considerable distress. They snap because they are in pain. As a result of depression, being burned out, an anxiety disorder, or post traumatic stress disorder, small annoyances feel overwhelming. Each new issue feels like the straw that broke the camel's back.

Frequently, but certainly not always, there are troublesome personality traits and ways of perceiving the world that foster the irritability. In particular, many volatile managers have a tendency to interpret all actions as being directed at them. For example, if someone fails to help them, they see it as a sign of the person's lack of consideration for them rather than simply a sign that the person was very concerned about other things. If they are depressed, they are likely to believe that people dislike them. If they are narcissistic, they may see others as being jealous or hostile.

A frequent reason that managers snap at someone is that someone has snapped at them or is pressuring them. Aggression, like electricity, takes the path of least resistance. I remember seeing a father yell at a six-year-old, who immediately slapped his four-year-old brother, who immediately hit his two-year-old brother, who immediately slapped his pregnant mother's belly. How many of us have come home after being given a hard time by a client or a superior on whom we could not readily push back and then snapped at our kids over nothing? When managers are given a difficult time by their superiors or a major client, they are likely to take it out on subordinates. The technical term is *displacement*.

Volatile managers are often moody and go through cycles of good days and bad days. They may also have times of the day when they are typically in good or bad moods. Knowing when they are more and less volatile can help you to avoid being caught in a downpour.

Volatile managers often feel badly after chopping someone's head off. Sometimes they make excuses to themselves for their behavior and argue that the person deserved it. Unlike bullies and sadistic managers, they do not enjoy attacking and demeaning others, and would rather not do it. They can't help themselves, however.

Borderline personality disorder drives the volatility of some people who have angry outbursts. Borderline personality disorder is related to narcissistic personality disorder. While people with narcissistic personality disorder go into a narcissistic rage that overwhelms their judgment in response to a threat to their self-esteem, people with borderline personality disorder fly into a rage when there is a threat to a crucial relationship. They become frantic when they feel they may be abandoned. Their moods are unstable and they have intensive periods of anxiety, depression, or irritability lasting a few hours or days. They generally have a chronic feeling of emptiness interrupted at times by brief euphoric periods when relationships are going well, and very painful mood when relationships feel unstable. They are often impulsive and abuse drugs or alcohol, drive recklessly, spend money they do not have, act in a promiscuous manner, or try to hurt themselves or others. Their relationships are unstable, and they vacilate between idealizing and devaluing people. Under stress, they may become paranoid or dissociate (feel that they or the world is unreal, as if they are living in a dream or a movie). Their anger is inappropriate, intense, and under poor control.

Factors Fostering Volatility

◆ Stress
◆ Medical problems
◆ Pain
◆ Difficulty sleeping
◆ Depression
◆ Anxiety disorder
◆ ADHD
◆ Alcohol and drugs
◆ Personality disorders
  • Narcissistic
  • Borderline
  • Paranoid
  • Antisocial

Organizational Impact of Volatile Managers

Volatile managers can have a very negative impact on an organization. One of the most malignant aspects of irritability is that it is highly contagious. Having someone frequently angry with you adds markedly to your stress level and can push you past your ability to contain your distress. Moreover, the behavior of one or more high-level volatile managers can negatively impact the culture and make it seem acceptable to snap at people. In time, the irritability can become an epidemic.

Faced with a volatile manager, many people seek to shield themselves by caring less about work and putting their energy elsewhere. Others stay committed but find themselves preoccupied with anxiety about being harshly criticized, and they are therefore unable to fully focus on productive activities. Many cease being creative and practice only tried-and-true, safe options that seem to carry less risk. People may also become less open to sharing information lest being the bearer of bad news will get them in trouble. Productivity, morale, retention, and recruitment all suffer.

An interesting observation, as long as you are not the one being yelled at, is that managers who are particularly skilled with clients may be very irritable with subordinates. It is as if they hold all of their frustration inside while working with clients, and it pours out later with subordinates. Sometimes, they have an authoritarian personality style that permits venting aggression on subordinates but calls for exemplary tact with those above them, including clients.

A Volatile Manager (or, How Frank Learned ▬▬▬ His First Lesson about Scapegoating)

Bill had a reputation for losing his temper, so much so that many people avoided contact with him. As a result, he often did not hear about things in a timely manner. He became angry when he did hear, which only led people to avoid him even more.

Liz should have called Bill to tell him that her team was doing work that affected his department. She probably hesitated because of Bill's reputation. In any event, she decided to have Frank make the call, thinking it would be a growth experience for him.

Frank had not yet heard about Bill's reputation. Frank called Bill to tell him about his team's activities. Upon finding out that work that related to him had been going on for a while without his being informed, Bill lost his temper and proceeded to yell incessantly at Frank. Bill then called Liz's superior and yelled at him. Angry that Bill was yelling at him, and unable to do much about it, he ordered Liz to fire Frank.

Emotional Intelligence Approach to Dealing with Volatile Managers

The first step in dealing with volatile managers is correctly assessing that the problem is irritability and not bullying or being frantic. The prescription for dealing with volatile managers is very different from the prescription for dealing with sadistic bullies or ruthless managers. In fact, tactics that will calm a volatile manager are likely to provoke a bully.

The second issue is to assess whether the person has a serious personality disorder and is therefore at risk for engaging in violence if his or her Achilles' heel is threatened. There is a great difference between the brief annoyed (but unfair) statements, or even the yelling, of a stressed manager and the potential violence of a narcissistic or borderline manager who feels threatened. It is important to know how bad things can get, as well as when such managers are likely to be angry. In addition, change is often very possible in a relatively brief period of time for an irritable manager who is having a hard time dealing with stress. A volatile manager with a narcissistic, antisocial, or borderline personality disorder usually needs years of therapy to make sustained, significant improvement.

Diffusing the Situation

The Institute of Mental Health Initiatives provides a brief list of ways to calm an angry person:

- Reduce the noise level.
- Keep calm yourself.
- Acknowledge that the irate person has been wronged (if true), or, at least, acknowledge their feelings without any judgment.
- Ask them to explain their situation (so you can tactfully correct errors).
- Listen to their complaints without counterattacking.
- Explain your feelings with non-blaming "I" statements.

Responding in a respectful, concerned, nonhostile way is often sufficient to diffuse a situation with a volatile manager who has become angry. Their anger is fueled by the belief that you are not concerned with their feelings and that you may even be hostile to them. If you are calm and respectful, they will calm down. If, however, you respond in a dismissive or annoyed manner, the situation is likely to escalate and become polarized. In polarization, the parties are arguing for diametrically opposed positions that neither of them actually believe in. When faced with an accusation, most of us have a gut reaction, generally learned early in childhood, to strongly assert our innocence even if we are guilty. Sometimes, we feel belittled if we do not push back and assert our innocence. Some of us can avoid taking the caustic comments of toxic people seriously and can therefore maintain poise and appropriate behavior. Your confidence will grow if you accept and practice this.

When someone is angry with you, noting that you had no intention of causing her problems can sometimes help diffuse the situation, since on some level this is what she fears. Apologizing for causing her inconvenience and noting that you will do things differently in the future is also generally helpful. Saying this does not mean that you think that you made a mistake, only that you regret they were inadvertently inconvenienced, and given what you know now, you will do things differently in the future. Allowing someone to vent without arguing with them, and finding reason to empathize with their distress, will calm most volatile people. If it does not, then the person is not simply stressed from anxiety and depression, but has some problematic underlying personality traits.

Defusing a Potentially Explosive Situation ▄▄▄▄▄▄

Lydia was irritable and frequently had minor temper tantrums that blew over as fast as they arrived. The damage done to subordinates, however, lasted awhile.

When Tom walked into the conference room, he could sense something was wrong. Lydia's face was tense and she did not say her usual, "Hello, how was your weekend?" Tom asked what was wrong. Lydia launched into a monologue about how Tom was not pulling his weight on the new project. Lydia complained that she had worked all weekend while Tom played. Moreover, Tom had failed to send Lydia the draft report he had promised to send.

Tom's initial instinct was to push back, to tell Lydia about all the work that he had done, how he had worked several evenings while Lydia went out with friends, and how it was unreasonable to have him work on weekends in addition to 14-hour days. Tom had seen Lydia lose her temper before with people and knew that it tended to blow over quickly. Tom decided not to push back and to just let it pass. He acknowledged how hard Lydia was working and that an unfair portion of the burden had fallen on her over the weekend. He also acknowledged having fouled Lydia by failing to send the report. He acknowledged without demeaning himself that Lydia had good reason to be upset. Tom then switched gears and asked how he could be most helpful now. What could he do to get things on track? He offered to stay over in town that night to put in extra hours. Lydia noticeably calmed down and told Tom that it was not necessary for him to stay overnight, that the work would get done.

Some of the greatest wisdom for dealing with angry people comes from Eastern philosophies. For example, rigid trees break and die in a storm, while grass bends and survives. In time the storm passes and the grass survives to grow stronger. Bending, being flexible and accommodating, is often a better way to handle an angry and aggressive manager than getting into a power struggle about the appropriateness of his or her behavior.

Often, we want to push back in order to show that we cannot be pushed around. The result is further anger and deterioration of the relationship. In the process, you create an enemy who may choose to stab you in the back at the worst possible moment. It is very easy to make an enemy; there is no challenge to it or sport in it. The fun of having "given someone what they deserve" fades quickly.

There is sport and challenge, however, in turning a difficult person into someone who treats you better than they treat others. Tactfully handling these situations in ways that maintain both sides' self-esteem and avoids actions that could escalate the conflict opens the way for a change in the relationship.

Assuming that the volatile manager is not particularly narcissistic and is not borderline, it is often helpful to find a time when he or she is calm to talk about how being yelled at and belittled interferes with your doing an optimal job. If he is narcissistic, confronting him will only make matters worse, and it is best to ignore his tantrums the best you can and to leave for another position if staying is too stressful. Meanwhile, you can look forward to the time when he will self-destruct. Unless he changes, he will sooner or later fall on his own sword as his reputation for anger grows.

Helping Someone Fall on His or Her Own Sword

Annie was growing tired of Phillip's tirades. She had once tried to address the issue with Phillip, only to have Phillip become angrier. Annie did not have the connections to be able to go over Phillip's head. She did, however, know Doug, who had connections with top management. She convinced Doug to join her on a project that Phillip would be heavily involved in. This time, instead of walking on egg shells to avoid Phillip's blow-ups, Annie did her job as she would with most executives.

As expected, Phillip repeatedly lost his temper. Doug talked with senior management about Phillip's temper. Annie and another manager placed complaints shortly afterwards. Senior management told Phillip to get an executive coach and to get his act together soon or to move on.

Sometimes, an irritable manager who will not listen to one individual who comes to him to discuss the impact of his anger will listen if confronted en masse. An irritable manager can more easily discount the complaints of one person than of five or ten people. It is also safer to have several people approach a volatile, aggressive superior than for one person to do it. One person can be fired or transferred. The entire team cannot.

An Irritable Manager Slowly Brings Himself Under Control

Stanley had a reputation for snapping at people. It usually had much less to do with what they had or had not done than with how he was feeling that day. On most days, he was irritable. Over time, people noted that some of the most talented people in his division had left—more than was the norm for the company.

One day, Stanley snapped at Ben one too many times. Ben simply walked out of Stanley's office. Later, he came back and said, "Look we have to talk. I don't deserve to be yelled at that way. We've lost good people because of your yelling." Stanley became very defensive and got into an argument with Ben over how much he yelled, whether it was called for, and whether good people had actually left because of him. In the subsequent months, Stanley kept Ben at arm's length and kept Ben off of the projects that he himself was directly involved in—the best projects. Meanwhile, his snapping decreased for a while but then returned to baseline.

Ben asked me to consult. I suggested he begin to talk with other people on his level to see if he could build support for a group confrontation. People were hesitant but agreed that they would consider sitting down with Stanley as a group if a good intervention could be planned.

The group convinced Stanley to call me in to discuss morale, retention, and motivation. I suggested that we get 360-degree feedback on all senior managers. Stanley thought it was an acceptable idea as long as he was not included. Attempts to convince him failed. This anonymous feedback would have been the gentlest way to confront Stanley. Not being able to follow this path, the group agreed to confront him en masse. The group tried to arrange for an all-day retreat to discuss morale and motivation. The retreat was held, but Stanley decided he was too busy to attend. On some level he probably knew that he was likely to be confrontated on his temper.

One last possibility remained. The most senior people in the group arranged a meeting with Stanley. They started by talking about what a great job he was doing, how much they had learned, and how the company was doing well despite challenges. They then talked about how they wanted more interaction with him but were at times intimidated. They also talked about their individual experiences with his temper and how it had adversely affected their morale. Stanley could no longer deny that the incidents were frequent or claim that only one or two overly sensitive people minded his temper. The group recommended that Stanley call me to help him work on his temper, and he acquiesced.

For a brief period after the confrontation, Stanley bit his tongue when he was angry. He asserted that the problem was solved. In time, however, he returned to his baseline rate of outbursts. We talked about what led him to become angry. We also talked about how his anger had cost him his first marriage and closeness with his children. We looked at how he interpreted situations that led him to explode. We talked about other ways of interpreting these situations and other ways of expressing his concerns and annoyance. He was suffering from a significant level of anxiety and depression. It abated somewhat as his temper cooled and people responded better to him. The anxiety and depression continued to be a problem, however. He agreed to try medication. In a few weeks, he had significantly better control of his temper, worried less, was more energetic, and was actually able to enjoy his work.

Dealing with Your Own Feelings

Anger directed at you can set off a fight-flight reaction. The fight-flight reaction can drive you to respond in ways that are not in your interests or that may be inappropriate. Several millennium ago, when mankind regularly faced wild beasts, the fight-flight reaction was very helpful. It would have been rather dangerous to simply stand there waiting for an animal to attack rather than running away or picking up a stone to throw. In modern business, however, remaining calm and helping the person who just yelled at you to calm down is usually the best response.

How you react to someone's anger determines how big a problem it becomes. Some people can be yelled at and not let it bother them. Others are unnerved by it but are able to go about their work. A third group is upset and not able to work at their best. A fourth group cannot contain the anger they feel in response, and respond in ways that fuel the fire.

How you respond depends upon your self-confidence, how you interpret your manager's angry behavior (including whether you take it personally), the models you learned over the years for how to deal with angry people, how you were taught to deal with superiors, your capacity to contain feelings and maintain self-control, and the sensitivities you developed over the years, particularly during childhood. For example, a child who was subjected to a great deal of anger is likely to be sensitive to expressions of anger forever after. As a result, the person may exaggerate the seriousness of someone's anger. If the person is also lacking in confidence and has an anxious temperament, facing the anger will be very painful. If the person interprets the anger as a statement of the manager's persistent negative feelings about him rather than the manager simply blowing off steam at whoever walks by, the experience will be even more painful.

In dealing with painful situations, it is important to challenge beliefs that intensify your anger and lead you to take counterproductive actions. For example, sometimes people feel that failing to respond in kind to aggression leads it to get worse, or that failing to respond is a sign of weakness and is demeaning. I would argue that strength is demonstrated by feeling that the attack is so meaningless that it warrants no response. It may also mean that you have the patience and self-control to select the time, place, and method of response that is optimal. Executive coaching or therapy can provide you with tools to increase your self-control.

Attitude is critical. If you avoid taking the anger of a volatile person personally, and if you expect that there will be some noise and anger pointed in your direction at times, you will be much less stressed than if you assume that people you work with will always treat you respectfully and that their anger is your fault. Developing a perspective that helps you to weather volatile managers more easily takes time and practice and often coaching. This skill, however, will be helpful to you in many situations for many years to come. Having a volatile manager is not only a major hassle, it is also an opportunity to learn useful skills that you can use for the rest of your life to control your feelings and deal with difficult situations. Make use of it.

Chapter 29, "Developing Your Emotional Intelligence" deals with enhancing your personal competence and discusses how to work to change automatic, painful reactions that we often have to toxic managers.

For HR and Senior Managers

If your company's culture is tolerant of displays of anger, many managers will express their frustration and stress in ways that are destructive to coworkers and to the company. On the other hand, a culture that is intolerant of displays of anger will encourage people to keep themselves under control.

Leadership can curb aggressive behavior throughout the organization by taking active steps to change the culture. A company's culture arises from the qualities that leadership looks for in hiring and promoting, what leadership measures and rewards, the myths and stories leadership tells, and the example leadership sets.

If a particular manager is behaving in an aggressive and destructive way, HR and upper management can insist that the person receive coaching or counseling to gain better self-control. Sometimes, the manager only needs to learn the difference between aggression and assertion, discuss situations in which aggression is likely to come out, and do some role-playing of new ways to deal with the situations. In other situations more is needed. For some people, the combination of their personality style and the stress they face leads them to lose their temper frequently. They interpret situations in ways that cause them to feel much angrier than others would in the same situation. For example, some people have a tendency to see others as being inconsiderate, domineering, or hostile, while most people would have more benign interpretations. Moreover, some people see catastrophes, while others see problems, and still others see opportunities. A skilled therapist can help us to see things in new ways.

Many people achieve significant reductions in their anxiety, depression, and resulting irritability through a brief period of cognitive behavioral psychotherapy. Selective serotonin reuptake inhibitors (SSRIs) are also frequently very helpful for depression, impulsivity, and anxiety. The improvement in their quality of life—and in the quality of life of those around them—can be substantial.

There is also a great deal that organizations can do to screen potential hires and promotions to avoid having volatile people rise within the organization and creating a culture and atmosphere that are stifling and destructive. Organizations can screen out many volatile managers by doing adequate background checks and, when the person is internal, doing 360-degree feedback. It is also important to create a culture in which subordinates are listened to when they have complaints about superiors.

Conclusion

Volatile managers are the most common variety of aggressive managers. They run the gamut from people who are irritable from stress, anxiety, or depression and who briefly yell at you when you do not deserve it, to people with borderline or narcissistic personality disorder who may lose all judgment and fly into a rage in which they may hurt or kill themselves or you.

Easily and frequently upset, they take out their frustration on whoever has the misfortune of walking into their office. They can make your life miserable on a daily basis. Although they generally have no desire to hurt you, constantly facing their anger can be destructive. Not knowing when your boss will blow up, you are likely to keep your head low, avoid taking any chances or showing initiative, avoid the boss even if you have information he should be told, and redirect your energy away from work.

If your boss is irritable, gently addressing the impact on your work of his yelling at you can both help him maintain self-control and decrease your sense of being a helpless victim. If the volatile manager is your subordinate, confrontation of the damage his irritability causes him and those around him is needed. There is a great deal that can be done with a combination of medication and therapy to help volatile people gain better self-control. In the meantime, do what you can to learn what pushes their buttons, and stay out of their way when they are likely to explode.

There is a great deal that HR and senior management can do to decrease angry outbursts in the workplace and thereby improve working conditions and improve morale, retention, and productivity. The first step is creating a culture in which temper tantrums are not acceptable behavior. Three hundred and sixty degree feedback and listening to subordinates' complaints are also crucial. Access to anger management and executive coaching through the company's EAP is also important. In addition, always consider what nonpersonality psychiatric issues might be at play. Is the manager depressed? Does the manager have an anxiety disorder? Does the manager have ADHD? Is she under too much stress, or has she been traumatized? Is alcohol use contributing to the problem? Recognizing one of these and encouraging an evaluation with a psychiatrist can lead to marked improvement and can be extremely helpful to you, the company, and the manager.

Your Turn

- What volatile managers have you observed?
- Give examples of their volatility.
- What made them more volatile?
- How did their behavior affect you?
- How did their behavior affect others?
- How did their behavior affect productivity?
- How did their behavior affect communication?
- What did you and others try to do to cope?
- What worked, and what did not? (What made things better, and what made things worse?)
- What did you learn?
- How would you do things differently in the future?

Table 12–1 Overview of Volatile Managers

Symptoms	Underlying Factors	Impact	Ways for Subordinates to Cope	Ways for Senior Management to Cope
Easily angered	Tendency to see people as hostile or obstructionist	Impairs morale	Avoid pushing their buttons	Be clear on destructive impact of their anger on their career and others' well-being
	Feels overwhelming pressure to perform and accomplish	Impairs retention	Avoid them during the times of the day when they are most volatile	Provide reassurance to decrease the pressure they feel
	Underlying frustration and anger	Leads people to focus on protecting themselves rather than on the work of the organization	Don't take it personally	Consider assignment to positions where their irritability will not be destructive
			Realize they are not out to get you	Cognitive behavioral therapy to decrease anger
			Let them know certain actions are hurting you and your ability to perform	Assess if treatable problems with anxiety or depression are exacerbating their behavior
			Offer support to decrease the pressure they feel	Foster a culture rejecting angry outbursts
			Let them vent; avoid arguing with them	
			Avoid angry responses which solidify conflict	
			Consider group confrontation of the angry person	
			Learn Zen or meditation	

◆ What advice would you give to someone facing a volatile manager?

◆ Do you at times act in similar ways?

  • How does it affect people?

  • How does it affect your team?

  • How does it affect your career?

Further Reading

Institute of Mental Health Initiatives, (202) 364-7111.

The movie *Fatal Attraction* provides a depiction of borderline personality disorder.

CHAPTER 13

Frantic Colleagues

I Can't Stop Racing Around

Some people become so frantic from the pressures of work and daily life that they cannot stop racing around. Some people are chronically in this anxious, agitated state. Others enter an overaroused state when the stakes are high and they are under unusual pressure. As a result of their frantic state they are either clueless or uninterested in how you are affected by their behavior. Like a bull in a china shop, they can do considerable damage, although they have no desire to hurt you. Constantly racing around out of fear that they are falling behind, they cut corners. In particular, they fail to consult with others and pay too little attention to what they know about the opinions and interests of colleagues. Complicating matters, the intense pressure that they feel predisposes them to feel frustrated by the normal give and take of business, leading to irritability.

A variety of factors can predispose someone to become a frantic manager. Some have an anxiety disorder, some have attention deficit hyperactivity disorder, and some are overwhelmed by stress. Sometimes, people become addicted to the excitement and intensity of a war-zone mentality. Their adrenaline flows, and they have an intense sense of being on a mission. The atmosphere is intoxicating. As a result, some people unconsciously, and unnecessarily, promote a sense of intense pressure around their work.

Frantic managers need to learn that the road to hell is paved with good intentions. Their willingness to do whatever it takes, including ignoring how they treat people, in order to "get the job done" interferes with the work. It is particularly damaging to future productivity since it damages team relationships and fosters burn-out.

A Frantic Manager

Alexa was a mid-low-level manager at a large company. People who liked her described her as hardworking, dedicated, and intense. Anyone who met her felt her anxiety pouring out. She spoke quickly and with a tone of urgency in her voice. She seemed fragile.

Those who worked with her did not soon forget the experience, however much they might want to. There was no indication that she used alcohol, but she clearly increased the consumption of those who worked with her. She had an amazing ability to say the wrong thing and to ignore the fact that you also had thoughts about how things should be done. Nevertheless, there was no indication that she wanted to hurt others. She was more clueless than ruthless.

An interdisciplinary team was created to redesign the process of developing and writing proposals for clients. The team consisted of five people: a team leader and four members of roughly equal rank. A computer consultant was also assigned on an as-needed basis. Brett was assigned to work in tandem with Alexa in developing a computer program that would be used to facilitate future proposal writing. Two weeks into the project, the team instructed Brett to gather best practices material on proposal writing and present it to the team. For reasons that remain a mystery, Alexa told Brett not to do the work. Brett replied that he would be happy to not do it if the team or team leader agreed. Alexa became very upset. She did not want him to do the work and objected to his saying he needed the team's agreement on this.

Meanwhile, in a key meeting with a high-ranking company official, Alexa usurped the position of the team lead and dominated the meeting.

Problems escalated. Alexa and Brett agreed that he would do the first draft of a Power Point presentation, send it to her, and she would give feedback. Instead of sending comments, however, Alexa did her own presentation and sent it out to the entire group without showing it to Brett. Around the same time, Alexa objected to giving Brett full access to the computer program they were developing. Alexa did not want Brett to be able to make changes in the program by himself, although she could. In addition, Alexa approached their technology consultant and sought to work with him without including Brett. Brett spoke with her about this, and Alexa replied that she learned better on her own and therefore didn't want Brett to join the meetings. Alexa did not relent until she was instructed to by the team leader herself.

A deadline was rapidly approaching for several work products. Alexa failed to make changes in the computer program she had agreed to do, leaving Brett to do it late the night before it was due. Alexa had become preoccupied with her daughter's birthday party and had therefore not returned any of Brett's calls, although they had agreed to speak over the weekend so they could coordinate their work and turn in the required materials Monday morning. When Alexa reviewed a write-up for the team, she cut all of the materials Brett had written on best practices, the same material he had been ordered to get by the team leader but Alexa had objected to his getting.

With Alexa becoming an increasing problem, the team leader began asking questions. She found out that Alexa had burned her bridges in every department she had worked in and that no one wanted to work with her. This project was her last hope. Nevertheless, she could not contain herself.

Her evaluation for the project was poor and the company let her go soon afterwards.

You will also come across colleagues who, although not frantic, fail to pick up on social cues and therefore step on your toes figuratively and literally. The more severe cases are diagnosed as Asperger's disorder. The milder cases are sometimes described as having a nonverbal learning disorder.

Most people intuitively pick up on social cues and know when someone wants to end a conversation, when someone wants to hear more, when someone dislikes your idea, and when they like it. People with nonverbal learning problems don't accurately read these signals. They also fail to pick up on and follow cultural patterns. Their eye contact, facial expressions, and body posture often seem odd. They are also often fixated on narrow interests and do not understand that you do not share the same intensity of interest. Changing from one routine to another can be very hard for them. They also often lack interest in others' emotional experience and needs.

These individuals are not narcissistic. They do not feel that they are better than others, and they do not devalue others. They simply do not understand others and do not realize that they do not understand. They also tend to have poor motor skills. Many gravitate toward engineering and computer science, where their ability for singular focus and their lack of people skills is less of a handicap.

Social skills training can be enormously helpful. They need to be carefully taught the skills that most people learn during their first years. They need to learn how close to stand with another person, how much eye contact to make, how to be a good listener, and how to read cues concerning whether others are interested or not interested, in agreement or not in agreement.

Never Fit In

Kyle was always different. When he was a child, people saw him as bright, interested in the world around him, and well-behaved. He never had many friends, however. The problem was more than anxiety in dealing with other children. He did not know how to start a conversation or to show interest in what others were doing. His limited social interaction did not seem to bother him a great deal. He was very focused on his computer, computer games, and searching the Internet. He was also fascinated with how things worked.

Not unexpectedly, Kyle went into engineering. In college, since he was not that interested in dating or hanging out with friends, he was able to focus very heavily on his studies and did very well. Near the end of college, he met a woman who was attracted by his gentle style and seriousness toward work and life.

She did not mind his weaknesses in social skills. The relationship went well, and they were married shortly after he began working.

Work went fairly well. Kyle was seen as a bit of an odd duck, but he was pleasant and not at all aggressive. In time, however, his good work led to a promotion, and he now needed to interact far more often with people. Problems now began in earnest.

People who needed to deal with Kyle on a frequent basis found his lack of social savoir faire discomforting. He could be very rigid in pursuing a point. He did not seem to pick up on negative feedback. He would ramble on and on about his ideas. He sometimes did not know when to take no for an answer. A victim of the Peter Principle, Kyle was almost fired.

Kyle was sent for executive coaching. Fortunately, this coach had special training and correctly diagnosed the problem. The coach provided concrete instructions on how to read vocal cues and how to enter conversations. They did a lot of role playing and videotaped their interactions. Kyle's skills improved markedly. It not only helped his work, but his social life improved. This provided more and more opportunities to practice his new skills and to become more comfortable with people. He would never be incredibly smooth and polished, but he was much better able to do the work the company wanted him to do and to enjoy life.

Emotional Intelligence Approach
to Frantic Managers

Dealing with Superiors

Frantic managers are so overwhelmed by anxiety and stress that they become clueless. Sometimes, if you catch them during a quiet period, they may be open to hearing that their frantic pace and failure to include people in discussions makes it difficult for people to work with them. You must avoid attacking or demeaning them, since this could lead them to become angry. You are, after all, talking to your boss, and rank has its privileges. Recognizing their heavy responsibilities and hard work is often helpful. Suggesting ways in which you can better support them and lighten their load can also be beneficial.

Dealing with Coworkers

The approach to frantic coworkers is similar. You can, however, usually be blunter with coworkers. Nevertheless, as much tact as possible, is still desirable.

The biggest problem in dealing with frantic colleagues is often our own reaction. We become angry at their inconsiderate treatment of us. We become even angrier if we interpret their behavior as hostile. An emotional intelligence (EI) approach entails, among other things, being aware of the feelings we have about others' actions and why we have those feelings. An EI approach has us question our interpretation and consider other possible interpretations. If we realize that frantic people's behavior is not aimed to hurt us, but that stress has wreaked havoc with their judgment and self-control, we are less likely to be angry. This perspective, in addition to helping us to contain our blood pressure and enabling us to avoid escalating the problem, has the added benefit of generally being accurate.

Dealing with Subordinates

In dealing with frantic subordinates, it is part of your job to help them learn about the company culture and effective ways of working. It is necessary for the well-being of the team, their career, and your own sanity to confront them with their behavior. In doing so, remember that the behavior is unintended and that they are likely to change once they are better aware of what they are doing. Clobbering them, which may be tempting if they have caused you and the team considerable frustration, is tempting but counterproductive. Bolstering their self-confidence and sense of security is far more helpful in the long run.

For HR and Senior Management

The EI perspective argues that awareness of our emotional state helps us to maintain better control. Therefore, the first thing that HR and senior management can do is to point out to such workers that they are overcharged and frantic. Moreover, it should be carefully explained to the frantic managers how their behavior is getting in the way of what they want to accomplish.

Decreasing the pressure managers experience and providing reassurance about the good work they are doing is often helpful. Decreasing their workload or getting them more support can also be helpful. People get into overcharged states when they think superiors expect large workloads from them or they feel that they need to do extra work to make up for weaknesses in their performance. A combination of reassurance, support for their strengths, and decreasing their workload will make it easier for them to cope.

Frantic managers can generally benefit from executive coaching. In addition, a psychiatric evaluation might reveal that a highly treatable condition, such as depression, anxiety, or ADHD, is exacerbating the problem.

Another part of the EI approach is helping frantic managers learn new skills for achieving their goals. They need to learn assertiveness skills to replace their aggressive style.

In assigning and promoting people who have a tendency to fall into hyper states or who function in them continually, senior management should be aware of the impact of their hyper behavior and presentation on coworkers and clients. It can be quite destructive. They are likely to come across as aggressive or dismissive. Your job is to assign people to positions in which they are most likely to succeed and to avoid placing them in situations that will lead to failure, unless you want them to self-destruct. You can also be clear with such managers that they need to develop better controls on their hyper presentation as a condition for promotion.

Conclusion

Frantic managers (see Table 13–1) become so hyper during the course of life and work that they fail to pay adequate attention to how their actions impact others and inadvertently step on your prerogatives and boundaries. Their lack of attention to colleagues' boundaries does harm, but far less harm than bullies who seek to intimidate, or ruthless managers who have a goal and are willing to destroy you if you get in the way, or volatile managers who periodically strike out angrily in response to frustration.

Whether they are your superior or your subordinate, you can often ameliorate the situation by gently pointing out the negative impact of their behavior and by helping to reduce their work load. Frantic individuals often have an underlying anxiety disorder or ADHD. They are always highly stressed. Treatment of the underlying anxiety disorder with therapy and/or medication, and of the ADHD with medication, often leads to marked improvement.

Table 13-1 Overview of Frantic Managers

Symptoms	Underlying Factors	Impact	Ways for Subordinates to Cope	Ways for Senior Management to Cope
Constantly racing around	Feel overwhelming pressure to perform	Impairs morale	Realize they do not mean to hurt you	Assess if treatable problems with anxiety or depression are exacerbating their behavior
Inadvertently step on people's prerogatives or are irritable with people	Fear of criticism	Fosters burnout in others	Let them know certain actions are hurting you and your ability to perform	Provide focused coaching to modify key problematic traits
			Offer support to decrease the pressure they feel	Provide reassurance to decrease the pressure they feel
			Understand their fears and limitations	Decrease their workload
			Avoid surprising them; keep them informed	Consider assignment to positions where their being frantic will not be destructive

Your Turn

- What frantic managers have you observed?
- Give examples of
  - How they behaved when frantic
  - Ways they violated people's boundaries
- How did their behavior affect you?
- How did their behavior affect others?
- How did their behavior affect productivity?
- How did their behavior affect communication?
- What did you and others do to cope?
- What worked, and what did not? (What made things better, and what made things worse?)
- Were there any effective ways to slow them down?
- What did you learn from the experience?
- How would you do things differently in the future?
- What advice would you give to someone facing a frantic manager?
- Do you at times act in similar ways?
  - How does it affect people?
  - How does it affect your career?
  - What can you do to slow yourself down?

Further Reading

On nonverbal learning disorders: http://www.nlda.org.

CHAPTER 14

Underpinnings of Aggression

Why Am I So Angry?

Understanding what drives aggressive behavior is crucial in designing measures to cope with it. The more you know about an aggressive individual's way of interpreting others' behavior, motivation in being aggressive, and ability to control aggressive impulses, the better able you will be to deter him or her from violating your space and prerogatives. Measures that would calm aggression in one person might exacerbate it in another, depending upon what is motivating and driving the person.

There are three major theories that attempt to explain why people sometimes try to hurt others in anger. Freud thought that aggression was an instinctual drive, like sex. He believed that there was a natural and progressive build-up of aggressive energy that eventually led people to aggressive actions. In marked contrast, the frustration-aggression hypothesis argues that aggression arises only when someone is frustrated in his or her attempts to achieve a goal. In contrast with these, social learning theory states that aggression is a learned behavior influenced by witnessing when and how people behave aggressively and seeing how others respond to aggressive behavior.

In addition to these basic theories of aggression, psychiatrists have learned that a variety of emotional problems increase our tendency to experience anger and/or to act on it. Psychosis, mania, PTSD, depression, and drugs can all predispose an individual to behave aggressively. Furthermore, certain problems decrease an individual's ability to constrain aggressive feelings. These include ADHD, a history of brain trauma, mania, substance abuse, and certain personality disorders—histrionic, borderline, and antisocial.

The differences among the theories are not simply of academic interest. Understanding the origins of anger enables us to take steps to decrease its likelihood and intensity. If someone's aggression is driven by depression or anxiety, these need to be treated. If the primary issue is poor impulse control, then the impulsivity should be the focus of treatment. If the aggression comes from high levels of frustration, the key is to take steps to decrease frustration. If learning theory is correct and people are aggressive when they have learned that it will get them what they want, we need to make sure that aggressive behavior is sanctioned rather than rewarded. If Freud was correct and aggression steadily rises until it is released, we need to provide nondestructive outlets for aggression.

Three Theories on Aggression

Frustration and Aggression

The classical frustration-aggression hypothesis holds that aggressive behavior always presupposes the existence of frustration and that frustration drives the organism until it performs hostile and aggressive acts. The main difference between the frustration-aggression hypothesis and Freudian psychoanalysis is whether aggression inevitably arises as time passes or only when we experience frustration. Later writers suggest that frustration can lead to nonaggressive actions as well as aggressive ones.

Aggression arises when someone or something threatens the values that are most important to an individual: power, wealth, respect, well-being, and intimacy. Over time, frustrations can build up from a variety of sources and eventually overwhelm your ability to contain it. Sometimes, the walls of the dam containing frustration are overwhelmed by an accumulation of disappointments and upsetting situations. Perhaps in a short period of time a work project runs into serious problems, a loved one decides someone else is more attractive, and a your stock's value goes so far south that the racetrack seems to be a better way to invest money. The combined weight of the various disappointments and frustrations can lead you to lose your temper over the next drop of disappointment that falls from the sky.

Some people go through life with a reservoir of frustration and pain that arose long ago from a traumatic experience. New frustrations and disappointments continually threaten to push the waters over the top of the dam. If a frustration resonates with very painful events from the past, it not only adds to the reservoir but stirs up the waters, creating waves that can burst over the top and sometimes crack the walls of the reservoir.

Psychodynamic Theories

Freud believed that aggression and sex are drives. They build up over time and periodically seek outlets. This is no longer mainstream thinking.

Self psychologists, heirs to the work of Heinz Kohut, argue that people experience "narcissistic rage" when their self-esteem is threatened. In this state, judgment and normal inhibitions collapse, and people strike out to destroy the person who hurt them, often doing things that are destructive to themselves. Such people seem to feel that honor requires attaining revenge, and that without honor life is worthless.

Certain things stir up a degree of narcissistic rage in most people, such as finding your spouse in bed with your best friend. This is not likely to happen during the normal workday. At work you are more likely to experience scapegoating, unfair evaluations, challenges to your authority, unfair criticism, and having someone steal credit for your work. These are upsetting to most people. For some people, however, one or more of these so threaten their sense of control or remind them of an abusive childhood that they go into a narcissistic rage. The result can be publicly throwing a temper tantrum, firing a crucial employee, berating a boss who can fire you, and in rare cases violence.

Social Learning Theory

Social learning theory argues that people learn much of their behavior by observing others. People try out behaviors that they have seen in others. If they get positive reinforcement, they will continue the behavior. If the world reacts negatively, they will drop it from their repertoire. From the perspective of social learning theory, aggression arises when someone sees others behaving aggressively and getting away with it, and when the person's own aggressive behavior leads to success in obtaining objectives rather than sanctions.

Factors Modulating Our Aggression

Aggression and Personal Values and Beliefs

What people value and how they interpret situations has a marked impact on when they become angry and how they deal with the anger. Understanding how people interpret situations and what they value most can help you to avoid "pushing their buttons" and to know how to defuse a situation once someone has become angry.

Some people seek smooth, collegial work relationships above all else. Some crave a chance to be creative and express themselves. Some want as much money as possible. Others desire to be needed or loved. Still others want to be the center of attention. People are at risk for behaving aggressively when things they value are threatened. Someone who desires a chance to express himself is not likely to be upset when someone else is selected to run a project, as long as he is given a creative task to fulfill and some autonomy in doing it. Someone in search of power and respect may not be bothered if assigned a project without creative opportunities as long as she is in charge and the company considers it an important endeavor. People who value maintaining amicable relationships above all else and desire to maintain a self-image as considerate and kind will rarely be outwardly aggressive.

People's ways of interpreting situations also have a great impact on what makes them angry. For example, if a friend walks past you on the street without saying hello, you might assume that the person was preoccupied and stressed. Alternatively, you might assume that the person was never really a friend and can't be trusted. Similarly, when a person's ideas are quickly rejected by a superior, he or she may think that the superior is currently stressed, while other people may think that this is simply the boss's style, and still others may think that the superior dislikes them.

Some managers see other people as primarily helpful and realize that they will at times have legitimate needs that conflict with their own. Some people see others primarily as competitors, who are getting in their way. Some see colleagues as largely hostile individuals who will take advantage of them whenever possible and hurt them for the fun of it. How you interpret people's motives and behavior has as much impact on how you feel as what people actually do.

Early life experiences have a remarkable impact on how we interpret current situations. For example, early experiences of being pushed around or ignored create a model in our minds of an unresponsive, hostile world.

Once the models are formed, they are relatively impervious to change without psychotherapy, since new experiences tend to be interpreted so that they fit the existing model.

Prisoner of a Lifetime of Small Hurts

Neil often saw people as obstacles. While growing up, his father was generally irritable and Neil felt threatened by him. His mother was highly anxious and oblivious to what Neil wanted, but not hostile as his father was. Neil was teased a lot by other children both because he was anxious and because he cared about grades and learning.

Over time, Neil began to stand out academically. Although he had friends, he saw most people as competitors or obstacles: that is, as people who might get better grades than he or who might tease him. In high school he tried hard to become more social, and he faced painful rejection. The accumulated experiences left a reservoir of hurt. He became fairly abrasive. He frequently got annoyed over small incidents in which people were not considerate or were interfering with something he wanted to do.

As time went on, he had some career success, had lots of therapy, and made more and more friends. He now entered into an upward spiral. The more positive feedback he got from people, the more he socialized, and the more he socialized, the better his social skills became. He was a good listener, interested in others, and even witty at times. Once he knew you, or if you were the friend of a friend, he would be very nice and go out of his way for you. Being generous and giving to people was what he liked most about himself.

At the same time, Neil continued to have a talent for getting into unnecessary struggles with people. If someone gave him a hard time over a small request, or tried to block him from doing work he felt was important without a good reason, or challenged his authority in an area that clearly was his to determine, he was thrown back into his image of people as obstacles and easily became annoyed with and very wary of them. It generally took a long time before he would be at all comfortable with the person again. Nevertheless, his ability to control his reactions grew. He often felt annoyed and needed to work to control his reaction, but it ceased to interfere with his work or career advancement.

Narcissistic individuals are particularly at risk for behaving aggressively. Their fragile self-esteem and preoccupation with their self-esteem leaves them vulnerable to narcissistic rage. Their devaluation of others and entitlement frees them from many of the inhibitions on behaving aggressively that most people feel. Under stress, they can slide into paranoia and see others' actions as deliberate attempts to hurt them. Finally, their poor treatment of others leads to poor relations with people and becomes a self-fulfilling fantasy.

Psychiatric/Emotional Problems Fostering Aggression

Chronic high stress, anxiety disorders, depression, and chronic pain or other medical problems all impair our ability to absorb any new stress that comes along. As a result, we are likely to strike out. Bipolar disorder markedly increases irritability as well as releasing our inhibitions and self-control.

Substance abuse is a very common problem in business. Alcohol and drugs weaken self-control at the same time that they impair mood, sleep, and judgment. The ability to control aggressive feelings is particularly undermined while intoxicated, while hung over, and while withdrawing.

ADHD is a common cause of poor impulse control. Generally seen as a problem in children, it is also common in adults. People with ADHD have a hard time containing their impulses, and it is difficult for them to pause and think before they speak. Therefore, they often interrupt others, answer questions before someone finishes asking the question, find it painful to wait their turn, and blurt out their thoughts and annoyance before thinking about the consequences.

Recognizing and treating these psychiatric problems can be enormously beneficial in helping someone contain their aggression. Without professional treatment, things are unlikely to substantially improve if someone is suffering from one of these problems.

Table 14–1 Psychiatric Factors Fostering Aggression

Difficulty being assertive	Unable to be assertive, the person is taken advantage of; frustration grows and eventually bursts out as aggression; alternatively, the person may behave passive aggressively.
Depression	Even low-level chronic depression can lead someone to feel picked on and therefore angry. It can also lead to low self-esteem and interfere with being assertive.
ADHD and other impulse problems	Impulsivity gets in the way of self-control. Person is unable to contain feelings.
Paranoid traits	They believe people are trying to hurt them. Some people are taught to interpret the world this way. The traditional psychodynamic understanding is that paranoid individuals are filled with anger, project it onto others, and therefore believe that they are being threatened.
Narcissistic personality traits	Very vulnerable to feeling slighted and goes into a narcissistic rage if their self-esteem is threatened. They also think they are better than others and are entitled to have whatever they want.
Borderline and histrionic personality disorders	These individuals experience tremendous emotional pain when there is a threat to important relationships. A significant other leaving them or simply being emotionally unavailable for a moment can send them into a rage.
Ruthless/ antisocial traits	Lacks empathic connections to others and lacks superego restraints on actions. These people think they should always have their way.
Oppositional traits	Desperately and constantly trying to defend their autonomy, like the two-year-old child, they reject what others want in order to prove to themselves that they are not being dominated and pushed around.
Compulsive traits	These individuals have a very limited capacity for warm feelings toward others. They are overly focused on work and have a rigid sense of what is right and wrong. They ignore the need to foster relationships and maintain cooperation, and they push hard to have their way in all matters.
Stress and burnout	Too exhausted to adequately think about the impact of action on others.
Authoritarian traits	Some people believe in rigid hierarchies and that the person in charge should dominate.
Substance abuse	Substance use can dull one's ability to think about the impact of actions or can induce agitation.
Group dynamics	Group dynamics often bring out the worst in people, including paranoid feelings and fight-flight reactions.

Culture and Aggression

Both the societal and corporate cultures have considerable impact on aggressive behavior. In some cultures it is acceptable to show anger, in others it is not. In some cultures it is acceptable to undercut those who are in your way. Other cultures do not tolerate this behavior. Most people are significantly restrained by their culture's expectations and the fear of sanctions if they violate the culture. Those who are not at all restrained will generally be extruded unless they have remarkable skills or connections.

Prisoner of Another Culture

Gabrielle was unable to make the transition from one office culture to another. Her living by the old culture's rules led her to alienate many people.

Gabrielle spent five years working for a mid-sized company. She had performed well, moved upward, and was ready for a new challenge. The culture of her prior firm supported directness. Directness included open confrontation and at times displays of anger. No one took such incidents very seriously. Most workers were comfortable with the rough and tumble style of the firm. On the other hand, backbiting was not tolerated.

Two or three weeks into her new position, Gabrielle heard that someone had said something negative about her behind her back. Feeling she had been severely fouled, she called the person into her office and blasted him. Taken aback, the person said little in response to Gabrielle's attack, but he began talking to others about Gabrielle's not fitting in. When Gabrielle became aware that people were speaking about her behind her back, rather than confronting her directly, she became increasingly irritable. She did not understand this new place or why people were not talking with her directly. The situation progressively deteriorated and she chose to leave before she was fired.

Group Dynamics

Group dynamics can be a formidable spur to aggression. Groups often elicit strong feelings and a sense of righteousness in their members. As a result, groups often scapegoat people. Understanding how and why groups do this can help you avoid becoming a target of a group's aggression.

To help maintain group cohesion, groups develop an invisible wall around themselves. Members develop a sense of us versus them. Group members tend to see the group as perfect, and all badness and negative perceptions are placed on outsiders. Tensions between groups are likely to become particularly difficult if the groups must work together but have different objectives and needs. For example, although production and sales both want the company to succeed, they have competing parochial interests in terms of how many models to sell and how frequently to make product changes.

Groups often turn on a group member who does not fit in or who has traits (such as insecurity) that the group does not want to accept as part of itself. In this setting, scapegoating can readily occur.

Another way in which groups can exacerbate aggressive behavior is by decreasing inhibitions. When part of a group, people lose a sense of personal responsibility for their actions and feel that aggressive actions are acceptable, since everyone else thinks that it is appropriate and it is really the group that is acting.

Why We Let Ourselves Become Aggressive

Despite the pressure of frustration and perhaps psychiatric problems, most people still have consciences that tell them not to hurt others. To get around their consciences, people use a number of excuses. People focus their attention on the importance of the cause that they are pursuing; they tell themselves that they were just following orders or that they just went along with the crowd. Another set of excuses entails degrading the victim; blaming the victim; or denying the harm done to the victim by the aggression. If you understand the excuses that people use to circumvent their consciences, you can sometimes head off the maneuver and help their conscience to stand firm.

Some people allow themselves to behave aggressively because they are ruthless and have little conscience. Several factors affect a person's strength of conscience. First, there may be inborn, biologically determined differences in how an individual responds to others' pain. Second, early childhood experiences impact whether someone feels warmly toward other human beings or sees others as objects to be used and discarded. Third, the cultures people grow up in, live in, and work in all impact the content of their conscience, their beliefs about which behaviors are appropriate and which are not.

Some people behave aggressively because they do not realize that they are hurting others. A variety of factors and situations can underlie their cluelessness. Most of us, when sufficiently stressed or depressed, lose touch with the feelings of others and the potential impact of our actions on others' interests and feelings. Some people either were never taught to understand how their behavior affects others or their ability to learn how their behavior affects others was impaired. Nonverbal learning disorder (a neurological dysfunction) can impair our ability to understand others' feelings. Various personality disorders can cause people to be so preoccupied with their inner struggles that they lack the inner emotional space to connect with others.

Conclusion

Aggression is often divided into two categories: (1) cold, calculated attempts to attain an objective regardless of the cost to someone and (2) emotions that overwhelm the person's judgment. Anger is now generally believed to come from frustration. Anger is set off by different things in different people. Both rigid and paranoid personalities feel their autonomy is under constant threat. As a result, they are often chronically tense and become very angry if they are not allowed to be in charge. People with underlying narcissistic issues will become enraged if their self-esteem is threatened. Individuals with borderline psychopathology are particularly vulnerable to loss of a major romantic attachment. Under stress, most people are "on edge," and when their aims are frustrated they become angry, but not enraged as do people with narcissistic or borderline personality issues. Alcohol drugs and depression can all increase irritability.

Aggressive behavior does not arise simply because there is a drive to be aggressive. There also needs to be a release of inhibitions. Those with narcissistic personality issues are predisposed to acting aggressively not simply because of the intensity of their anger, but because their devaluation of others decreases their inhibitions. Group dynamics, certain cultures, alcohol and drugs can all reduce inhibitions constraining the use of violence.

Now that we have discussed what lies underneath aggression, we are ready to move on to ways of containing it.

Further Reading

Albert Bandura. *Social Foundations of Thought and Action: A Social Cognitive Theory.* Prentice Hall. 1986.

Margaret Rioch. "The Work of Wilfred R. Bion on Groups." *Psychiatry*, 33: 56–66, 1970.

Margaret Rioch. "'All we like sheep—'(Isaiah 53:6): Followers and Leaders." *Psychiatry*, 34: 258–2732, 1971.

L. Berkowitz. "Whatever Happened to the Frustration-Aggression Hypothesis?" *American Behavioral Scientist*, 32: 691–7082, 1978.

Howard A. Bacal. "The Essence of Kohut's Work and the Progress of Self Psychology." *Psychoanalytic Dialogues,* 5(3): 1995.

Paul H. Ornstein and Anna Ornstein. "Some Distinguishing Features of Heinz Kohut's Self Psychology." *Psychoanalytic Dialogues,* 5(3): 385–391, 1995.

The movie *The War of the Roses* provides a terrifying example of how a struggle can escalate out of control as people become locked in a power struggle and of how people can go into a narcissistic rage and behave in self-destructive ways when they feel their self-esteem is threatened.

CHAPTER 15

Surviving Aggression

Strengthening Your Defenses

Organizations and Aggressive Managers

Aggressive managers and executives can do significant damage to an organization's productivity and long-term development. They damage the morale and motivation of subordinates and peers, divert their energies from useful tasks, and drive away the most talented people.

There is much that leadership can do to establish a culture limiting destructive behavior at work, and thereby remove a significant obstacle to productivity and retention, as well as create a more humane, safe environment.

The basic steps in reforging aspects of an organization's culture are:

- ◆ Leaders act as role models and walk the talk.
- ◆ Leaders tell stories and myths supporting the desired culture.
- ◆ Align measurement and reward systems with the desired behavior.
- ◆ Hire and promote those whose behavior supports the desired culture.

Culture Change to Contain Aggression

Dawn was delighted to accept the offer to be CEO of the company. Not only was she moving up from a senior VP position, but the new company was larger than the one she was in.

Dawn quickly began meeting people and listening to their interests, perspectives, hopes, and ideas for the company. As she listened to people, she was surprised by the amount of back biting. She wasn't used to this. In group meetings, if she did not take rigid control, her senior executives would bash each others' ideas, make personal attacks, and try to push each other aside to dominate the meeting. As she read people's files to learn more about them, Dawn often saw fairly harsh complaints about their weaknesses rather than suggestions for ways to grow. Dawn wondered if she wanted to be in this culture.

She called in a consultant who looked into the origins of the current culture and devised a game plan to change aspects of it. Dawn's predecessor, who had founded the company, had been an excellent strategist but was also very aggressive. He was critical of others and not infrequently his voice produced a remarkable number of decibels. His style had worked, and so no one had challenged it. Even if it hadn't worked, challenging a company's founder is difficult, and when he has a bad temper, it's dangerous.

The first step Dawn took was to announce that there was a five-dollar penalty for insulting or yelling. The money went toward the firm's Christmas party. Anyone could call the penalty on any other person. There was no court of appeals. Dawn staged a scene in which she was aggressive, was called on it, and promptly paid the fine. She began telling stories about great motivators who never yelled. She went out of her way to be polite and respectful to others. She had the consultant teach HR how to do behavioral-event interviewing to better screen both new hires and managers for bad tempers. She was very careful not to hire or promote angry people. The use of 360-degree feedback was instituted as part of the performance measurement system and became a significant part of the measurement and compensation system. The culture changed markedly.

Aggression Versus Assertiveness

Aggression and assertiveness are often confused. Their impact on people and on organizations is very different. *Assertiveness entails making clear statements of what you want.* You remain within the realm of assertiveness when you say why it is appropriate for you to obtain what you want and what your next steps will be if the person refuses. For example, stating that you will go to someone's superior to have your request reviewed at a higher level, if they fail to agree, is being assertive.

Aggression involves destructive behavior. Once you step away from stating the logical reasons that make your recommendation preferable, and you begin attacking the person who disagrees with you, you have crossed the line into aggression. Taking steps to undermine another person because you are upset that he does not support you is aggressive. Phrasing comments with the intent to incite people against him and to permanently damage his reputation is highly aggressive.

In most cases, the distinction between assertiveness and aggression is relatively clear. Telling someone that her idea is not as strong as another course of action or that she is not yet ready for a certain position because of X, Y, and Z is assertive. Insulting her or generally disparaging her work or abilities is aggressive. Writing a poor but accurate evaluation that prevents the company from giving responsibilities to someone who cannot handle them is assertive, not aggressive. Writing a poor evaluation because you are upset with the person for not supporting you is aggressive. Going through proper bureaucratic channels to oppose someone's actions that you honestly believe would be bad for the company is assertive. Going out of your way to damage someone's reputation, either to decrease his ability to compete with you or to get revenge, is aggressive.

There are situations that do not fit nicely into one category or the other. Going to someone's supervisor both to bring pressure on her to do her job and to get revenge by hurting her is both aggressive and assertive.

For many people, learning the difference between assertiveness and aggression is a crucial step in containing their aggression. Many people think that the only way to speak up is the aggressive way that they are used to. Learning how to be appropriately assertive, and to recognize the boundary line between assertiveness and aggression, can be enormously helpful in containing their aggression.

Assertive Versus Aggressive

When I was in my third year of medical school, at the beginning of my first rotation, my senior resident told me that no one had ever taught me to do a medical write-up. He added that this was fine, since he would teach me that evening. In reality, he was well aware that I had had a course on doing medical write-ups. The senior resident had lots of things to do besides remedial work on medical write-ups. Nevertheless, either because he was an unusually patient person or because he was a wise leader or because someone had once done him a good turn, he avoided expressing anger and frustration, and assertively said what needed to be done. As a result, I did not crawl into a shell of insecurity; I worked very hard on the rotation and did above average work, and I remember him to this day.

On another occasion, I was working on a project with a half dozen people. The head of the project was a very capable individual with whom I wanted to build a relationship. When she called one day I took the opportunity to thank her for all of her great work. She complained that almost no one had come to the last meeting and that I had missed two in a row. When I would not guarantee I would never miss again, she threatened to remove me from the project. The incitement of the red flag she was waving in my face was stronger than my discretion. I was particularly offended because I had previously gone out of my way to help her. I told her she was being a bulldozer. She informed me that our conversation was over. I then ate a fair portion of crow in order to get back on good terms. I had meant to be assertive but had slipped over the line. I had had other alternatives. I could have told her that I felt hurt and left it at that. I could also have spoken to others in the group to rally support. I could also have done nothing, since I knew she did not have the authority to remove me. By responding needlessly to a challenge and adding an attack on her, I passed the line into aggression.

Tensions between groups can incite difficulties and flare-ups between individuals. Groups have a strong tendency to see themselves as superior to others. This helps to maintain group unity and to avoid tensions between the members of the group. The stronger the group identity and the more confidence that your group is doing things the right way, however, the greater will be the rejection of outsiders and how they do things. The resulting tension hampers cooperation between groups.

Problems become particularly serious if groups have competing objectives but are forced to cooperate. For example, sales, marketing, and production need to work together to sell products, but their preferences are often in conflict. Sales often wants to make changes in products to meet customer needs and to make multiple versions of a product to meet the needs of different customers. Production, however, will lose economies of scale and markedly complicate their processes if they make many different models. Each group is likely to see the other as not understanding its needs and as being unnecessarily oppositional.

Once tension exists, contact is likely to lead to problems rather than improved relations. To decrease tensions, you need to create a common goal so that people must cooperate in order to succeed.

Containing a Battle Between Groups

The merger between the two mid-sized companies had been in the works for more than a year. People were apprehensive but hopeful. They had different strengths in research and development, and different distribution systems. If the merger worked, they had a shot at making it into the first rank of their industry. At the same time, people worried about the changes that would be forced on them and who their new coworkers would be. Their cultures were actually rather similar. This would help to avoid many of the problems that generally plague mergers. Considerable care was taken in dealing with political issues. Raises were given and new titles created to minimize the number of people who would be angered by losing status. Some people were let go with golden parachutes.

Two change management consulting companies were called in to consult. One company suggested a series of large and small social gatherings to help people get to know each other in informal settings. The culmination would be a huge weekend retreat. The other company said that people should be given new, challenging tasks that could be accomplished only by combining the expertise and strengths each company brought. If real tasks were not available, they should be created.

The first recommendation seemed to be much more fun. The idea of making work where none existed seemed absurd. A series of small and large get-togethers were arranged. People wore badges identifying their company of origin so that others would know who to approach and get to know. People enjoyed the social events; however, they gravitated toward people they already knew. At the weekend retreat, things turned sour. The baseball and soccer games turned into competitions between groups representing the two original companies. When tension arose over questionable rule violations, spectators chose sides according to their original company. Over dinner, people spent most of their time complaining about the lack of honesty and sportsmanship of people from the other company. Back at work the next week, the antagonism continued.

Feeling desperate, upper management called the consulting company that had recommended cooperative work projects. The consultants noted that their job was now considerably more complicated. The leadership of the merged company was surprised to hear that these consultants wanted to send people away again. This time, however, it was to a combination of outward bound experiences and working weekends. No more multistar resorts. They were in cabins or tents. Rather than good times and play, people would be required to work together. If they did not work together on the outward bound weekend, they would be rather cold, and as the weather would have it, wet. Those lucky enough to be in cabins were given business challenges that required the skills and resources of both companies to solve. Upper-level managers were given the challenge of finding projects that they could not have accomplished prior to the merger, areas in which they previously would not have been competitive but now were. Those below them were given the task of outlining how to accomplish these new projects.

The projects continued after the group returned from the working weekend. People were encouraged to consult with others outside of their own group but were told that they needed to consult with three people who were new to them before they could speak to someone from their own company. Generally, one of those three people had better advice than the person from their own company and therefore made them see the benefit of the merger. As coworkers struggled with their new tasks, the anger from the first retreat vanished. To help motivate people, management offered significant bonuses for actionable projects that could not have been accomplished before the merger. People began to identify with the new company and the new name. As recommended, the merged entity hired a number of new people, people who would identify only with the new company. After a couple of years the new company moved into the top tier of its industry.

Coping with Aggressive People

The first step in coping with aggressive people is assessing what lies underneath the aggression (Table 15–1). Only then do you design a game plan.

Table 15–1 Addressing Different Types of Aggression

Type of aggression	Most effective responses
Frantic	Help the person to calm down. Decrease his or her workload.
Irritable	Help the person to solve problems and resolve conflicts; wait for the storm to pass—it won't last long.
Bully	Avoid the person at all costs.
Ruthless	Help the person understand the negative impact of his behavior on things he values and how he will benefit from altering his behavior.
Passive-Aggressive	Set clear expectations for what needs to be done and when. Avoid long discussions in which the person can drain you with his or her negativism. Avoid making yourself vulnerable by giving the person work products that are crucial and must be done by a certain date.

Containing Our Aggression: Avoiding Self-Sabotage

Much of the general wisdom about how to deal with our anger is inaccurate. Talking about our anger with a friend or therapist does not necessarily lead it to decrease. Rumination tends to increase our anger as we continually replay the hurt. Talking is useful if it leads us to look at the situation in ways that are less upsetting, such as by seeing the perpetrator's actions as not intended to hurt us. Talking also helps if it leads us to find assertive/constructive ways of fixing or at least coping with the frustrating situation. Behaving aggressively toward someone who has angered us may make us feel better, but it also decreases our inhibitions on being aggressive toward people in the future. It can also lead to a cycle of retaliation and counter-retaliation, increasing our frustration and weakening our inhibitions.

Our beliefs about situations, rather than the situations themselves make us angry. If we think that someone is being callous and inconsiderate, we are much more likely to become angry than if we think that the person is overwhelmed and preoccupied. We often jump to incorrect conclusions about why someone is behaving in a certain way. More careful consideration, or accepting that we do not know the reason, will often help us to calm down and no longer seek revenge.

Our anger can often be lessened by trying to understand the other person's position and thinking of factors that may be leading the person to behave in the offensive way. For example, New York City bus drivers are taught that passengers who repeatedly ask questions, such as, "How far is 49th Street?" may be suffering high anxiety or may have language or hearing problems. Similarly, we can try to understand those we work with. What in their culture, their fears, their childhood, their stresses, their perceptions of the world may have contributed to the behavior we dislike in them? How can we use this understanding to persuade them to do what we want? Moreover, it is often helpful to ask if the person has redeeming characteristics. When we are angry with someone, we equate the action with the whole person rather than saying that we disliked this particular action. Moreover, we should ask ourselves if we ever made a mistake or if we have characteristics that sometimes make things difficult for others. If so, should we be burned at the stake?

Many people become angry with others in order to deny that they had any hand in a problem that exists. In childhood they learned that it was not acceptable to make mistakes. To protect themselves from their own harsh criticism, they lay all blame for problems on others. To reinforce the idea that the other person was totally at fault, they become very angry with them. Appreciating that we are falling into this pattern helps us regain control.

If we decide to take concrete steps to change a situation that is making us angry, there are several principles that can help to make us effective in getting what we want. We should avoid acting impulsively. We should make sure that our anger is justified and be clear on what we want to change. We should prepare in advance what we want to say. Rehearsing what we will say with someone else is often helpful. We should focus our energy on how to fix things and what we want done in the future rather than complaining about the past and finding fault. To the extent that we do talk about what was done that we did not like, we should use "I" statements and say how something made us feel rather than focus on how the person's actions were inappropriate. It is also helpful to think about the likely consequences of acting on one's anger. What will it do to the long-term relationship, the person's motivation, to our own reputation, and to our own health? Francis Bacon noted that, "By taking revenge, a man is but even with his enemy; but in passing it over, he is superior."

Some people find it hard to forgive because they believe that to cease being angry lets the person off the hook or shows that it is acceptable for people to treat them in ways that are painful to them. Forgiving someone, however, is not a promise to forget or to believe that the other person was not responsible, nor is it a statement that what was done was not serious, nor is it permission to repeat the offense. Forgiveness is certainly not a reward to the other person. Forgiving is only a decision to no longer hate, to let go of your anger in order to heal yourself, to give yourself some peace. Ask yourself if you have ever let someone down or hurt someone.

The basic wisdom for dealing with anger has been around for many years. Seneca was a Roman philosopher-educator who served several Emperors until Nero executed him in 65 AD at the age of 61. He wrote that "hostile aggression" is to avenge an emotional injury. He noted that anger often arises because we attribute evil to the other person or because the other person has hit a weak spot, lowering our self-esteem. Seneca suggested a number of things to help people control their anger.

1. Avoid frustrating situations by noting what made you angry in the past.
2. Reduce your anger by taking time, focusing on other emotions (pleasure, shame, or fear), weapons of aggression, and attending to other matters.

3. Respond calmly to an aggressor with empathy or mild, un-provocative comments or with no response at all.

4. If angry, concentrate on the undesirable consequences of becoming aggressive. Tell yourself, "Why give them the satisfaction of knowing I am upset?" or "It isn't worth being mad over this."

5. Reconsider the circumstances and try to understand the motives or viewpoint of the other person.

6. Train yourself to be empathic with others; be tolerant of human weakness; be forgiving; and follow the "great lesson of mankind: to do as we would be done by."

Seneca also advocated child-rearing practices and humanistic education designed to build self-esteem, model nonaggressive responses, and reward constructive, nonviolent behavior.

Helping an Executive to Cease Exploding

Kent had learned over the years how to control his anger. Those who knew him found his stories of his younger, volatile self hard to believe. When he was in high school, he had been in more than his share of fights and would smash things when he was frustrated. When he first entered the business world, yelling at people was so common for him that he could only estimate the frequency and not the number of incidents. In time, a woman he was in love with told him that either his temper would go or he would go. She could not imagine raising children in a house with someone who periodically exploded.

Kent went into therapy. He began learning anger control techniques. He tried to count to ten and take some slow breaths before yelling or breaking something. He tried to think about the consequences of yelling or breaking something before he did it. He tried to decrease some of the pressure he was under and exercised in the morning to burn off some tension. He tried to recognize what things upset him and to think about new ways of looking at them. All of these helped, but the process of figuring out what upset him and learning to see them in new ways was going more slowly than he wished. He wanted medicine to make it better immediately before his relationship collapsed. He was prescribed an SSRI, one of the new-generation antidepressants that works by increasing serotonin levels in the brain. In addition to being good for depression, it helps decrease several types of anxiety and decreases irritability and impulsivity in some people. Within a few days, he was doing much better. He agreed to keep looking at the things that upset him, the reasons they upset him, and to try to look at them in new ways. Always enjoying a challenge, he accepted a new one: staying in control. Over time, it became easier and easier, and the medication was no longer necessary. He not only saved his relationship, but his newfound self-control helped his career, his health, and his happiness.

Conclusion

A number of factors can drive aggression. Some are internal to the person, including vulnerable self-esteem, pleasure in dominating and hurting, a reservoir of frustration, depression, poor impulse control, high stress, or an image of the world as hostile. Organizational factors can also drive aggression. These include cultures in which aggressive actions are sanctioned, and organizational problems fostering conflict between groups within the organization.

An Emotional Intelligence approach to aggression begins with understanding what lies underneath someone's aggression, what is motivating it, and what decreases the person's inhibitions. You can then design interventions to decrease the person's motivation to be violent and increase his inhibitions and ability to control his behavior.

Further Reading

Lucius Annaeus Seneca (John W. Basore Translator). De Ira (On Anger) in *Seneca: Moral Essays,* Volume 1. Harvard University Press, 106-355, 1988.

Lewis B. Smedes. *Forgive and Forget: Healing the Hurts We Don't Deserve.* HarperCollins Publishers, 1996.

PART IV

RIGID MANAGERS

You Will Do It My Way

Many managers are rigid. They insist on doing things their way to such a degree that we wonder if they are allergic to compromise and change. They are resistant to learning new ways of doing things and are major obstacles to organizational change and improvement efforts. Working with them can be very frustrating as we see resources wasted on outmoded, inefficient methods. They are the last people you want around if you want to cut through red tape and get things done quickly or in a new way. Rigid managers also tend to be unresponsive to others' wishes and needs. When dealing with subordinates and peers, they tend to micromanage, giving excessive directions on the details of how to carry out a project rather than giving general directives and trusting their workers to find the best way to reach their goals. They seem to constantly be in control struggles with others, and when their anger is not bursting forth, it is just under the surface.

There are many rigid managers. People with these personality traits are often attracted to management positions rather than to teaching, research, or entrepreneurship. Management provides greater predictability, clearer relationships with others, and does not require the creativity or risk taking of the other fields. Management is certainly not the only profession with rigid individuals. Law and medicine are filled with rigid people, and there are many compulsive teachers, researchers, and entrepreneurs. Nevertheless, management is a haven for many compulsive, educated, work-oriented individuals.

Some aspects of rigid managers can be very helpful in some managerial positions. In particular, the meticulousness and hard work of compulsive individuals is often valuable. These traits may not bring high efficiency or leaps in performance, but they can bring high quality. More creative and flexible individuals may not have the patience to ensure that every detail of a project is in place. If you want someone to ensure that the details of the bureaucratic process are carried out, managers with compulsive traits are ideal. Perhaps most important, their tendency to work very hard and eschew leisure time can benefit a company. Similarly, if you want someone to carefully carry out your orders and to see to it that their subordinates follow suit, someone with authoritarian traits is useful.

Nevertheless, the difficulty of rigid managers in accepting change and their tendency to control others creates many problems. Understanding what drives the rigidity, what limits the manager from trying new things, can both help us tolerate the behavior and sometimes provide us with the tools to modify it.

The Many Flavors of Rigid Managers

A number of factors and personality types can underlie rigid behavior. Some rigid managers have compulsive personality styles, some have authoritarian personality styles, some are oppositional, and some are narcissistic. Some are rigid because they believe that a coercive managerial/leadership style is most effective. Understanding what lies underneath the rigid behavior of a manager is crucial to finding the most effective way to modify the behavior.

Compulsive managers, like most toxic managers, exist on a spectrum (Table IV–1). Some compulsive managers are mildly rigid. They push for things to be done their way, they tend to micromanage, and they compromise only reluctantly and with discomfort. They are hampered in their ability to develop the people under them to lead, and they do not get the best out of people. Assuming that they are otherwise competent to do their job, however, they are usually able to perform reasonably. Those who are very compulsive tend to be perfectionists, which seriously compromises their ability to make decisions and finish projects and work tasks. Their performance is much more seriously hampered if they need to be creative or produce in a rigid timeframe. If you pour narcissistic traits into the mix, the problem grows exponentially. You now have a control freak who demands that everything be done their way and can be offended if you even suggest that you have a useful idea.

Table IV–1 Spectrum of Compulsive Managers

	Healthy Narcissism	**Narcissistic**
Very compulsive	Perfectionist	So impaired they are unlikely to rise
	Serious problems in making decisions and finishing work	
	Very uncomfortable doing things as others wish or even unable to do so	
Moderately compulsive	Presses to do things their way	Control freak
	Micromanages	

Compulsive Managers

People with compulsive personalities have a constellation of problems, including being uncomfortable with change and doing things in new ways, discomfort with spontaneity and warm feelings, a tendency to be very critical of themselves and others, avoidance of leisure and a continual focus on achieving and accomplishing, and dogmatism. This personality style has sweeping impact on the person's life both in and out of work. It is rooted in a fear of chaos and a tendency to harshly criticize mistakes.

Authoritarian Managers

Authoritarian managers believe in hierarchies and tradition. When outside of a bureaucratic or political system, they can be very warm and nice.

Oppositional

Oppositional managers are forever protecting their autonomy from dangers real and imagined. Every interaction is an opportunity to prove to themselves that they will not be pushed around. Every interaction poses the threat that they might be. In the process of protecting themselves from being dominated they often seek so much control that they wind up dominating others.

Passive-Aggressive

Passive-aggressive managers are frequently negativistic or oppositional in their dealings with people. Forever protecting their autonomy from dangers real and imagined, they dig their heels in on any issue they can find.

Dictatorial

Dictatorial managers believe that a coercive style is the appropriate way to run a team. The assumption underlying their use of coercive leadership is that people respond to sticks and not carrots, and that subordinates have little to offer other than carrying out their superiors' orders to the letter. Another path to dictatorial leadership is that the manager believes he or she has great expertise and knows far better than anyone else how things should be done—a belief more often based in excessive narcissism than reality.

Some managers are dictatorial because they lack expertise and fear admitting it to themselves or others. By rigidly demanding that things be done their way, they hope to hide the fact that others may know more about how to do things and have greater competence in the area.

At times, business decisions need to be made and carried out very quickly. Making the perfect decision is less important than making a good one and implementing it. In such a situation, a good manager may transiently behave in a dictatorial fashion. However, to avoid damaging the culture and atmosphere of the company, the manager should explain to subordinates that this is an unusual situation.

Control Freaks

The rigidity of some managers is driven by an underlying narcissistic personality. Feeling that they are superior to others, they see little reason to adjust their preferred way of doing things to meet the concerns and preferences of others. They feel entitled to have things done just the way they wish. If you challenge their rigid control and micromanagement you inadvertently threaten their self-esteem and they are likely to go into a narcissistic rage and seek to destroy you.

Rigid Managers and Aggression

Passive-aggressive individuals, like most rigid individuals, have problems with anger, but their means of dealing with it are unusual. While compulsive individuals deal with their anger by becoming rigid, and by letting their righteous indignation pour out, passive-aggressive people are uncomfortable with expressing anger. Rather than directly saying no or attacking someone's ideas, they become oppositional and negativistic, and they drag their feet. Their difficulty with being assertive leads them to feel that others dominate them much of the time. As a result, they frequently are oppositional. Unlike narcissistic individuals, they do not have an exaggerated sense of their abilities; they simply think that others are even more incapable than they are.

Table IV–2 summarizes key characteristics of the oppositional personality types underlying rigid behavior: compulsive, authoritarian, passive-aggressive, narcissistic, and dictatorial.

Part IV Overview

The section begins with a chapter on compulsive managers. Compulsive managers are an extreme form of rigid managers, in which both work and play situations are dealt with in a rigid, unyielding style. Authoritarian managers are bureaucratic monsters who believe that people should do as they are told, follow convention very rigorously, and at times express considerable anger. Dictatorial managers are primarily following a belief that coercive leadership is best. Other areas of their lives will generally not have them in rigid control of others. Passive-aggressive managers could easily have been discussed in Part III, "Aggressive Managers." These managers are negativistic, and they drag their feet in order to sabotage others' plans. Finally, Part IV has a chapter discussing the general impact of rigid managers on organizations. An important type of rigid manager not discussed in this section is the narcissistic manager.

- ◆ Chapter 16—Compulsive Managers: Slaves to Work and Perfection
- ◆ Chapter 17—Authoritarian Managers: Bureaucratic Monsters
- ◆ Chapter 18—Dictatorial Managers: I'm in Charge
- ◆ Chapter 19—Oppositional Coworkers: Any Way but Your Way

Table IV–2 Traits of Rigid Managers

Personality Type	Approach to Tasks	Force Driving Rigidity	Treatment of Subordinates	Treatment of Superiors	Self-Image
Compulsive	Feels there is only one right way	Discomfort in doing things in new ways	Controlling; micro-manages		Moderate to poor
Authoritarian	Will do what he's told	Believes in hierarchies	Controlling, expects obedience	Obedient	Moderate
Oppositional	Will reject your suggestion	Feels autonomy threatened	Controlling, an-noyed if challenged	Oppositional, some-times contentious	Moderate
Passive-Aggressive	Passively blocks activities	Feels autonomy threatened	Undermines people if upset	Grumbles, drags feet	Moderate to superior
Control Freaks	Feel they know better than others	Arrogance	Demeaning	Amicable if treated as special, scornful if not	Grandiose
Dictatorial	Task oriented, get the job done	Need for coordina-tion and rapid decision making	Generally respectful	Respectful	Confident

- ◆ Chapter 20—Passive-Aggressive Managers: You Can't Make Me
- ◆ Chapter 21—Organizational Impact of Rigid Managers: Innovation Stymied

Further Reading

David Shapiro. *Autonomy and the Rigid Character.* Basic Books, 1981.

CHAPTER 16

Compulsive Managers

Slaves to Work and Perfection

Compulsive managers are the ultimate rigid managers. They insist that things be done their way, not because it is the best way, but because it is the only way they can tolerate. Change and flexibility are outside of their skill set. Preoccupied with details and unable to see the big picture they cannot distinguish between what is important and what is not. This leads them to micromanage others.

Preoccupied with critical thoughts about themselves and everyone with whom they deal, they are continually on edge and insist on controlling those around them lest something go wrong. Trapped in a world of "shoulds" and "should have" they have little pleasure and often become depressed.

Obsessed with working and accomplishment, they have a hard time relaxing, having fun, and being spontaneous. Worried about wasting time, they are uncomfortable with leisure time and approach it as a task that needs to be organized. They excessively plan their activities and cannot deal with changes or spontaneity. Pleasure comes not from spontaneity and play, but from a sense of satisfaction in accomplishing tasks, no matter how insignificant the achievement.

Working or living with a compulsive manager may feel more like being with a robot than a person. Sometimes this means Commander Data from

"Star Trek: The Next Generation," and sometimes the "Terminator,". Compulsive individuals seem almost allergic to warm feelings and demonstrate little compassion for others. Warm emotions and spontaneity require releasing controls and trusting the world. They tend to be stiff and are uncomfortable in demonstrating or receiving warmth. They are obsessed with work, turn play into work, and attempt to fill every moment with useful activity.

They tend to hoard both money and objects. Hoarding objects is not tied to sentimentality, but to not wanting to waste things. Money is also hoarded to prepare for future catastrophes. They generally live well below what they could afford.

Their dogmatism and rigidity can turn casual conversations into frustrating experiences. They are far more interested in telling you what they know than finding out what you think. They are not interested in sharing ideas and thinking together about issues. Whatever interest they have in hearing your thoughts is to be able to find fault with you. Their dogmatism leads them into arguments over trivial things. They feel undeterred in expressing extremist opinions and are generally unable to realize how their statements will make others feel. Discussing politics and religion with them is a risky endeavor (unless you are looking for a fight).

Interpersonal relationships are significantly compromised for compulsive individuals. People may feel that they are walking in a minefield, never knowing when they will upset the compulsive individual and suffer a verbal harangue. Their dogmatism, lack of warmth, and critical comments make people very uncomfortable. Friendships are tenuous, both because compulsive individuals frequently offend people and because they are so easily offended. They spend their play time criticizing and correcting people they are supposed to be playing with.

A compulsive personality style can markedly impair work effectiveness. While superiors may appreciate their meticulous behavior, they will also find compulsive individuals poor at innovating, unable to distinguish between what is important and what is not, expending resources on the wrong things, and slow to finish work. Subordinates are in an even more difficult position, since managers with compulsive personalities both micromanage and fail to provide the support subordinates' need to perform at their best. Subordinates are also intimidated by the compulsive manager's righteous indignation and unpredictable anger. The atmosphere these managers create is stifling.

The compulsive personality style of a manager, peer, or subordinate has a wide-ranging impact on your work. It affects how he interacts with you, what he wants from you, how he evaluates your work, how he does his own work, and what could lead him to become angry with you. The more you understand about how compulsive individuals see the world, process information, find value in certain things, and fear other things, the better able you will be to survive and succeed when working with one.

The core characteristics of an *obsessive-compulsive* personality are

1. Excessive focus on details and rules that interferes with the real objective.
2. Rigid insistence that his or her own way should be followed.
3. Difficulty with spontaneity and warm emotions.
4. Exaggerated focus on work and achievement.
5. Indecisiveness.

All areas of their personal lives and work are impaired by the combination of their difficulty with warm feelings, spontaneity, and play; their excessive focus on details to the point that they lose sight of important issues; their indecisiveness; and their difficulty in accommodating other people's preferences.

Underlying Psychodynamics

High levels of anger and fear of its destructive capacity leads to a general sense that things are not going well and creates an obsession with maintaining control. They fear and seek to control both the chaos of the world and of their own feelings. The fear is so great and the solution so rigorous that they lose all flexibility and spontaneity. Warm feelings toward people and engagement in playful activities require spontaneity and a loosening of controls and are therefore eschewed. Their intense desire for control and perfection leads to preoccupation with details, rules, lists, order, organization, and schedules to the extent that the major point of activities is lost.

Their anger often leads to explosions of righteous indignation at those who do not do things as they feel things should be done. Compulsive managers may take a perverse pleasure in being wronged by someone, since it gives them license to attack with righteous indignation. Venting their anger can give them a brief respite from their chronic tension. Focusing their anger on someone else also provides a respite from their eternal self-criticism.

Compulsive individuals have an unusual perceptual style. They excessively focus on details and are unable to see the big picture. They are also weak at knowing which details are important and which are not. The excessive focus on details leads them to be very critical and to feel negatively about things that are not perfect. Lost in a sea of details and unable to judge what is important they can squander huge amounts of time on trivia while important issues, such as deadlines, are missed.

Their tendency to engage in black and white thinking, rather than recognizing shades of gray, fosters rigidity. In a black and white world, there is only one way to do things. Other ways are unacceptable, since there is only a right way and a wrong way. Being unable to see value in others' perspectives and having a profound sense that their way is the only reasonable way leaves compulsive individuals stubborn, rigid, and unable to compromise.

A hyperactive, harsh conscience, intensified by a tendency to see things in black and white terms, colors their experience of the world overriding all else. They often have a sense that they are basically good people, but hate themselves for making so many mistakes. They work obsessively and eschew pleasures in an abortive attempt to prove to themselves that they are good people. Their pervasive fear of making mistakes leaves them anxious, serious, and tense, and leads to indecisiveness and procrastination undermining the success of their hard work.

Origins of Obsessive-Compulsive Personality Style

Compulsive individuals are rigid as a result of an internal struggle to control their feelings. They have a constricted lifestyle with very limited ability to enjoy things and be close to people. The need for order in all aspects of their lives enslaves them.

A variety of factors come together to lead an individual down the path to a compulsive personality style. The perceptual style of excessive focus on details without the ability to see the relative importance of those details may be inborn. The focus on control (rather than affection) and tendency to aggression may be partly inborn as well as a result of problems in parenting and development when the child was two years of age and beginning to establish control of his or her own body. A vicious cycle can develop in which the parents' attempts to control the child angers the child. The child is scared of his or her own angry feelings and therefore eschews feelings and spontaneity and seeks rigid self-control. The preoccupation with power, control, and anger blocks out warm, tender emotions. Play is also inhibited by the fear of spontaneity and the loss of control that arises when we feel warm, tender feelings. Work activities markedly predominate over play.

A Compulsive Manager ▬▬▬▬▬▬▬▬▬▬▬▬▬▬▬▬▬▬▬

Colleen was very bright and more than a little frustrated that the people around her were not equally dedicated or hardworking. But she did her best. Wanting the HR department to do first-rate work she put in long hours and went out of her way to give good opportunities to those close to her. She bragged about how well people who had worked for her had done in their careers. At the same time, she seemed very distant. She neither made small talk with people nor asked about the personal lives of those she worked with. When a subordinate noted he had a new child on the way Colleen literally said nothing. It wasn't that she did not like children—she was very invested in her own two children. But, she never talked about her family, what she liked to do. No one knew if she had any fun times or hobbies other than collecting mementos. Her one pleasure seemed to be in the growth of the responsibility of the HR department under her stewardship.

Colleen liked everything in its place. She wanted to know where people were and what they were doing, and she became annoyed when they did not spontaneously provide this information, even though she never asked for it. She frequently changed her mind about things she had said. The one consistency was the definiteness with which she always said things. She probably did not remember that she had said the opposite a few days earlier. More than a little intimidated by her, people rarely questioned her decisions or changes in decisions. They just went with her most recent assertion. Colleen expected that things would be done exactly the way she wanted. People never questioned this expectation. Fortunately, she was highly competent, bright, and skilled.

When Nancy came into the department, Colleen saw that she was a significantly harder worker and more talented than most of her subordinates. Colleen helped Nancy network and learn new skills. She gave her many opportunities but never provided praise. While others would say that work Nancy had done was excellent, Colleen would say that it was acceptable. Nancy was quite worried until she was told that the word "acceptable" was high praise from Colleen. They never went to lunch, talked about life outside of work, or discussed their families. When Colleen met Nancy's husband, she barely said hello. Nevertheless, Colleen seemed committed to fostering Nancy's career and went out of her way to do so.

At some point, Colleen seemed to change and avoided contact with Nancy. Nancy tried to find out what was wrong, why Colleen seemed to be distancing herself, but Colleen would say almost nothing. Someone suggested that Nancy had started to become too independent, was not checking in with Colleen or keeping her adequately informed. Then Nancy was called to a meeting in which Colleen expressed serious concern about Nancy's work. Nancy was told she needed to get her act together. Nancy was stunned. She listened to the complaints. They were not true. Nancy tried to explain things to Colleen, but Colleen was not interested in discussing the issues. When Nancy had clear evidence that an accusation was without merit, Colleen interrupted and said whether or not it was true, there were many other problems. Nancy's major accomplishments faded away and were of no importance in the face of a number of small problems of dubious validity.

Nancy wanted to fight each accusation but saw that Colleen was not interested and that nothing she said would change Colleen's mind. When she was younger, she would have tried to argue. Nancy had learned, however, that in some situations people are simply not interested in the truth, only in fortifying the opinions they hold. To try to convince them that they are wrong only creates increased tension and makes them even more negatively predisposed to you. Nancy decided that the best she could do was to stop talking, apologize for having failed Colleen, promise to do better in the future, and begin looking for a new position.

Compulsive individuals have difficulty separating important bits of data from unimportant aspects. If they see several small problems and a few great strengths, the small problems may weigh in more heavily, since there are more of them. Compulsive individuals tend to see things in black and white terms. They hate ambiguity and shades of gray because they mean that there is no clear answer and one might make a mistake.

Once you get on the bad side of a compulsive individual, it is very difficult to redeem yourself. Once someone has a negative image of you, they tend to read all information through a filter that trivializes positive information and magnifies negative information. Psychologists use the word *schema* to refer to the models people have of the world. In other words, once people have a solid impression of someone or a situation (a schema), they will distort their reading of data to fit the existing schema. *Schemata* are crucial because they help us make sense of the world. When they become rigid, however, we get into the situation of a person who says, "I know what I know; don't confuse me with the facts."

Emotional Intelligence Approach to Compulsive Managers

Dealing with Compulsive Superiors

Compulsive bosses can make your life miserable. In addition to insisting you do things their way, their way is often wrong, since they are not good at learning new things, tend to excessively focus on details, and cannot see the forest for the trees.

Their disinterest in the opinions of others is also very frustrating, if not degrading. Creativity and initiative are damaged. They are stingy with compliments, allocation of needed resources, and salary increases. They have very limited interest in your emotional needs for support, praise, and encouragement or in your hopes and aspirations. They will not understand your family needs or hobbies or desire for a life outside of work. Their excessive focus on work and rejection of leisure time will generally lead them to pressure you to do the same.

There are several things that you can do to limit the problems they cause you. One of the most important is to understand their values and their fears, and to be responsive to them. They value long hours, seriousness, and meticulousness. Phrase things in the words they understand and can relate to. You will get further by telling them that it is crucial for the team to be punctual with an assigned task than you will by saying that it is good enough and is due. Talk about how important work is and not about whether or not you enjoy it. When you need or want to attend to your family, it is better to talk about your family responsibilities than about wanting to spend time with your family. They can understand responsibilities more than the need for time to rest, relax, and have fun.

Compulsive individuals fear chaos and things being out of control. They also have limited trust in others. Therefore, they generally want to be filled in on the details of what you are doing. The micromanagement may seem silly and even annoying to you, but it is better to go along with it. Compulsive managers often prefer the information in written form for efficiency sake. This has the added benefit of enabling you to prove that you had, in fact, kept them informed. They dislike changes of plans and spontaneity. If changes need to occur, let them know well in advance. You should also seek clarification of assignments and periodic check-ins to make sure that you know exactly what they want and can give it to them. A compulsive manager may well be unhappy if you give him a product that is ultimately better than, but not exactly what, he had wanted. Therefore, check in with him as you do the work to make sure you are providing exactly what he wants.

Follow rules to the letter. Never come in late or leave early. Never complain about staying late. Never say that you want to spend time relaxing or having fun. They will see you as not committed to the company and the work and perhaps even as unreliable. Instead, talk about how a brief break would enable you to work more effectively.

It is also important to do things the way these managers are used to having them done. Changing their minds or showing them the error of their ways is guaranteed to lead to disaster. Never get into debates; they have an overriding need to be in control. Avoid discussing politics and religion with them unless you happen to share their strongly held views or are able to listen and agree with anything people say.

Get your positive strokes elsewhere. They will not be effusive with you. Moreover, reset your gauge for measuring compliments. Whatever positive statements they make will mean more than a big compliment from someone who goes around complimenting everyone. Also avoid getting bent out of shape when they criticize. They have a need to vent aggression. Often, they mean relatively little by it. Do your best to see it as their way of making conversation, although it may be unpleasant to you. In addition, do not let on that you are upset. They do not really care. Using "I" statements about how their behavior bothers you will backfire. They are not sympathetic creatures, although they may have learned some of the socially acceptable responses.

You also need to protect yourself from excess demands. You need to be careful to not burn yourself out by working endless hours, worrying about perfection, and receiving limited praise.

Dealing with Compulsive Coworkers

Compulsive coworkers are difficult, but not as difficult as compulsive superiors. Compulsive coworkers can be overly focused on details and interfere with your finishing a project. They can be overly critical and give too much advice. They can also pass criticism on to others if they are in competition with you. Keep a bit of a distance, and don't take their criticism personally. Don't give them ammunition to pass on to others. Divide up work so that you can at least get yours done and so that superiors will see that you are effective. Without attacking your colleague, make sure your superiors know how things are divided and that you are getting your part done.

Dealing with Compulsive Subordinates

The primary problems compulsive subordinates present is that they do not understand the big picture and may be late on work products because they are trying for perfection in ways that are unimportant. With each project, you need to tell them what the key parameters are and why these factors are important. It may be readily apparent to you what is and is not important, but it is not clear to them. You need to tell them. It is also important to frequently check in to make sure that they are moving forward and not becoming impossibly bogged down in unimportant details. In giving directions, remember their values. Instead of saying something is good enough, talk about how punctuality in finishing the deliverable is key.

It is also important to select their work tasks carefully, utilizing their skills and avoiding their weaknesses. Giving them work that needs to be done very quickly or that requires creativity and innovation is setting them up to fail. You may choose to do this if you want to document their failures and fire them. You don't want to do this if you want them to stay around. Give them work in which meticulousness is important. They can, for example, be very good at planning a conference or keeping records. They are not the people you want to send as liaisons to a new group with whom you want to build a relationship because their interpersonal skills are limited. They present a higher risk than the average person for offending others as a result of their having rigid, extreme views and their tendency to voice them. It is your job as a senior manager to place people into the positions and work tasks in which they will have the greatest chance to succeed.

It is important to remember their strengths. It will help you tolerate their weaknesses with less frustration. Remember their willingness to work long hours and their dedication. This can be very helpful at times. Providing them with positive feedback is important. These people are insecure under the surface. Positive feedback may lessen their rigidity.

For HR and Senior Management

The hard work and perfectionism of compulsive managers is very appealing. However, their difficulty in separating the forest for the trees, and their rigidity, ultimately compromise their work.

Perhaps the most crucial aspect of working with compulsive managers is being clear on their strengths and weaknesses, and on the depth of their weaknesses. Compulsive managers are particularly unlikely to change. Compulsive managers are likely to learn the technical skills necessary for a new job. They are very unlikely, however, to acquire the people skills needed to improve morale and motivate people. They are also unlikely to be innovators, since they dislike change. You may be able to convince them of the priorities in a new project, but they are unlikely to be able to walk into a new situation themselves and be able to figure out what is important and what is not. They will also have a hard time doing things new ways.

Place them in a position in which their hard work and meticulousness are needed and in which flexibility and supporting/encouraging others is not. It is also important to provide lots of oversight so that you do not suddenly find out that their rigidity, lack of understanding of the big picture, and poor emotional intelligence has seriously compromised a project. Be clear yourself on where their weaknesses may compromise a project and provide the coaching and guidance necessary to succeed.

A good executive coach may be able to help them be better aware of the areas where behavioral change would help them. Significant change, however, is unlikely to come without a coach who is also a trained therapist who can help them free themselves from some of their anger and find new, less destructive ways of dealing with it.

Conclusion

Compulsive personality traits (see Table 16–1) can seriously undermine the work that a manager is trying to do. Their rigidity concerning how to accomplish work tasks impedes innovation, and their insistence on having

Table 16–1 Overview of Compulsive Managers

Symptoms	Underlying Factors	Impact	Ways for Subordinates to Cope	Ways for Senior Management to Cope
Rigid insistence on having one's own way	Desire for control over all else	Impairs creativity	Understand their fears and limitations	Assignment to positions where their detail focus and rigidity are helpful (quality control) and not destructive (creative endeavors)
Excessive focus on details and rules over big picture	Perceptual style that sees details rather than big picture	Impairs productivity	Avoid surprising them; keep them informed	
		Impairs morale		
Excess perfectionism	Negative view of people, including self	Impairs initiative	Focus discussions on work	Oversight to continually assess performance
Difficulty with spontaneity and warm emotions	Fear of chaos		Demonstrate diligence	
	Fear of criticism		Do things the way they like them	Focused coaching to modify key problematic traits
Hypercritical	Difficulty trusting people		Don't debate with them	
Nonsupportive			Seek emotional support elsewhere	Assess if anxiety or depression are exacerbating their rigidity
Exaggerated focus on work/achievement				
Indecisiveness				

their way and lack of attention to their subordinates' needs for support damages relationships with people. Compulsive managers' difficulty in seeing the big picture, along with their rigidity, makes them particularly unsuited to hold the top position in an organization.

Differentiating compulsive managers from other types of rigid managers is important in designing the best way for dealing with the problem and in assessing the long term impact of the problem. Compulsive managers are more globally impaired in their ability to relate to people than are authoritarian and dictatorial managers. They are very limited in their ability to respond to people's feelings and needs. They most resemble narcissistic managers. Significant differences exist, however. The rigidity of compulsive managers arises from their intense fear that they will make a mistake, while the rigidity of control freaks comes from feeling that they are better than others. Narcissistic managers are risk-takers rather than highly cautious like compulsive managers. They can also enjoy themselves and be spontaneous. The self-dislike of compulsive managers is very close to the surface and usually sticks out into the fresh air where all can see. In contrast, the fragility of the narcissistic manager's self-esteem is well hidden in subterranean caverns. It is primarily evidenced by periodic earthquakes of anger when the narcissist's self-esteem is challenged.

The first step in dealing with compulsive managers, whether they are your superiors or your subordinates, is deciding what aspect of their behavior you most want to change. You are unlikely to effect a major personality change in someone, whether you are his or her friend, spouse, boss, subordinate, or therapist. You can, however, often soften the rough edges in his or her behavior. This is often enough to effect a major improvement in your own quality of life. There are many aspects to personality. Only a limited number of personality traits directly affect your interactions with the person, and even fewer have a major effect on you. The trick is to decide which traits you most want to modify in the person and to focus efforts on those.

If your superior is compulsive, you will have the least difficulty if you remember their focus on details and need to feel in control. Keep them well informed, and be meticulous in your work. Do not expect them to be interested in you or to praise you. If you need these things, look elsewhere for them. Follow rules to the letter. Show them that you are very focused on work and that you take your responsibilities seriously.

If the compulsive manager is your subordinate, place him or her on projects in which details and meticulousness are key to success and in which a supportive style in dealing with people is not needed.

It is important to assess compulsive managers for depression and anxiety problems. These problems are common in people with this personality style and lead to a significant worsening of their maladaptive personality traits.

Your Turn

- What compulsive managers have you observed?
- Give examples of their
  - Excess focus on details, rules, and achieving perfection that gets in the way of the major point of the activity and decision making
  - Rigid insistence that his or her own way should be followed
  - Difficulty with spontaneity and warm emotions
  - Exaggerated focus on work and achievement
  - Indecisiveness
- How did their behavior affect you?
- How did their behavior affect others?
- How did their behavior affect productivity?
- How did their behavior affect communication?
- What did you and others try to do to cope?
- What worked, and what did not? (What made things better, and what made things worse?)
- What did you learn?
- How would you do things differently in the future?
- What advice would you give to someone facing a compulsive manager?
- Do you at times act in similar ways?
  - How does it affect people?
  - How does it affect your team?
  - How does it affect your career?

Further Reading

David Shapiro. *Neurotic Styles*. Basic Books, 1972.

CHAPTER 17

Authoritarian Managers

Bureaucratic Monsters

On first glance, authoritarian managers can be difficult to tell apart from compulsive ones. Both are rigid and controlling in their dealings with subordinates. In addition to their making all decisions and micromanaging you, both authoritarian and compulsive managers have limited interest in listening to your ideas. They insist that there is only one right way to do things and will be happy to tell you what it is, even if you assure them they should not go to the trouble. In addition to these hallmark traits of rigidity, they both have a tendency to engage in angry outbursts.

Despite the similarities, there are important differences between the two. Understanding the differences and being able to assess which type of rigid manager you are dealing with increases your chance of successfully managing their toxic behavior and avoiding unnecessary problems.

There are three central characteristics of the authoritarian personality style:

1. Strong adherence to social convention.
2. Submission to whomever they see as legitimate authority.
3. Tendency to act aggressively, particularly when it is sanctioned by authority figures.

Fear of chaos and criticism are the demons that underlie and drive the behavior of authoritarian managers. Rigid adherence to social convention and the dictates of authority figures provides authoritarian managers with some protection from their own unyielding and punitive consciences. They want to believe that the answers are simple and clear, and that there is one right way. For authoritarian individuals, everyone has a proper role to play in life, including a stereotypic gender role. If only everyone followed social conventions, people would get along well, and we would all know what to expect in interactions. Without clear roles, things become messy, tensions develop, and people are not clear on what they should do.

Preferring clear and simple answers, their thinking tends to be simplistic and avoids complexities that can leave them unsure of the best action to take. When answers are clear and simple, they know what to do and what not to do in order to avoid being in trouble. They also avoid introspection, since this could undercut their confidence that they are doing things the right way.

Although harsh, controlling, and even contemptuous of those who report to them, authoritarian managers are generally submissive, obedient, and loyal to those above them. Their eagerness to submit to authority figures sets them apart from compulsive managers. A particularly interesting aspect of authoritarian managers is that they may not recognize the same authority that you do. They may decide that their boss is in control, or that the technical expert should have final say, or that the outside consultant should have final say. I was once working on a project designing a new software tool. My counterpart from another team was being difficult about how to do things. When I said that a certain decision needed to be made by the entire team or by our team leader, she strongly objected and said that she would do whatever our technology expert (another team member) advised. She had her own, idiosyncratic sense of what was right and appropriate, and no one could convince her differently.

In addition to rigidly insisting that their subordinates do things their way, authoritarian managers are often irritable and aggressive. A number of things can rouse their anger. They become frustrated and angry when their subordinates fail to show them the deference they feel they deserve. They also become angry when other people do not observe social customs as they believe they should. In part, this upsets them because people failing to follow custom interferes with their ability to know what to expect and threatens their security that there is only one right way to do things. Their frustration and stress also builds because of their failure to live up to their own expectations. Negative feelings about others and harsh condemnation of others provides an excuse for them to vent some of their pent-up aggression. Ruminating about the faults and mistakes of others also serves to put a Band-Aid on their own tarnished self-image, since seeing others as "bad" means that at least they are not the worst. This psychological solution has a cost, however. Their negative assessments of people reinforce their fear of chaos and their desire for strict rules, law and order, and rigid hierarchy.

As a result of their rigidity and aggression, authoritarian managers are often difficult and possibly even toxic to work with. How difficult depends upon how extreme their traits are, your ability to adjust to their style, and whether they push your emotional buttons.

Authoritarian managers grew up in a home or community that valued obedience to authority and conventional values above all else. Moreover, it is likely that when they were growing up, adults were harsh with them and administered ample verbal and physical punishment. Parents and teachers discouraged them from having their own ideas and making their own decisions. They identified with their parents and came to admire power and those who wield it. They developed contempt for those whom they saw as weak. They were less concerned with how power was used than with having it. Parents and teachers impressed upon them the importance of a rigid hierarchy, order, and control. They learned that the world was dangerous and needed to be rigidly hierarchical, with those above barking orders to those below. Now that they are adults, they continue to be obedient to those above them and to take their aggression out on those below them, as their parents did to them. Power and submission rather than warmth and caring was the cornerstone of their childhood relationships, and so they tend to glorify power and toughness.

Authoritarian Manager

Victor saw himself as liberal, but his friends knew he was not. He dressed conservatively, was monogamous, was uncomfortable with having more than one drink of alcohol, and was politically moderate. He rebelled against his parents by rejecting their atheism and going to church. Throughout his life, he wanted to go to a good college, have a solid job, and raise a family.

As a child, he was relatively socially ill at ease and felt pushed aside by others. Having great respect for expertise, and having intellectual gifts himself, he hoped that he would eventually learn enough that people would finally listen to him. Although Victor accepted that "rank has its privileges," he was very angry with those who abused their power and trod on the weak. He worked actively to protect people who could not speak for themselves.

After college, he held various jobs. In each he felt a fair amount of anxiety. He wanted to do things the best way. He felt that superiors held the right answer to each situation, and he wanted to find it and carry it out. Meanwhile, Victor felt that those below him should take his advice on every issue, not because he ultimately had the best answer (he felt his superiors did, not him) but because he was more likely to be correct than those who reported to him.

Victor puzzled many who knew him. His tendency to ask overly simplistic questions left some thinking that he did not have sufficient intelligence to know how to put his pants on in the morning. Others, however, saw his intelligence and promoted his career. A major breakthrough in his style occurred when a senior manager took him under his wing, extensively coached him, and clearly pointed out the problems with his presentation. In his next job, and ever after, no one questioned his intelligence.

As he moved up the ranks, Victor often experienced superiors as being blunt, if not harsh, in their comments. He often followed suit with those who reported to him. A degree of social blindness, along with a belief (rationalization) that feedback should be given and received with clarity and a lack of emotions, drove his style. He irritated many people. When the problem was pointed out to him, he felt awful. It totally violated what he felt was right. He worked on it and began rounding off his rough edges. Nevertheless, for a long time, the abrasive/dismissive side could slip out when he was under pressure. When he was rushed, and he felt that his extensive training and intelligence gave him the answer to problems, he tended to tell others what they should do rather than listening to them. In the culture of his organization, this sometimes did not go over well.

Despite his rigidity, periodic anger, and attempts at dominance, he had neither a compulsive nor narcissistic personality. Unlike the compulsive individual, he enjoyed many things and had a very warm side. He liked to play. With people he knew, he was sensitive, supportive, and generous. Although a strong believer in morality, he was not scrupulous as a compulsive individual would be. Particularly important in terms of his work style, he always had his eyes on the big picture and was not obsessed with details. He would not have stood around rearranging the deck chairs while the *Titanic* went down. He was not a perfectionist and in fact needed to work hard to make sure the details were sufficiently taken care of before he moved on to the next challenge. He also did not have a narcissistic personality. This was clear both in his concern for others, at least those he knew outside of work, and in his self-devaluation, something well hidden from those who saw him as arrogant. He had more fantasies of self-destruction than of grandiose accomplishments.

Emotional Intelligence Approach to Authoritarian Managers

Dealing with Authoritarian Superiors

Rigid, authoritarian bosses are common. If you have not yet had one, you will. You will also face far worse. Authoritarian managers submit to their superiors and expect you to submit to them. It is generally best to play the game. Show them some deference and do your job competently, and they are likely to treat you well. Above all, do not go around them or over their heads. They value hierarchy above all else and will be furious if you circumvent it.

Do your best to roll with the punches. They probably do not mean as much by their criticism as you take it to mean. They do it to everyone. It is their way of saying hello. Remember what is important to them: convention. Follow convention and the rules. Beyond that, you can be creative.

Rigid, authoritarian bosses tend to be harsh, but they are not sadistic. If they are sadistic, then you are dealing with far more than simply an authoritarian personality. Go back and rethink the personality structure and dynamics of your boss.

The most crucial issue is working on your own reaction. It is essential to avoid letting them destroy your morale, initiative, and creativity. By doing good work, you maximize the opportunity to move to other positions. If you let your work quality decline along with your morale, your options for obtaining a more desirable position will also decline. If you become angry, resentful, and difficult to work with, you will provide the authoritarian manager with concrete examples of poor work quality that can damage your performance rating. How hastily you need to exit a situation depends on whether you can continue to do decent work and whether the authoritarian manager basically likes or dislikes you.

Dealing with Authoritarian Subordinates

Authoritarian managers are easier for superiors to deal with than are other problematic managers because of their deference to authority. They believe in hierarchy, and you are above them. They can present serious problems for you, however, if they decide that the "real" or appropriate authority is not you, but someone else, perhaps someone they see as having greater expertise. The risk of this happening can be minimized by making sure that experts speak directly with you, rather than give their opinions and preferences to the authoritarian manager under you.

For HR and Senior Management

Authoritarian managers tend to be limited in their creativity. They have a particularly detrimental impact on the groups they lead by damaging subordinates productivity and creativity. Coaching can ameliorate the problems they cause. Senior managers and HR need to impress upon authoritarian managers that the culture of the organization is different than that which they are used to and that they need to accommodate themselves. In particular, they need to allow those under them more freedom in decision making. They also need to not vent anger toward those under them.

In coaching an authoritarian manager, it is useful to obtain 360-degree feedback—having superiors, peers, and subordinates evaluate the manager—to gain an understanding of the situations in which the authoritarian manager becomes rigid and when the rigidity is most destructive to the work process. It is often helpful to observe the manager in meetings and on the phone, and to read evaluations and memoranda he or she writes in order to gain a more detailed understanding of how he or she interacts with people. Providing concrete suggestions for doing things differently will help. Because patterns developed and used over years can silently come back to us and reassert themselves unless we are vigilant, it is important to periodically assess how they are doing and provide ongoing feedback and recommendations.

Conclusion

Some rigid managers have authoritarian personality styles (Table 17–1). They believe that people should submit to authority figures and follow conventional morality. They share many similarities with compulsive managers. Authoritarian managers, however, are willing and eager to submit to authority figures, while compulsive managers want to do things their way. Moreover, unlike compulsive managers, they are able to enjoy things and sometimes relate warmly to people. Managers with authoritarian personalities are more amenable to suggestions and are likely to change their style than are compulsive managers.

There are significant differences in the rigid styles of compulsive and authoritarian managers. Both authoritarian and compulsive individuals expect to have their way when dealing with subordinates and are likely to be dismissive of subordinates. But, while authoritarian managers are generally comfortable in following the lead of their bosses, compulsive managers are not. Compulsive managers are only comfortable doing things their own way, while authoritarian managers want the hierarchy to be followed. While compulsive managers dislike the uncertainty and confusion of doing things in new ways, authoritarian managers dislike the uncertainty of equality and lack of hierarchy.

If your superior tends toward authoritarianism, it is best to not struggle with them. Remember that their being domineering is neither personal nor a statement that they think they are better than you. It is simply a statement that they believe organizations and society function best if there is a hierarchy.

If your subordinate is authoritarian, you are generally in luck: You have a loyal supporter. Problems can, however, arise if you have an authoritarian supporter who recognizes someone else as the real authority. In this case, limit their contact with this person and have the person speak only with you about major work issues.

Table 17–1 Overview of Authoritarian Managers

Symptoms	Underlying Factors	Impact	Ways for Subordinates to Cope	Ways for Senior Management to Cope
Rigid adherence to social convention	Belief in hierarchies	Aggression and excess control impair morale, initiative, and innovation	Avoid surprising them; keep them informed	Limit their contact with people they may see as an authority other than you
Submission to what they see as legitimate authority	Fear of chaos	Can undermine legitimate authority and cause chaos	Demonstrate respect for their authority	Assign to positions where their personality traits will do the least harm
Tendency to act aggressively, particularly when sanctioned by whom they see as legitimate authority	Fear of criticism		Do not go over their head	Oversee to continually assess treatment of others
Prone to scapegoating and bullying	Underlying anger		Follow conventions	Provide focused coaching to modify key problematic traits
			Do things the way they like them	Utilize their respect for authority to foster change
			Don't debate with them	
			Avoid letting them damage your work (and thereby your reputation)	

Your Turn

- ◆ What authoritarian managers have you observed?
- ◆ Give examples of their
  - • Rigidity
  - • Obedience to an authority figure (who was the person to them?)
  - • Aggression
  - • Strong adherence to social custom
- ◆ How did their behavior affect you?
- ◆ How did their behavior affect others?
- ◆ How did their behavior affect productivity?
- ◆ How did their behavior affect communication?
- ◆ What did you and others try to do to cope? What worked, and what did not? (What made things better, and what made things worse?)
- ◆ What did you learn?
- ◆ How would you do things differently in the future?
- ◆ What advice would you give to someone facing an authoritarian manager?
- ◆ Do you at times act in similar ways?
  - • How does it affect people?
  - • How does it affect your team?
  - • How does it affect your career?

Further Reading

Theodor Adorno, E. Frenkel-Brunswik, Daniel J. Levinson, & R. N. Sanford. *The Authoritarian Personality.* Harper and Row, 1950.

Bob Altemeyer. *The Authoritarian Specter.* Harvard University Press, 1996.

CHAPTER 18

Dictatorial Managers

I'm in Charge

Dictatorial managers are the least problematic of the rigid managers. Their behavior is limited to wanting to make all key decisions themselves. They fail to seek and make use of real input from those reporting to them. The behavior of dictatorial managers is not driven by problematic personality traits. Rather, they hold the old fashioned belief that a dictatorial style is the best way to manage.

Although this leadership style is sometimes efficient, it carries a significant cost to the team's morale and the development of future leaders. When people do not participate in decision making they are more likely both to fail to whole heartedly support decisions and to succumb to stress and burn-out. Team members feel that the decisions are being imposed on them (and indeed they are) rather than being a product of the group's efforts. This interferes with team members becoming committed to and excited about projects. Instead, oppositional and passive-aggressive behavior become likely.

Dictatorial leadership also carries a cost in terms of creativity and making the best decision. Group decisions take longer than decisions made by a single person. But, these decisions are usually the best informed and most creative. Group participation is not the same as decision making by consensus.

Consensus decisions are political compromises rather than well thought through analyses of problems.

Another problem with a dictatorial style of leadership is that it fails to develop future leaders. In order to learn how to analyze problems, develop options, and to someday fill the shoes of your manager it is important to have the experience of working together on solving problems.

For a manager to use a dictatorial style for a brief period during a crisis is usually not a serious problem. For a manager to use it for a long time is.

A Dictatorial Manager

Josh was a dictatorial manager. Outside of work he was not particularly rigid. He certainly was not compulsive, authoritarian, or narcissistic. He enjoyed play time as well as work. He was not wedded to conventional values. He did not think that he was particularly brighter or more capable than others. He did, however, feel that efficiency called for quick decision making and that in most cases a rapid decision was better than a slow one. He was concerned that long group discussions used up enormous resources and time that were better expended on implementation.

People who worked with him were sometimes frustrated that they did not have a bigger input in the decision-making process. They were uncomfortable with the degree to which he took charge and forged ahead with plans without consulting with them. Nevertheless, they felt that Josh was interested in them and respected their work. If someone needed a day off for personal issues or needed to go home early, she knew she could count on Josh to give it to her. He gave people feedback on their work and was generally positive and sensitive in his interactions with them. He would talk with people about where they wanted to be in five years and what they needed to do to get there. The one thing he would not do was include them in decision making.

Things changed suddenly. The company faced a major reorganization. Plans had to move ahead more rapidly than usual. Josh now had even less time for and interest in conferring with the people on his team than he usually had. As he started giving out assignments, he failed to adequately explain the big picture to people. They had a basic idea of the company's thinking about the change. They did not, however, feel connected to it or to the steps their team was making to support it. As a result, they did not feel very motivated to work the extra hours that were needed. It was one thing to put in long hours one week, knowing that Josh would pay them back the next. It was another thing to mobilize the energy to put in long hours week after week with no payback in sight. If Josh had normally engaged them in decisions and now was unable to, he would have earned their loyalty and could have gotten away with it. He had not, however, earned this type of loyalty and faith. People saw little reason to markedly put themselves out for Josh or the company, since they had never felt that connected to the company as a result of never having been part of the decision-making process.

Josh saw that his team was not putting in the effort needed. He talked to people and saw that their motivation was seriously lacking. He did not understand why. His people had always produced for him before.

Emotional Intelligence Approach to Dictatorial Managers

Dealing with Dictatorial Bosses

Dictatorial bosses are less destructive than most of the toxic managers discussed in this book. They can, however, be very problematic to deal with, especially if they push your buttons. Some people cannot cope with someone who fails to show the normal courtesy of seeking and considering their input.

Because their dominance of decision making is based on a misplaced belief that it is efficient, rather than a pathological need for control, dictatorial bosses are more likely to be able to talk to you about your concerns over having input.

After expressing an understanding of why they have centralized decision making, you can talk about the benefits of wider participation. If they become very upset, either you were not tactful or they are not simply dictatorial.

For HR and Senior Management

There is a right time and place for managers to make quick decisions without wide input from their teams, but to routinely exclude teams from all decisions is counterproductive. Managers who do so either have some problematic personality traits that are getting in the way, or have gotten lazy about bringing greater participation into decision making, or are unaware of the importance of greater participation. Education along with ongoing monitoring and some coaching to encourage practice and persistent change should be enough to solve the problem. Finding the problem is often harder than solving it, since people are hesitant to complain about a superior.

Conclusion

Dictatorial managers believe that highly centralized decision making is the best option. They seek relatively little input from others. Although efficient, there are serious costs in terms of accessing all of the information and ideas relevant to a decision, innovation, harnessing the energy of team members, and growing new leadership.

Changing the behavior of dictatorial managers is generally not that difficult. If it is, the manager is more than simply dictatorial. Effecting change can usually be accomplished by having superiors encourage the change, providing some executive coaching, and keeping an eye on how the measurement-reward system and messages sent out by senior leadership inadvertently support dictatorial styles.

We now continue on our journey through the land of rigid managers. To review, narcissistic managers want things done their way because they know what is best; compulsive managers want things done their way because they are uncomfortable with new ways; authoritarian managers want things to be done their boss's way, and dictatorial managers want a good decision to be made quickly, since that is most efficient. As we will discuss in the next chapter oppositional managers are obsessed with defending their autonomy and object to doing things your way in order to prove to themselves that you will not dominate them.

Table 18-1 Overview of Dictatorial Managers

Symptoms	Underlying Factors	Impact	Ways for Subordinates to Cope	Ways for Senior Management to Cope
Insistence on how something should be done	Belief that central control is the best way to run an organization	Excess control can impair morale, initiative, and innovation	Proactively give them information and ideas before decisions are made Understand that they are only trying to be efficient and do not mean to disempower you Try talking about the benefits of greater team participation Find a mentor to teach you what this manager will not Avoid letting them damage your work (and thereby your reputation)	Oversight to continually assess treatment of others Provide focused coaching to modify key problematic traits Assignment to positions where their leadership style will do the least harm

Your Turn

- ◆ What dictatorial managers have you observed?
- ◆ Give examples of their
  - Insisting on having their way
  - Limiting discussion of decisions
- ◆ Why were they acting this way?
- ◆ Could they be something other than dictatorial?
- ◆ How did their behavior affect you?
- ◆ How did their behavior affect others?
- ◆ How did their behavior affect productivity?
- ◆ How did their behavior affect communication?
- ◆ What did you and others try to do to cope? What worked, and what did not? (What made things better, and what made things worse?)
- ◆ What did you learn?
- ◆ How would you do things differently in the future?
- ◆ What advice would you give to someone facing a dictatorial manager?
- ◆ Do you at times act in similar ways?
  - How does it affect people?
  - How does it affect your team?
  - How does it affect your career?

CHAPTER 19

Oppositional Coworkers

Any Way but Your Way

Oppositional coworkers are contentious. They argue with you about anything and everything. It is not because they dislike you; it is the only way they know how to interact.

Desperately and constantly trying to defend their autonomy, they reject what others want in order to prove to themselves that they are not being dominated and pushed around. They are not looking to have a certain option adopted; they are looking to prevent your option from being adopted. In the process, what they actually prefer may be lost.

To protect their self-esteem they deny their responsibility for problems and blame others whenever possible. The feeling that they are always being dominated leads to a reservoir of anger. This leads to chronic irritability. They can lose their temper relatively easily. Those with less self-control and more anger will deliberately annoy others and be resentful, spiteful, and vindictive.

An Oppositional Colleague

Many people have traits that make things difficult for others. Some are self-centered, some are irritable, some are overly confident in their opinions, some are very pushy. Harold was at times

247

all of these and more. A couple of people on the team said that
he reminded them of their children during the terrible twos.

It wasn't that Harold insisted on what he wanted; it was that
he objected to whatever you wanted, even if he had been advo-
cating for it himself a week before. He didn't just argue about
how to go about a project, he seemed to argue about everything:
where to go for lunch, how to raise children, whether a movie
was good or bad, and any other issue that might come up.

Particularly puzzling, he did not seem to mind the arguments. Others found them pointless and draining. Harold, after
speaking forcefully and attacking your opinion, would be calm
and happy while you were trying to keep your blood pressure
under control. He seemed to be rejuvenated by the fight.

Emotional Intelligence Approach to Oppositional Coworkers

Dealing with Oppositional Superiors

Oppositional traits in superiors are unlikely to come out in full force
with subordinates, since subordinates expect superiors to be in charge and
to have their way on most issues. Oppositional managers have little need
to prove they cannot be dominated by subordinates, since they generally
cannot.

Managers with oppositional personality traits, if challenged by subordinates, become indignant. If this happens you need to quickly move into
a more deferential posture.

Dealing with Oppositional Peers

Oppositional peers can be very draining. You go out for lunch and wind
up in debates about anything and everything. You try to make decisions on
a project, and they argue with whatever you think. Invoking your mutual
superior may not work, since your peer is quite willing to fight with him
or her as well.

Sidestepping arguments is the best way to conserve your energy and
your sanity. If they ask for you opinion on something you can say that this

is not the time to discuss the issue or that you haven't formulated your opinion yet. If a decision must be made and your oppositional peer insists on struggling, defer the issue to your boss. Let him struggle with your oppositional peer; your boss is paid more than you.

Dealing with Oppositional Subordinates

While most toxic behavior is directed at subordinates, oppositional behavior is primarily directed at superiors. An oppositional manager will find reasons to argue over almost anything, no matter how trivial. You have several choices. One is to transfer her to someone with whom you are annoyed. Another option, and the best one if she has valuable skills, is to support her sense of autonomy as much as possible. Solicit her input. Go along with her preferences as much as possible. Pick your battles.

Perhaps most important, avoid getting caught in protracted debates. With most people, a debate will go on for awhile and then they will slowly back away from it, even if they do not agree. After awhile, most people have no desire to rehash their opinions or waste their time. The oppositional person, however, reinforces their sense of autonomy by arguing and is likely to continue until overcome by hunger or sleep. While the healthy person has nothing to lose by giving in except the issue at hand, the oppositional person is threatened with a loss of autonomy and will defend this for as long as necessary. Her stamina will generally outlast yours.

For HR and Senior Management

Oppositional coworkers can be very trying. Nevertheless, a good therapist is likely to be able to help them achieve better control of their feelings and behavior in a reasonable period of time.

Conclusion

While narcissistic and compulsive managers want things to be done their way, and authoritarian and dictatorial managers believe the hierarchy should be followed, oppositional individuals are primarily interested in not doing it your way. Close relatives of those who are passive-aggressive, oppositional people are able to speak up and push for an option. Nevertheless, they are preoccupied by the need to prove that they cannot be pushed around, and therefore, gratuitously object to what others want.

Table 19–1 Overview of Oppositional Coworkers

Symptoms	Underlying Factors	Impact	Ways for Subordinates to Cope	Ways for Senior Management to Cope
Opposes whatever others want	Desperately defending their autonomy	Slows decision making	Avoid arguing	Psychiatric assessment to see if depression is driving or intensifying the oppositional behavior
Contentious, argumentative	Feels pushed around	Drains others' energy		
Denies blame, blames others				Send for executive coaching or therapy
May be angry, touchy, spiteful				

Your Turn

- What oppositional managers have you observed?
- What oppositional traits did they show?
- How did their behavior affect you?
- How did their behavior affect others?
- How did their behavior affect productivity?
- What did you and others try to do to cope?
- What worked, and what did not? (What made things better, and what made things worse?)
- What did you learn?
- How would you do things differently in the future?
- What advice would you give to someone facing an oppositional manager?
- What advice would you give to someone facing an oppositional subordinate?
- Do you at times act oppositional?
  - In what ways?
  - How does it affect people?
  - How does it affect your team?
  - How does it affect your career?

CHAPTER 20

Passive-Aggressive Managers

You Can't Make Me

The term *passive-aggressive* refers to behavior that interferes with someone else's goals without directly opposing them. Negativism and procrastination are the key weapons in the passive-aggressive individual's arsenal. No matter how good your plan of action is, they will find reasons to be negative about it. Once a decision has been made to follow a course of action they will drag their feet no matter how clearly you convey the urgency of the situation. The more you push, the more they dig their heels in.

If you find someone infuriating and you do not know why, there is a good chance that he or she is being passive-aggressive. They engender a great deal of frustration and anger in others. The negativism and foot-dragging of passive-aggressive people is generally far more frustrating than the behavior of those who openly oppose you.

Unable to be assertive, they constantly feel that others are dominating them. As a result, they are filled with silent anger and respond in the only way they know how. Desperately and constantly trying to defend their autonomy, they reject what others want in order to prove to themselves that they can't be pushed around.

When you tell them that a need is urgent, they do not really believe you. They believe that you are simply trying to be bossy. Priding themselves on their relaxed style and ability to remain calm when others are flustered, they are likely to move even more slowly as you become harried and put pressure on them to get things done. After failing to meet a deadline, they will rationalize that the demands were unreasonable or unclear.

Passive-aggressive individuals are generally not aware that their behavior is a problem. Rather, they see you as the problem. The passive-aggressive individual is not sitting across the table from you thinking, "Boy, will he be upset if I trash every idea he has," or "If I move slowly enough, we will be late for the movie she wants to see that I don't really want to go to." All of this is unconscious to people who are passive-aggressive. From their perspective, they feel pushed around and are voicing important concerns or trying not to be harried in their getting ready. They feel they are doing you a favor, since they are going along and don't understand why you are so unappreciative of this.

Passive-aggressive individuals can be a serious problem for a team. In failing to get their work done, they can stall the work of the entire team and leave people with nothing productive to do with their time as they wait for a crucial step in the team's project. Their negativism can seriously damage morale and enthusiasm just when the team needs these most. They are also inevitably late to meetings and returning from breaks, leaving everyone sitting around waiting. They are also high-maintenance and draining. They tend to complain about being unappreciated or misunderstood, often envy others, and complain about their personal misfortunes. They often become depressed, and when depressed, their behavior is likely to be at its worst.

A Passive-Aggressive Manager ▬▬▬▬▬▬▬▬▬▬

Alex could give lectures on how to be passive-aggressive and irritate people. He was a lower level manager at a mid-sized company, supervising four people. They worked together and did similar things. When new people came to the department, Alex was initially nice. He seemed to like people at first and would help them learn the ropes. In time, however, he would invariably become disgruntled. He did not try to damage people's careers or reputation, or to avoid blame. He only sought to inconvenience people and to avoid doing work.

Once, for example, when Alex was annoyed with a client, he said a report was not finished when it actually was. Only after four days did he finally release the finished report. When told to do things he did not want to do, he would ask for such obsessive details that the person would generally decide to do it themselves, since that was easier than giving step-by-step directions. Alex often failed to relay phone messages, sometimes even telling callers—falsely—that the person for whom they had called was out of the office.

A very capable employee joined Alex's group. She was not very tall. Alex began putting supplies on the top shelf out of her reach. He had not done this before she joined the group. Her predecessor had been taller and it would not have inconvenienced him significantly. At times he sabotaged office supplies so that someone would be inconvenienced if in a rush to finish a project. One employee needed to keep the blinds near her down so the sun would not stream into her eyes. Whenever he passed her desk and she wasn't there, he would open the blinds, mumbling that the plants needed light and forcing her to reclose the blinds. He would also abruptly kick boxes, leading people to wonder if he might suddenly explode and making them wary of him. When superiors tried to speak with him about problems and mistakes, he became clueless, seeming not to understand what they were saying, and refusing to acknowledge that any mistake was made.

In time, most people grew to hate him. When layoffs occurred in his department, he was cut, since he was doing so little work. He did much better at a new position. He saw that his behavior had cost him his job. In his new position, he avoided getting into an escalating power struggle with people.

Emotional Intelligence Approach to Passive-Aggressive Managers

Dealing with Passive-Aggressive Superiors

Passive-aggressive superiors can sit on your raise or rush you to hand in a report and then sit on it until it is overdue, making you look bad. Pressuring them or telling them you are upset will only annoy them and lead to increased foot-dragging. Failing to remind them, however, will also not work. You need to muster every bit of tact you have when you talk with a passive-aggressive superior. As tempting as it is to call them on their inappropriate behavior, doing so will only backfire. Instead, it may help to casually toss out a statement explaining why it is so important to you that something is taken care of. Noting that you appreciate how they are overloaded with work and offering to help them either with this or another task to lighten their burden often helps.

If you are seeking to advance your career, a passive-aggressive manager is not the person to work for. He is unlikely to do much to help you. Moreover, he is unlikely to go far himself and be able to take you along.

When you do work or finish a report for a passive-aggressive manager, make sure you date it and, using any excuse you can, let others know it is done. Therefore, if your boss sits on it, you will not be fully to blame. Nevertheless, if your boss sits on it for too long, he will find an excuse, such as your spelling errors or poor grammar that he had to fix, to make you look bad when he gets it out late. When there is a conflict between their ability to protect themselves and their having integrity about who made a mistake, rest assured they will always protect themselves. If you have an excuse to circulate your report, or even just your ideas, to senior people early on, it is generally a good idea. You can use the excuse that you want their input and feedback as early as possible. This protects you both from the passive-aggressive manager blaming you for the report being late and from having him steal credit for your ideas.

Dealing with Passive-Aggressive Coworkers

Coworkers who are passive-aggressive will also cause you pain. If you become their friend and confidant, they will drain you and shift work to you. If you become the target of their passive-aggressive behavior, they will interfere with your work and career. It is best to keep them at a gentle distance. Do not make excuses for them to try to protect them. You will only go down with them. Do not take responsibility for getting their work done; they will not learn and you will not be able to do the things you need to. In time, the friendship will collapse and you will resent having done so much for them for no good reason. In the long run, they won't thank you. Rather, they will find a reason to resent you, no matter how good you were to them. This experience can interfere with your being able to trust others and to build positive relationships in the future.

Passive-aggressive people can be dangerous in other ways as well. They complain a lot, which in itself is draining. Far worse, however, if you agree with their complaints or even nod to show that you heard them, they may cite you as agreeing with them and compromise your relationship with superiors and colleagues.

Perhaps the most important guideline to use when dealing with a passive-aggressive coworker is not to count on them. If you do, you will get yourself in trouble sooner or later—and probably sooner. No matter how clear you are on a deadline, they will find a way to not get the work done and to be puzzled that you are annoyed. I once worked with a colleague under a tight deadline. My colleague had more to gain than I did from the success of the project. Perhaps he was bothered that I had been given the lead role. We divided up the work, agreed we would review each others' work, set a deadline for the first deliverable, and noted we needed to be in touch every other day. Then I made my big mistake: I sent my colleague a draft of my part. My colleague disappeared and missed the deadline. When he reappeared, he had totally rewritten my work and not done any of his own.

Dealing with Passive-Aggressive Subordinates

Passive-aggressive subordinates are very frustrating. The quick answer on how to deal with them is to transfer them to someone you dislike who has limited ability to retaliate. Barring that, you should find those areas of their behavior that are most problematic for getting the job done and focus attention on ameliorating them. Make a silent note to yourself of what they are doing that is most problematic. Are they negativistic on ideas? Do they drag their feet? Do they "yes" you to death and then not deliver? Make these behaviors a major part of their assessments, and give them continual feedback when you feel they are engaging in negativistic and oppositional behavior.

Interpreting their behavior will not be helpful, and subordinates are likely to see it as an invasion of their space and to respond by increasing their passive-aggressive behavior. Rather, focus on the need for everyone to cooperate in certain ways and on how cooperation issues are evaluated by the company.

It is also important to decrease their tendency to be oppositional. You can do this by proactively seeking their opinion and input on things. If you get their buy-in, they are less likely to feel put upon and to therefore be oppositional. You can sometimes also help them to learn more appropriate ways of being assertive. For example, suggest how they can tell you that they need more time to complete a task so that they will not feel the need to promise to meet your schedule and then fail to do so.

If you have any insecurity or tendency to reflect on yourself, passive-aggressive subordinates can undermine your self-confidence. They will always be certain that you were unclear or that your demands are unreasonable. If you stand your ground, they are likely to express regret and promise to do better, only to repeat the problems many times in the future. Avoid letting them see your frustration. Your becoming angry can be positive feedback for passive-aggressive managers and may encourage them to continue their infuriating behavior.

Document the problems in their work products so that if the time comes, you will be able to fire them without excessive difficulty. In the meantime, avoid getting into debates about whether they did or did not do the work you instructed them to do and whether or not a problem was their fault. The debates will drag on endlessly, draining energy you need for other tasks.

For HR and Senior Management

Many people who appear to be passive-aggressive actually have treatable psychiatric problems. It is important to assess this both out of fairness to the person and because it is much more cost-effective for the company to encourage the manager to get treatment for problems with anxiety, stress, depression, or ADHD than it is to find and train a replacement.

People with ADHD are disorganized and distractible, and often do not finish tasks on time or as instructed. Managers and workers who are under a great deal of stress from either work or personal issues, or who have post-traumatic stress disorder, will have great difficulty concentrating and focusing and may therefore exhibit the outward symptoms of passive-aggressive personality traits. Depression and anxiety are also distracting and drain people of their energy. Depressed individuals have low energy, cannot concentrate, and may find it impossible to motivate themselves to get tasks done or show up to meetings on time. Their tendency toward pessimism and worry may come out as negativism.

All of these can often be readily ameliorated if the person is seen by a competent psychiatrist and follows through on treatment. You do not want to lose a good manager who simply needs to take a pill every morning. Managers with passive-aggressive traits, however, are another matter. They often need extensive coaching and therapy for their behavior to improve and remain better. Executive coaching can help them realize the impact of foot-dragging and negativism on others. Therapy is needed to help them recognize the aggression that lies underneath the oppositional behavior and develop better assertiveness skills to replace their passive-aggressive patterns.

Conclusion

Passive-aggressive managers, like other rigid managers, are inflexible, dislike compromise, and will not go along with the wishes of others (see Table 20–1). Rather than outwardly insisting that things be done their way, however, they try to block others' plans by procrastination and negativism.

Passive-aggressive managers and employees are very frustrating to deal with. We intuitively feel that they are sticking it to us. Their wasting our time and interfering with our work can be infuriating. It is helpful to remember that their negativism and foot-dragging is generally unconscious to them. Moreover, it is driven by their sense of powerlessness. Imagine them as young children trying to protect themselves and not knowing how. One way or another, it is important to find a way to not let them get to you, since you have better things to do with your energy than become furious with them. Most of all, do not count on them to do things on time or according to your instructions. The more crucial it is that they follow directions and meet deadlines, and the more pressure you put on them, the more likely they are to sabotage you. Do not give them the weapons to blow you up.

It is very rare for passive-aggressive managers to rise in organizations unless they have some very unusual connections or talents. Their negativism and procrastination generally prevent them from succeeding.

If you have a passive-aggressive subordinate, it is important to set clear expectations, warn him or her of the consequences of failing to do the work, document the failures, and avoid becoming tangled in debates about why he or she did not do the work the way you instructed.

Finally, take the time to assess if the person is truly passive-aggressive or if a treatable psychiatric problem is impairing the manager's performance.

Your Turn

- ◆ What passive-aggressive managers have you observed?
- ◆ Give examples of their
  - • Negativism
  - • Foot/dragging
  - • Sabotaging people

Table 20–1 Overview of Passive-Aggressive Managers

Symptoms	Underlying Factors	Impact	Ways for Subordinates to Cope	Ways for Senior Management to Cope
Negativistic	Problems being assertive	Fails to get work done	Date your work, circulate it, let people know you finished it on time	Assess whether ADHD, depression, or anxiety are contributing; if so, treat it
Oppositional	Filled with anger	Frustrates and infuriates others		Set clear expectations
Procrastinates	Believes others are pushing him around			Warn him or her of the consequences of failing to do assigned work
				Document failures to do work
				Avoid debates about what to do and excuses about why they did not do the work
				Make oppositional behaviors a major part of performance assessments
				Give them continual feedback on their oppositional behavior
				Seek their input to increase their buy-in
				Executive coaching or therapy to teach them appropriate assertiveness skills

- How did their behavior affect you?
- How did their behavior affect others?
- How did their behavior affect productivity?
- What did you and others try to do to cope?
- What worked, and what did not? (What made things better, and what made things worse?)
- What did you learn?
- How would you do things differently in the future?
- What advice would you give to someone facing a passive-aggressive manager?
- What advice would you give to someone facing a passive-aggressive subordinate?
- Do you at times act in similar ways?
  - How does it affect people?
  - How does it affect your team?
  - How does it affect your career?

CHAPTER 21

Organizational Impact of Rigid Managers

Innovation Stymied

How Rigid Managers Impact Companies

Rigid managers are obstacles in the way of organizational learning and productivity. The energy that people expend in dealing with them is lost to the real work of the company.

The meticulousness of rigid managers has value in certain situations. For example, when following or enforcing safety protocols, legal requirements, and customer service standards, it is valuable to have someone who cares about details and will not give in to temptations to cut corners. You want the person tuning your car to follow prescribed procedures, and even more importantly, you want the daycare center taking care of your child to follow guidelines. At other times, however, rigid adherence to rules serves little beneficial purpose and can markedly interfere with finding efficient ways to solve problems, produce products, and deliver services.

Rigid managers impair productivity in a variety of ways. While the best managers know when to follow the protocol to the letter and when to cut through red tape, compulsive managers often cannot appreciate the difference. Moreover, rigid managers can be slaves to their own internal rules for dealing with situations. Their way is often not the most efficient or efficacious way, and they are resistant to changing and learning. The top-down decision making of rigid managers and their lack of interest in the input of the team interferes with creativity and motivation. Rigid adherence to rules can also easily alienate clients and suppliers as well as place unnecessary burdens on staff.

Compulsive managers are particularly destructive to morale. They do not understand human needs for support, for self-expression, and for participating in decision making. Rigid managers are generally handicapped in their ability to show interest in their subordinates as people with needs, hopes, and feelings. Their lack of interest in their workers markedly undercuts their team's ability to fully apply themselves. In particular, organizational citizenship behavior—volunteering to go beyond normal responsibilities, sharing information, going out of the way to help others—suffers when people do not feel they are part of the decision-making process.

All varieties of rigid managers have problems with their aggression. Rigid managers expect everyone to be thick-skinned and to be able to hear blunt feedback and deal with periodic angry outbursts without having their work affected. This is not, however, the case.

A final problem is that the quality of people in a unit tends to decline over time when a dictator is at the helm. The best people tend to leave. Good people avoid joining the department. Unexceptional people stay. The average ability of the workers slides into the sunset.

How Rigid Managers Can Rise in Organizations

Rigid individuals are often able to rise within organizations despite their serious limitations. Sometimes, their strengths enable them to perform adequately in one assignment, and their superiors fail to appreciate their inability to meet the needs of a new position.

In many situations, compulsive behavior is rewarded. For example, strict adherence to safety protocols is generally valued, or at least valuable. Meticulous behavior in developing presentations, putting on conferences, and accounting for cash flows and resources is generally a positive. The willingness of compulsive individuals to work long hours, eschewing personal pleasures and family time, is lauded. The respect for authority of the authoritarian individual also wins praise. Superiors often fail, however, to realize the flip side of their rigid traits: their inability to support, grow, and motivate people; their inability to learn new and more efficient ways of working; their lack of creativity. As a result, the Peter Principle is frequently in effect as people rise until they reach a position in which they perform poorly and then stay there.

Organizational Factors Promoting Rigidity in Managers

Certain cultures, recruitment and promotion practices, and leadership practices are particularly likely to foster rigid managerial behavior.

Culture. If an organization values compulsive work behavior and authoritarian hierarchical behavior, then rigid managers will thrive. Sometimes, this culture fits the actual needs of the company's work processes and market niche; sometimes, it is an anachronism that is dragging it down.

Recruitment and Promotion Practices. Sometimes, companies fail to pay attention to the personality traits of managers and the potential impact on their ability to succeed at their next position. When this is the case, rigid managers are able to move on and up until they reach the level of their incompetence.

Leadership Behavior. Leadership behavior has tremendous impact on the behavior of people within the organization by the role model they present, their encouragement of certain behavior through telling stories, by their tendency to promote certain people, and by what parameters they measure and performance/behavior they sanction.

Work Processes. If a company supports the use of bureaucratic processes and rigid hierarchies, rigid managers will thrive. However, rigid behavior will cause problems in organizations that are trying to be highly innovative in their work processes and responsive to their customers. Whenever bureaucratic obstacles are a problem, rigid managers will get in the way.

Rise of a Rigid Manager

Ted wanted his company to be creative, and he spent a considerable amount of money on consultants and workshops to encourage creativity. Somehow, nothing worked. He tried instituting awards for creativity. He heard some good initial ideas and provided support, but none panned out. One of the consultants recommended screening better for creativity in hires, and he did that.

As Ted told me the story, my interest grew. Since so much effort had gone into driving creativity and nothing had worked, I guessed that there was an invisible obstacle that needed to be removed. I asked about the measurement and reward system for the organization. Ted assured me that it had been adjusted to encourage innovation. I asked how he dealt with mistakes, since few will stick their necks out and be creative if making a mistake will lead you to the help wanted section of the papers. He noted that at one time he had been very hard on mistakes, but he had lightened up. After interviewing other people, I found that although he had lightened up, people remained very wary of taking risks. Moreover, the management style throughout the company was rigid and bureaucratic. Creative people became frustrated and gave up trying to be innovative. Several good people who were committed to innovation or who had exciting new ideas had left.

The long-term solution was to work on the gatekeepers of the organization. Hiring and promotion criteria had to de-emphasize self-assuredness and a commanding presence and had to focus more on flexibility and responsiveness to others. Meanwhile, managers who had compulsive or narcissistic personalities were moved to a function in which their personality traits would not get in the way of organizational creativity, or they were convinced to move on. Those who were authoritarian or dictatorial were given a weekend workshop and ongoing, frequent coaching. Flexible managers who tended to use a democratic leadership style in which they actively sought and promoted the ideas and initiatives of group members were placed in key positions over creative teams. Managers who had a history of coming up with creative ideas but had rigid styles were made members of teams rather than team leaders. Within six months, a noticeable change had occurred.

Ameliorating the Problem

You cannot eliminate all rigid managers from a large organization. If you did, you would not have enough people to staff it. Moreover, if all companies did it, the welfare rolls would swell, and our unemployment taxes would skyrocket. You can, however, avoid a situation in which a very rigid manager who cannot develop the needed skills is placed in a role in which he or she can do a lot of damage.

The key to doing this is assessing early on who is rigid and what limitations they have (see Table 21–1 and Table 21–2). Authoritarian managers are unlikely to be good leaders for creative teams or for units that have been accustomed to relative equality of staff. The shock could wreck morale and lead many to leave. The details of the authoritarian style are also important. In particular, does he or she express a lot of anger? Moreover, is the manager flexible and able to respond to coaching?

A compulsive manager is more of a problem. The interpersonal and analytic deficits are broader and deeper. Although it is time consuming to assess the specific strengths and weaknesses of the manager and the specific skills needed to succeed in a given position, not doing so with a compulsive manager will be very costly in the long run. In general, you want the compulsive manager in a position in which meticulousness and hard work are the primary keys to success. Moreover, you want to avoid placing him or her in a position in which you need a warm, supportive, outgoing individual or a creative individual able to try new things. You don't want a compulsive manager to be in charge of designing a change management initiative and motivating people to change. You might, however, want a compulsive manager to monitor and track the multitude of components that go into the initiative. Sometimes, compulsive managers can be effectively utilized by pairing them with managers who have complementary skills—for instance, an outgoing big idea person. They can be the director or codirector of a project or division.

Passive-aggressive managers are not likely to rise very far within organizations, since they are unlikely to perform well at any point. The key to dealing with them is to recognize the problematic traits and to see if coaching or therapy can ameliorate the deficits and enable them to make use of their other skills. If their deficits are significant and they do not improve, you need to be very careful that you do not move the manager to a new position in which his or her deficits would create increased problems.

The most prominent feature of a quiet narcissist is rigidity. Executive coaching may ameliorate some of the roughest edges they have and improve

Table 21–1 Characteristics of Rigid Managers

	Control Freak (narcissistic)	Compulsive	Authoritarian	Dictatorial Management Style	Oppositional	Passive-Aggressive
Reason They Insist on Their Way	Certain her way is best; often complains about superiors		Hierarchy must be obeyed; obeys superiors without problems		Feels pushed around; needs to defend autonomy at all costs, in all places, at all times	
Aggression Style	Rage if basis of self-esteem challenged	Often critical	Angry if authority challenged	Not angry	Contentious	Passive, procrastinates, negativistic
Emotional Style	Grandiose self-image	Overly serious, unemotional	Varies	Varies	Irritable	Sullen, withdrawn
Treatment of Authority	Subservient to their face, possibly mocking behind their back	Neutral	Respectful	Respectful	Contentious	Negativistic, grumbles
Treatment of Subordinates	Expects admiration	Insists their way be followed, possibly micromanage	Expects things to be done as they state	Fine if things are done as they state	Dislikes being challenged	Expects to be listened to

Table 21-2 Rigid Managers: Ways to Cope

Type	Crucial Assumption	Underlying Dynamics	How to Cope
Compulsive	Her way is the only way, since trying a new way would be very hard	Fears being wrong	Show her that many respected people do it this way and that this way will work out in this particular situation; avoid arguing about what way is best
Authoritarian	The boss's way is the way it should be done	Fears the world being out of control unless someone is rigidly in charge	Show him an authority he respects who does it this way
Dictatorial	Believes coercive leadership is most effective	Had role models who behaved this way	Respect her authority, give her credit, and explain ideas on how to do things
Oppositional	People are trying to dominate him and he must speak up	Feels that he is always being dominated and needs to push back	Let him feel a part of the decision
Passive-Aggressive	People are trying to dominate him, and he can't speak up	Feels pushed around	Encourage his participation
Control Freak (narcissistic)	"I know better than anyone, others are incompetent"	Covering over fragile self-esteem by a rigid, grandiose self-image	Feed her ego, don't cross her, explain how your ideas fit into her plans

their ability to motivate those under them as well as their ability to function in a team. They are unlikely to become wonderful team players or leaders, but not all positions call for this. The key to working with them is to accurately assess their strengths and weaknesses in dealing with people and to place them in a position in which there is a good fit and no expectation of significant growth of interpersonal skills.

Conclusion

Rigid managers come in a variety of flavors: compulsive, authoritarian, dictatorial, oppositional, passive-aggressive, and narcissistic. On the surface, each type displays similar behavior; for example, each insists on doing things his or her own way. You can differentiate between rigid managers by observing the rest of their behavior. Are they emotionally constricted and unable to engage in anything but work (compulsive)? Are they grandiose and think that they know better than anyone (narcissistic)? Do they believe that quick decisions from above are necessary for efficiency (dictatorial)? Are they primarily strong believers in hierarchy and convention but otherwise normal people (authoritarian)? Are they gratuitously negative, and do they drag their feet unless they get their way (passive-aggressive)? By taking an emotional intelligence approach—by understanding what lies beneath rigid behavior—you will be much more effective in coping with the problem and less likely to try a solution that may backfire.

PART V

IMPAIRED
MANAGERS

I'm Not at My Best

Many people unnecessarily suffer under a burden of treatable psychiatric problems that significantly impair their performance. Failure to recognize and treat common problems such as attention deficit hyperactivity disorder (ADHD), anxiety disorders, depression, emotional trauma, burnout, and alcohol or drug abuse costs businesses billions of dollars a year in lost productivity. Unfortunately, most of the time, the nature of the problem and the relative ease with which it can be ameliorated is not recognized.

These problems are also important because they can markedly exacerbate, or even mimic, the various personality disorders discussed in Parts I through V. When this is the case, treating the problem can lead to marked improvement in the toxic behavior. When people with narcissistic personality traits become depressed or anxious they become even less capable than they usually are to respond to others feelings. Moreover, they become desperate in their attempts to reinforce their fragile self-esteem, and so their toxic behavior increases. When rigid individuals become anxious or depressed their fear of chaos increases and their desire to be in control increases. Moreover, their cluelessness increases further impairing their ability to treat others considerately. Frantic and volatile managers, when anxious or depressed, become even more frantic and volatile than usual.

There are a number of reasons that the problems are missed. First, rather than realizing that anxiety, depression, or ADHD are making it hard for the person to function, people assume that there are personality traits leading to the aggression, rigidity, disorganization, impulsivity, and poor motivation that they see. Many therapists, and even many psychiatrists miss the treatable anxiety/depression/ADHD problem underlying what appear to be problematic personality traits. Many people burdened by these problems fail to go for assessment or treatment because they feel that there is a stigma attached to seeing a psychiatrist. In reality, their superiors, subordinates, coworkers, and families would rather they have treatment and function well than continue to be stressed and not be at their best. People also assume that the problems will somehow go away on their own. Sometimes they do ease in time on their own. They also sometimes get worse. Meanwhile a great deal of unnecessary suffering occurs. Many fail to go for treatment because they, and even their medical doctors, do not realize that there is a treatable psychiatric problem. People become used to a certain level of anxiety or depression and think that it is normal or inevitable. They do not realize that they could feel and perform much better. They also do not realize the toll that the anxiety and depression take on their physical health, relationships, and productivity.

Table V–1 Overlapping Symptoms of Various Types of Impairment

	Distractibility, Poor Concentration	Hyper/ Anxious	Loss of Enjoyment	Irritability
ADHD	++++	++++	+	++
Anxiety	+	++++	++	++
PTSD	+++	++++	+++	++++
Depression	++	+	++++	+++
Burnout	++	+	++++	++++
Alcohol Abuse	+++	+++ if detoxifying	++	++++

ADHD, anxiety, PTSD, depression, burnout, and substance abuse share many symptoms. They all impair concentration, induce anxiety, impair the person's ability to enjoy things, and cause irritability. The relative intensity of the different symptoms varies across the different problems. Fortunately, the medication for anxiety and depressive symptoms is the same, so that even if the exact diagnosis is unclear, the treatment is clear.

Part V Overview

The section begins with a discussion of attention deficit hyperactivity disorder (ADHD). The distractibility, disorganization, and impulsiveness that result from ADHD can significantly impair work function and can give the impression of self-centeredness. The problem is generally fairly responsive to medication, increased awareness of the problem, and mild adjustments in work environment. The next two chapters cover anxiety disorders and depression. Both anxiety and depression not only cause significant discomfort and impair work ability, but their presence generally exacerbates any existing personality problems. Both can often be ameliorated or completely controlled by medication and cognitive behavior therapy. Posttraumatic stress disorder (PTSD) has prominent anxiety and depressive symptoms. It can also give a presentation similar to ADHD. Burnout resembles depression and arises from experiencing high levels of stress. Bipolar disorder entails a combination of depression and manic/hypomanic episodes. During a hypomanic episode, a manager, as a result of grandiose feelings and a collapse of judgment, can make disastrous business decisions that cost the company considerable damage and expense. Alcohol and drug abuse are, unfortunately, very common. They impair judgment and functioning, and can cause problems with anxiety and depression.

- ◆ Chapter 22—ADHD: Distracted, Disorganized, Impulsive
- ◆ Chapter 23—Anxiety: Nervous, Frightened, Worried, Preoccupied
- ◆ Chapter 24—Depression: Pessimistic, Exhausted, Irritable, Unhappy
- ◆ Chapter 25—Posttraumatic Stress Disorder: I Can't Believe This Happened and I Can't Stop Thinking About It
- ◆ Chapter 26— Burnout: Used Up
- ◆ Chapter 27— Bipolar Disorder: Invincible to Depressed and Back
- ◆ Chapter 28—Alcohol and Drug Abuse: Only the Bottle Takes Away My Stress

Further Reading

R. Lubit, C. Kellner, B. Ladds, & S. Eth. *Five-Minute Psychiatric Consult.* Lippincott Williams & Wilkins, 2004.

CHAPTER 22

ADHD

Distracted, Disorganized, Impulsive

People with ADHD (attention deficit hyperactivity disorder) are easily distracted, impulsive, and disorganized to an extent that significantly impairs their functioning. When they take medication for the first time, the improvement in functioning can be remarkable. Being able to concentrate and get their work done is only one important change. They may now be able to sit and listen to people for the first time. They may significantly calm down, since they are now able to focus and are no longer continually distracted by a barrage of stimuli from the world that they could not previously filter out. Their ability to be organized in their work markedly improves, since they are no longer continually distracted from what they are doing and they can now carry through on tasks. Friends, family members, and colleagues are likely to find them much easier to deal with, calmer, and better organized. They no longer incessantly interrupt or talk nonstop. They are less irritable and impulsive. They no longer appear self-centered.

Although ADHD is common in adults, the problem is rarely diagnosed and treated. People assume that the person's difficulties are due to personality traits rather than to a readily treatable medical condition. The failure to treat has a serious impact on the person's life. Those with untreated ADHD are unlikely to go as far as they would if the disorder were treated, and the condition will have a significantly adverse effect on their relationships and enjoyment of life. They have to work harder than those around them just to keep pace. I've seen highly intelligent people who became doctors and lawyers and businessmen despite having ADHD, but they had to work much harder than those around them. Their social lives were seriously impaired by the impact of ADHD and by their needing to work so much harder than others. They irritated many people at work and did not perform anywhere near their capabilities. At the same time that some people recognized their high intelligence and potential, others felt that they were a disaster and should be asked to leave. It did not make for a happy life.

ADHD affects 5 to 10 percent of the population. There are two broad categories of symptoms: inattention and hyperactivity/impulsivity. Most children have both symptoms, but a significant number have problems only with inattention. As they move into adulthood, the hyperactivity tends to improve, but the distractibility continues.

Typically, those with ADHD have a hard time with school work, become frustrated, and stop trying to achieve. They do poorly in school due to difficulty concentrating and limited effort. Many get in trouble with the law as a result of impulsivity. Once they are out of school, they find a simple job that does not require much concentration.

Some children with ADHD are very hard working and bright, and they become professionals. They face constant struggle and rarely reach their true potential.

Adult ADHD Characteristics

◆ Restlessness: Always on the go, uncomfortable when inactive.

◆ Attention problems: Forgetful, tends to lose things, has difficulty concentrating on reading or conversations, is easily distracted.

◆ Unstable mood: Shifts from normal mood to excitement, depression, or boredom.

◆ Irritability/temper: Prone to outbursts that damage relationships.

◆ Emotionally overreactive: Easily stressed out.

◆ Disorganized: Poorly organized in work and time management.

◆ Impulsive: Interrupts, talks excessively, speaks before thinking, acts on feelings before thinking things through, and then says or does things that are ill advised.

Impact of ADHD on Managers

People with ADHD are handicapped in several ways. They have difficulty filtering out distractions, focusing their attention, and completing tasks. Unable to easily filter out the flood of stimuli from the environment, they become anxious or hyper. Tension can build as they try to force themselves to concentrate. It is particularly difficult for them to pay attention to tasks that are mundane or boring. Only novel and very engaging things can hold their attention. They are not lazy; they simply cannot focus on things that are not highly engaging, and they become distracted by external events or their own scattered thoughts.

People with ADHD are often poorly organized. In part, they have a very difficult time engaging in the relatively boring task of organizing papers and files. Also, their problems with attention interfere with their being able to hold things in their mind long enough to fit the pieces together and remember all they have to do. Their tendency to become distracted and move from one activity to another also interferes with finishing work in an organized way.

ADHD makes it difficult to inhibit your first reaction and select the most appropriate reaction to a situation. Managers with ADHD have difficulty pausing and thinking about how to deal with a situation. They tend to just react. They also tend to be easily frustrated. These problems cause difficulties in relationships as well as in work.

Managing ADHD

The first step in managing ADHD is recognizing it. Many of the symptoms resemble other problems. Correctly diagnosing ADHD often requires seeing a psychiatrist who is particularly familiar with the problem. Frequently, the problem is misdiagnosed as a personality disorder.

Distractibility is less of a problem when there are fewer distractions to deal with. Finding a quiet place to work is therefore helpful. Those with ADHD are less stressed and more successful if they find work that does not require sustained attention and that permits them to frequently get up and move around or to change activities.

Medication can make a marked difference in people. Stimulants— Dexedrine and Methylphenidate—are the classic medications for treating ADHD. The risks and side effects are usually minimal, far less than the impact of not treating the problem. Strattera is a new medication for ADHD.

All of these medications can significantly help people to focus their attention and avoid distractions. They no longer face a flood of incoming, unfiltered stimuli. They can stay on task and finish tasks. As a result, they often calm down and are less anxious or hyper.

Dealing with ADHD

Tracy had ADHD, but no one had ever diagnosed it. She was very bright and did well in school, even though her concentration was poor and her mind often wandered in class and while reading. She had learned to study in very quiet places with few distractions and to take frequent breaks.

She was warm and friendly and was well liked. Nevertheless, she had irritated many friends by her tendency to talk a lot, interrupt, and make comments unrelated to the subject under discussion. When she had dinner or coffee with a friend, her eyes often darted across the room. People sometimes thought she wasn't interested in them. In reality, she was readily distracted by changes in her environment, and someone walking by would inevitably catch her attention.

Tracy was very disorganized. She wasted considerable time sorting through the mess on her desk trying to figure out what had to be done each day and what could wait. She was also poor at prioritizing. She could become engrossed in an unimportant task and lose track of the more important ones that she needed to tackle. Or, in the midst of an important task, she might get a phone call and forget what she was doing. Rushing to make an appointment, she might be distracted by a letter on her desk and forget about her appointment until she was certain to be late. She frequently left her umbrella, hat, or pocketbook at restaurants or stores. When leaving for work or to run an errand, she invariably had to run back to her apartment before she'd even started her car to pick up something she'd forgotten

Tracy decided to go into sales, since she liked to be with people and preferred being on the go to sitting at a desk. Her energy, intelligence, and desire to please helped her to be successful. In time, she was promoted, and that's when serious problems began. Managing ten salesmen presented new challenges and required new skills. The demands on her to organize work schedules and activities exceeded her organizational abilities. No longer were her outgoing style and energy level enough to succeed. Organizing presentations to superiors was torture and not very well done. Her interrupting superiors and members of marketing and manufacturing at meetings was seen as arrogant and disrespectful.

Serendipitously, she was dating a child psychiatrist who enjoyed her energy but disliked being interrupted all the time. He was also becoming a bit impatient with needing to return to the apartment because she had forgotten something. As he heard about Tracy's work difficulties, he suggested she consult someone about possibly having ADHD. The psychiatrist she saw gave her a trial of medication. Her concentration rapidly improved, she got much more work done, felt less frazzled, and had more time for play. She was able to concentrate better on what people were saying, was less distracted by her own thoughts, and interrupted less. Her ability to organize her activities also improved.

Dealing with Managers with ADHD

Dealing with managers with ADHD can be very frustrating, whether they are your superior, subordinate, or peer. Realizing that the problem is ADHD, and not lack of respect, can decrease your distress.

Understanding the spectrum of issues posed by ADHD and knowing what skills are not impaired can help a manager to assign tasks that play to the individual's strengths and avoid weaknesses. In particular, you should avoid giving people with ADHD tasks that require high levels of organization, prolonged concentration on mundane tasks, and attention to details. Rather, assign tasks that enable them to often get up and move around and that depend on skills that they are strong in.

If the manager with ADHD is your superior, provide gentle help to keep conversations on target and assist with organizing projects and remembering due dates.

Conclusion

ADHD is a chronic, lifelong problem. The hyperactivity of ADHD tends to significantly decrease after adolescence, but the problems with inattention and impulsivity persist. Untreated ADHD will significantly impair work performance. The issues go beyond distractibility and include impulsivity, talking too much, interrupting people, snapping at people, being disorganized, forgetting to do important tasks, and avoiding tasks that are not engaging. People may see individuals with ADHD as anxious, not that bright, not that interested, or simply as difficult people. Once the biologically based problem with attention is treated, these symptoms go away and the ability to work and maintain good relationships improve dramatically.

Further Reading

P. H. Wender. *Attention-Deficit Hyperactivity Disorder in Adults.* Oxford University Press, 1995.

R. Lubit. "ADHD." In R. Lubit, S. Eth, B. Ladds, & C. Kellner (Eds.), *Five-Minute Psychiatric Consult.* Lippincott Williams & Wilkins, in press.

CHAPTER 23

Anxiety

Nervous, Frightened, Worried, Preoccupied

Anxiety can seriously impair performance, drain energy, and make people difficult to work with. As people become anxious, their ability to be flexible and to respond to others' ideas and wishes wanes. Anxiety is often seen as an indelible part of someone's personality when in fact it is often a treatable condition. Treating it can rapidly help the person to become much easier to work with and more productive.

Anxiety is a painful emotion accompanying a feeling that something bad will happen or is happening. Some people have more of an anxious, apprehensive state characterized by a great deal of worry, while others have anxious arousal with significant physical symptoms. In both cases, anxiety is painful and can significantly impair functioning. Anxiety interferes with concentration. Anxiety also impairs the ability to carefully and efficiently study a situation and come up with a solution. It can lead to muscle tightness, upset stomach, and headaches. The dry mouth, trembling hands, and hesitant presentation that can arise from high levels of anxiety does not come across well and does not inspire confidence in people. Being anxious requires a great deal of energy. People with performance anxiety or generalized anxiety disorder can become physically exhausted long before they have finished their day's work. People often become frightened of the anxiety as well as of the situation or object that triggers the anxiety, and they withdraw from experiences. As a result, they fail to have experiences that could help them grow, learn, and become more confident.

Generalized Anxiety Disorder

Anxiety comes in many different forms. In *generalized anxiety disorder,* people experience high levels of anxiety about a wide range of daily activities that pose no real threat. They are continually anxious and worry about whatever they are doing and whatever they are facing. They not only worry about whether they will be fired during a company downsizing, or if the mark on their skin is cancer, but they worry about whether their friends will be satisfied with the meal they are cooking for them or if people will be upset if they are late to dinner. Everything becomes a source of worry and trepidation. This leads to exhaustion as well as continual discomfort.

Generalized Anxiety Disorder ━━━━━━━━━━

Betty was always worried, always tense. Coworkers often avoided her, since her continual worrying was draining. One day she worried if the division vice president would be upset with her for being late to a meeting; the next day she worried about whether her team would be able to finish its project on time; the following day she was preoccupied with whether her child would get into the right private school.

She also complained a lot about how she was feeling. She often had headaches or felt stiff. By the afternoon, her energy seemed to collapse. It was exhausting to be nervous all of the time. Once and sometimes twice a week she came into work with bags under her eyes after not being able to sleep, since some worry had kept her awake. She was also often distracted in meetings from being preoccupied with whatever was currently worrying her.

The vice president of the division ordered her to see a psychiatrist; he thought she had attention deficit disorder. His son had just been treated for it and had gotten much better. Like his son, Betty was hyper and had a hard time concentrating. The psychiatrist said it wasn't ADHD, but a generalized anxiety disorder.

The psychiatrist offered her a choice of a 12-course of cognitive behavioral therapy (CBT) or a medication called a serotonin reuptake inhibitor (SSRI). Betty wanted whatever would work fastest and chose the SSRI. In a few days, she was less tense and stopped snapping at people. In the weeks ahead, her whole personality seemed to change. In reality, what changed was that the burden of excess anxiety was lifted from her shoulders, and her real personality was finally able to come out. She was no longer carrying a 50-pound pack on her back, draining her energy and making her feel bad. She was much easier to be with, and her energy and concentration improved, as did the bags under her eyes.

Betty was satisfied and wanted to continue with the medication and come back only for rare medication follow-up visits. Her psychiatrist, however, convinced her to try a period of CBT in the hope that she could then get off of the medication.

Social Phobia

People with social phobia experience marked and persistent fear in a social or performance situation in which they may be under scrutiny or exposed to new people. Typical examples include giving a talk, performing at a music recital, or meeting new people. They generally try and avoid such situations.

Social Phobia ━━━━━━━━━━━━━━━━━━━━━━━━━━━━━━━━

Erin was capable at her job. She was neither a star nor a dunce. Each month, however, she would dread the cross-departmental meetings. One hundred people were present, and every now and then she was called on to make a comment, never with forewarning. She feared she would not know the answer or would say something stupid and that her boss would forever hold it against her. She was especially worried because her boss chaired the meetings.

Under pressure from a friend, Erin talked to an executive coach. He taught Erin relaxation techniques and talked with her about the times she felt anxious. The coach suggested that Erin speak with her boss a few days prior to the meetings, tell him she wanted to be sure to give good answers, and would like to know in advance if he was going to ask her a question. Her boss agreed, and meetings ceased to be so terrifying.

Although the most anxiety-provoking situation was now under control, her difficulty speaking in public was still a problem. She tried a course of CBT. She and her psychiatrist looked at the things she said to herself about speaking in public. They looked at her fears of being embarrassed and her expectations that people would look disparagingly at her and that she would say something inappropriate. This helped, but not as much as she needed it to.

Before Erin could complete the course of therapy, she had an opportunity to give a talk that could be very good for her career. Her doctor gave her a beta blocker. This class of medication is primarily used to treat high blood pressure. It prevented her from having the physical aspects of anxiety and thereby prevented her from getting into an escalating cycle of feeling anxious, becoming tense, and becoming more anxious as she sensed her body's tension. Many people use beta blockers prior to giving talks or musical performances. Erin's speech went well. She saw how valuable public speaking would be to her career. Rather than chronically using beta blockers, she decided to continue therapy.

Her psychiatrist taught her progressive relaxation techniques. After relaxing herself, Erin imagined scenes of progressively more stressful speaking opportunities. Each week, she used her relaxation exercises to be able to imagine the stressful scene but stay relaxed. Her ability to perform in public without high levels of anxiety continued to improve.

Panic Disorder

In panic disorder, people experience half-hour bouts of severe anxiety, including a number of somatic complaints. The anxiety seems to come out of nowhere. Panic attacks sometimes lead to agoraphobia, a fear of being away from home without help lest a panic attack occur. As a result, the lives of people with panic disorder become increasingly restricted.

Panic Disorder ────────────────────────────────

Ted had been a good performer, a nice guy. Now he often seemed on edge, somewhat withdrawn and hesitant. He no longer went out after work and started missing a lot more work than usual.

One day a colleague found him in the men's room, sweating, looking terrified, and with his heart pounding. Assuming Ted was using drugs, the colleague told Ted that he needed to talk to the EAP (employee assistance program). Ted agreed. Ted explained he was having these attacks about once a week. They lasted a half hour and seemed to come from nowhere. He was preoccupied with them and avoided being away from home except when he absolutely had to.

The doctor diagnosed panic disorder and gave Ted an SSRI (a type of antidepressant). Ted objected, saying he wasn't depressed. The doctor explained that these medications boost serotonin levels in the brain and are helpful in depression and several types of anxiety. After a month, Ted's panic attacks ceased and he was back to the person he had once been.

Simple Phobia

A *simple phobia* entails having persistent and excessive fear of a specific object or situation that presents no realistic threat. The person is fine except when faced with having to deal with the feared object.

Simple Phobia ━━━━━━━━━━━━━━━━━━━━━━━━━━━━━━━━━━

Barry worked for a mid-sized advertising firm. He performed well and got along with people. Married, with two children and a love of outdoor activities, all aspects of his life seemed to be in place. The one thing about him that made people chuckle was that he always took the stairs rather than the elevator. He claimed he wanted the exercise. This made reasonable sense, except on occasions when they were late and needed to rush to the meeting. He would respond that he did not want to break his routine.

When his company decided to move to new headquarters on the 28th floor, Barry almost panicked. He decided to see a psychiatrist. He explained that for as long as he could remember, he was terrified of elevators. The psychiatrist diagnosed him as having a phobia and recommended behavioral therapy.

After Barry learned progressive relaxation techniques, he and the psychiatrist created a hierarchy of increasingly anxiety-provoking images, starting with thinking about taking an elevator, looking at an elevator, getting into an elevator with the door staying open, getting into the elevator and having the door briefly close, going a couple of flights on an elevator, and going on a long elevator ride. Each week, they practiced relaxation and then imagined progressively more stressful situations. After six sessions, Barry was able to imagine being in an elevator without feeling flooded with anxiety. The next step was "in-vivo" exposure: real-life practice. Accompanied by his therapist, Barry tried using an elevator. Having had the imaginary exposure, the experience was much less stressful than expected. As he practiced, his anxiety continued to decline and he was able to stay with the company.

Obsessive-Compulsive Disorder

Obsessive-compulsive disorder is the most difficult of the anxiety disorders to understand, since it is significantly removed from our typical experience. The sufferer is subject to either obsessions or compulsions.

Obsessions are intrusive, inappropriate, and persistent ideas, thoughts, or impulses that cause the person distress. They come to mind against the person's will and desire. It could be an image of something bad happening or an urge to do something the person finds unacceptable, such as hurting someone.

Compulsions are repetitive behaviors without instrumental value that are carried out to limit anxiety. These include excessive hand-washing, checking, counting, hoarding, or arranging objects. People with obsessive-compulsive disorder may feel compelled to wash their hands dozens of times a day, check to see that the stove is off or the door is locked five or six times in a row, count the ceiling tiles wherever they go, or have the objects on their desk in exactly the right order. If blocked from doing these activities, the sufferer becomes very anxious.

Obsessive-Compulsive Disorder

Mark was always a little rigid, a little tense, but it had never gotten in the way of work. One day, however, he began to be uneasy that unless he lined up the objects on his desk, something terrible would happen. What that terrible thing would be was unclear. He then became concerned that his hands were not adequately clean and that he might have touched something that could give him a horrible disease. He stopped what he was doing and washed his hands. To feel reasonably comfortable, he had to wash his hands several times an hour. His hands became raw and chapped. After leaving his office, he often returned to check if he had locked it. Going back to check once was rarely enough; he routinely checked four or five times to feel comfortable.

The rituals took up increasing amounts of time. He worried that he had lost his mind and was crazy. He kept the problem to himself. Then he saw Jack Nicholson's performance in *As Good As It Gets*. He recognized himself. He went to a psychiatrist and was given an SSRI, a drug that boosts serotonin levels. His symptoms began to abate, and he felt much better. Behavioral therapy helped to control some symptoms that had persisted despite the medication.

All of the anxiety disorders (see Table 23–1) impair performance and interfere with a person's rise within a company. Most people can obtain a significant improvement in symptoms in a relatively brief period of time. Combinations of cognitive behavioral therapy and an SSRI are usually most effective.

Table 23–1 Symptoms of Anxiety Disorders

Type	Symptoms
Generalized anxiety disorder	Excessive worrying and chronic feelings of anxiety not tied to a specific threat
Panic disorder	Brief episodes of severe anxiety and multiple somatic symptoms
Social anxiety disorder	Excessive fear of performing in public
Agoraphobia	Fear of being alone in a place from which escape is impossible in the event of a panic attack; leads to progressive staying at home
Simple phobia	Persistent and excessive fear of a specific object or situation that presents no realistic threat (heights, snakes)
Obsessive-compulsive disorder	Either obsessions or compulsions Obsessions are intrusive, inappropriate and persistent ideas, thoughts, or impulses that cause anxiety or distress Compulsions are repetitive behaviors without instrumental value that are carried out to limit anxiety, such as excessive hand-washing, checking, counting, hoarding, arranging

Treatment of Anxiety Disorders

Effective treatment exists for many people with anxiety disorders. Cognitive behavioral therapy and selective serotonin reuptake inhibitors (SSRIs) are generally the treatments of choice for all anxiety disorders.

Cognitive behavioral therapy entails a few months of weekly meetings in which people are helped to look at the conscious ideas they have that lead them to feel uncomfortable, and to practice doing the things that make them anxious. For example, a therapist may have you question whether the world will really collapse if you arrive late for a dinner party, or may encourage you to not wash your hands more than once before each meal, or to not line up the items on your desk in terms of height, and to see if the dread things you fear actually come to pass.

SSRIs have been around in the United States since about 1990. They affect serotonin levels in the brain and can treat depression, anxiety, and impulsivity.

Conclusion

Anxiety can make people tense and uncomfortable, drain their energy, and impair their performance. As a result of the toll that anxiety takes and the things people do to avoid becoming anxious, many will find anxious coworkers difficult to deal with. People may wonder if the anxious person is using drugs, is depressed, has a medical problem, or is simply a difficult person with an unpleasant personality. When recognized, anxiety disorders are often very treatable. Doing so can markedly improve productivity, relationships, and happiness.

Further Reading

Eric Hollander & Daphne Simeon. *Concise Guide to Anxiety Disorders.* American Psychiatric Publishing, 2002.

Jack Nicholson, in *As Good As It Gets,* provides a good example of obsessive-compulsive disorder

Woody Allen, in *Play It Again Sam,* provides a good example of generalized anxiety disorder.

CHAPTER 24

Depression

Pessimistic, Exhausted, Irritable, Unhappy

A Common Problem Often Ignored

Depression is a very common and costly problem for business. The National Comorbidity Study found that each year 6.6 percent of people need treatment for depression. The number may well be higher among top executives as a result of their high levels of stress and insatiable drive to achieve. Only half obtain treatment, and most of these people are not adequately treated. Depression costs the economy $44 billion a year in lost productivity.

Depression has tremendous costs for the individual, the company, and society. Depression feels awful, decreases productivity, and impairs the morale of a manager's team. Depression also increases the risk of heart disease and may cause diffuse physical symptoms that lead to expensive medical evaluations. The resulting healthcare expenses can be very expensive for the company.

Current treatments for depression are generally highly effective and often have few side effects. The primary problem in treating depression is that people often fail to come for treatment, either because they fear they will be stigmatized by seeing a psychiatrist or because they do not realize how helpful professional treatment can be. Encouraging a depressed person to get help, and being open to getting help yourself if you need it, can increase productivity and decrease suffering.

Impact of Depression

Depression is a combination of sad mood and hopelessness. In addition to feeling awful, you feel that the current situation will never improve. The negative perspective colors much of your view of the world and of yourself. You see the world as empty and sad, and you see yourself as undesirable. When depressed, it is difficult or impossible to find pleasure in anything. Depression can also cause changes in sleep and appetite and impair your energy level, concentration, and ability to make decisions. Both withdrawal from people and irritability are common.

Symptoms of Depression

- ◆ Feeling depressed
- ◆ Loss of interest in activities
- ◆ Loss of energy
- ◆ Slowed speech or thinking
- ◆ Irritability
- ◆ Change in sleep pattern
- ◆ Change in eating pattern
- ◆ Loss of self-esteem
- ◆ Difficulty concentrating or making decisions
- ◆ Persistent thoughts about death or suicide
- ◆ Withdrawal
- ◆ Pessimism
- ◆ Increased sensitivity to being criticized or rejected

These symptoms markedly compromise your ability to function effectively. Productivity and creativity suffer when your energy is low and you cannot concentrate. You also become easily fatigued and cannot work as many hours as you could in the past. Difficulty making decisions can bring work to a standstill. Your ability to effectively deal with others suffers as a result of irritability and a desire to withdraw. Your lack of enthusiasm and pessimism are a drag upon others' initiative and work. Increased sensitivity to being rejected and criticized can lead to further withdrawal or anger that deepen problems in getting along with others.

Origins of Depression

Depression usually arises from high stress and/or a biological vulnerability to becoming depressed. It can be difficult to know which came first, the depression or the stress. Someone may tell a story of how his marriage deteriorated, then his work deteriorated and he lost his job, and then he became depressed. A closer look may show that the person was beginning to become depressed and that the resulting withdrawal and irritability led to problems in his marriage and work. This led to an increase in his stress and a major depression.

For some people, mood fluctuates regardless of the stresses in their life. For others, stress that would lead some to temporarily feel down sends them into a prolonged tailspin of feeling awful, being unable to concentrate, and generally functioning poorly. Another group seems to be chronically pessimistic and unable to find enjoyment in life.

People who become depressed often have a tendency to "black and white thinking" and to "catastrophize." Black and white thinking is a tendency to see things as either very good or very bad. There are no shades of gray in the world. A project is either a complete success or it failed. A person is either totally supportive or is neither trustworthy nor a friend. The depressed person himself or herself is either a wonderful success or a dismal failure who could not make the grade. Since the road is never without some bumps in it, people who engage in black and white thinking are often faced with negative images of themselves and their world. Catastrophizing is the tendency to expect that problems you are facing will have the worst possible outcome. For example, when catastrophizing, not only do you see yourself as a poor manager because your last project did not go as well as hoped, but you expect to lose your job and never find another one.

Black and white thinking often develops because one's parents saw the world that way: Problems were not seen as things to be overcome but as signs that they and the world were in a very bad state. Black and white thinking can arise in depressed people from being taught that they should expect to have a life filled with failure and disappointment, or from having too many losses and problems in childhood. Parents may have taught them that no matter what they did, they were a disappointment to them. They may have had difficulty in making friends and now see themselves as unlikable. They may have suffered losses (death of a parent, their own illness, a community catastrophe) and come to feel that no matter how good things are, a disaster can suddenly occur and turn the world upside down.

Some people are biologically predisposed to depression and see things in a very negative light. In all likelihood, the biological and psychological issues interact to create a downward spiral.

A Depressed Manager

Roger was very serious about his work, worked hard, and was not that interested in leisure time. He was rarely if ever spontaneous or relaxed. Some wondered if he had a compulsive personality.

He often worried about whether he was doing a good job and whether people liked him. He sometimes had fun, but was often a bit down and did not enjoy things as much as others did. In the back of his mind there was always a worry. He was never really satisfied with his accomplishments and often worried that in the end he would fail. Little things bothered him, and he would become irritable and withdraw from people.

When he faced a combination of disappointment in his personal life and at work, he slid into a serious depression. His concentration crashed; he woke up early in the morning; he disliked himself more than usual; and felt that living was not worth the pain. He spoke to a professional and was given an antidepressant. Three weeks later, he felt better than he ever had. Until then, he did not realize that people could wake up each day, feel good, and look forward to the day. His concentration was better than it had ever been, he was cheerful, and life was fun. When there were problems or disappointments, he now felt down for an hour and then bounced back instead of staying down for a couple of days. He began to like himself. His work efficiency and relationships significantly improved. He was much less irritable and ceased feeling the need to withdraw from people.

Bereavement

After the loss of a loved one, people experience bereavement. People commonly think that the process of grieving and getting over the loss should take a couple of months. In reality, it generally takes two years. People generally feel sad, tend to be preoccupied with the loss, often experience physical complaints, suffer a loss of interest or pleasure in daily activities, and withdraw from people and activities.

Dealing with Depression

Depression is a highly treatable problem. Nevertheless, many people do not seek help for fear that they will be stigmatized by going to therapy. Some avoid therapy for fear that once they begin, their therapist will never let them go. In reality, the new evidence-based therapies for depression, cognitive behavioral therapy, and interpersonal psychotherapy, are time-limited and with a maximum of 16 sessions.

Research has shown that medication, cognitive behavioral therapy, and interpersonal therapy are effective in treating depression. Mild-to-moderate cases of depression respond equally to one of these therapies or to medication. A combination of medication and psychotherapy is generally best. The more serious cases of depression should be treated with medication.

Mild Chronic Depression ▬▬▬▬▬▬▬▬▬▬▬▬▬▬▬▬▬▬▬▬▬

Paul was often pessimistic, tended to feel down on himself, didn't seem to enjoy life as much as others did, and worried a lot. When problems came up, he tended to slip into feeling very depressed. His concentration decreased, he lost interest in things that he usually enjoyed, and his sleep suffered. He sometimes lost interest in living.

His pessimism, lack of enthusiasm, and limited energy chronically affected his performance and his relationships. When he was depressed and could not concentrate, his performance would crash. People could not count on him.

When he was feeling particularly down, he spoke to his EAP and was referred to a therapist for cognitive behavioral therapy. His therapist explained that how we think about things affects our feelings. Paul began to explore with his therapist how he tended to interpret things, particularly his tendency toward black and white thinking and catastrophizing. When problems arose, rather than seeing them as challenges to be overcome, Paul saw them as insurmountable obstacles that would inevitably lead to disaster. He also tended to see things in extremes. He tended to think that his career would be either a brilliant success or a disaster. Whenever things did not go perfectly, he saw his future career crashing and burning. There was no room in his thoughts for the idea that he could make a contribution and live well without necessarily making it to the top.

Paul's therapist worked to help him see shades of gray in life and to question himself when he started expecting certain disaster to occur. She encouraged him to keep records of how he was feeling and what events and thoughts led to those feelings. His mood improved, and he spent less time feeling depressed. He was able to develop a more positive self-image and was better able to deal with disappointments.

Dealing with Depressed Colleagues

The most important step in dealing with a depressed superior, subordinate, or peer is to realize that the problem he or she is having is indeed depression. Often, people only see the irritability or low energy and pessimism and think that the problem is the individual's personality. Realizing that the problem may be depression and that help exists can literally change the person's life. People with mild, chronic depression may have marked improvement in their functioning and their ability to enjoy life after receiving treatment.

Conclusion

Depression is a serious health issue affecting more than 20 percent of women and 10 percent of men during their lives. Some people develop severe episodes that last months to years with several of the following symptoms: difficulty enjoying things, loss of energy, loss of concentration, loss of self-esteem, changes in sleep and appetite, thoughts about death, and difficulty making decisions. Some people have mild, chronic depression that lasts years. In these cases, pessimism is often a major symptom. For some people, stress seems to set off the depression. For others, the depression seems to come from nowhere.

In many people the classic symptoms of depression will not be obvious. Instead, there will be a marked exacerbation of problematic personality traits such as irritability, rigidity, and narcissism. As a result, many will simply think that the person has a difficult personality and not realize that treatment for depression could rapidly improve the person's performance, quality of life, and the quality of life of coworkers.

Depression is among the most treatable of psychiatric problems. The biggest problem in successful treatment is generally getting the person to seek therapy—cognitive behavioral or interpersonal—or to take antidepressants, or to do both.

Your Turn

- ◆ What examples can you think of, of people who might have been depressed?
- ◆ What were the signs and symptoms of depression?
- ◆ What other types of problems did it look like?
  - • A personality problem?
  - • Irritability?
  - • Burnout?
  - • Anxiety?
- ◆ How did their depression affect their work?
- ◆ How did their depression affect you and other people they worked with?
- ◆ If they did not get treatment, what got in the way? How could someone have convinced them to get treatment?

Further Reading

Keith G. Kramlinger. *Mayo Clinic on Depression: Answers to Help You Understand, Recognize and Manage Depression.* Mayo Clinic Kensington Publishing Corporation, 2001.

M. M. Weissman, J. C. Paulowitz, & G. L. Klerman. *Comprehensive Guide to Interpersonal Psychotherapy.* Basic Books, 2000.

The International Society for Interpersonal Psychotherapy (ISIPT) provides information on the application of interpersonal psychotherapy: *http://www.interpersonalpsychotherapy.org/*

Aaron T. Beck et al. *Cognitive Therapy of Depression.* Guilford, 1987.

CHAPTER 25

Posttraumatic Stress Disorder

I Can't Believe This Happened
and I Can't Stop Thinking About It

At some time during our lives, most of us are exposed to an event that poses a threat of severe injury or death (assaults, car accidents, natural or manmade disasters), or a threat to bodily integrity (rape). Exposure to one of these situations often causes a number of very disruptive emotional symptoms that last at least for a brief period. In some people the symptoms last more than a month, and we say that the person has posttraumatic stress disorder (PTSD). After such events, victims are often plagued by memories of the event. They continue to think about it, although they try to block it from their minds. They may have nightmares, feel as if the event is recurring, or be flooded with anxiety whenever reminded of the event. Many victims feel numb and withdraw from people and activities they used to enjoy. Victims also typically become hyper-aroused and are irritable, can't sleep, are easily startled, and feel continually on edge. After a serious car accident, perhaps one-third of people develop PTSD. Some people develop these symptoms after witnessing or hearing about the traumatic incident of someone close to them.

When after a trauma someone has these symptoms—persistent re-experiencing of the event; avoidance of stimuli associated with the event and numbing of general responsiveness; and persistent symptoms of increased arousal—psychiatrists make the diagnosis of PTSD.

- ◆ Re-experiencing symptoms
  - Distressing, recurrent, and intrusive recollections of the event. In young children there may be repetitive play of themes or aspects of the traumatic event.
  - Recurrent distressing dreams. In children the dreams will be frightening but may not have recognizable content.
  - Acting or feeling as if the traumatic event was recurring.
  - Intense psychological distress at exposure to cues that symbolize or resemble an aspect of the traumatic event.
  - Physiological reactivity on exposure to cues that symbolize or resemble an aspect of the traumatic event.
- ◆ Numbing/avoidance
  - Efforts to avoid thoughts, feelings, and conversations associated with the trauma.
  - Efforts to avoid activities, places, and people that arouse recollections of the trauma.
  - Inability to recall an important aspect of the trauma.
  - Markedly diminished interest or participation in significant activities.
  - Feeling of detachment or estrangement from others.
  - Restricted range of mood (e.g., unable to have loving feelings).
  - Sense of a foreshortened future (e.g., does not expect to have a career, marriage, children, or a normal life span).
- ◆ Increased arousal
  - Difficulty falling or staying asleep
  - Irritability or outbursts of anger
  - Difficulty concentrating
  - Hypervigilance
- ◆ Exaggerated startle response

After suffering a traumatic incident, many people develop only some of the symptoms of PTSD, or may primarily suffer from anxiety or depression. Although they do not fulfill the criteria for PTSD, they have been traumatized, their functioning is impaired as a result of the trauma, and they need treatment.

Trauma reactions can markedly impair someone's ability to work and maintain relationships. Both the withdrawal and the irritability of PTSD are very difficult for other people to deal with. It is hard to cope with someone who is generally either distant and unresponsive or irritable and annoyed. The difficulty concentrating and tiredness from lack of sleep impairs work performance. The loss of interest in the world and preoccupation with memories of the event interfere with motivation and energy, and further impairs work performance.

Posttraumatic Stress Disorder (PTSD)

Bill was a hard-working manager at a Fortune 500 company. One day while driving home from a meeting, he had to jam on his brakes to prevent running into the car in front of him. Meanwhile, the car behind him crashed into him. Bill heard the metal crunch and his head flew back into the headrest. It seemed to take forever for the car to come to a halt. He was shaken but did not seem to be injured. He slowly got out of the car. He saw that the people behind him had not done as well. A boy who looked about his son's age was badly hurt. The driver was in worse shape. His mind flashed back to being 15 and the car accident he had been in with a good friend. His friend had not survived.

Everyone went to the hospital. Bill was examined and released. That evening he was shaky but all right. He thought a lot about the accident. He kept wondering if he could have stopped more slowly. If he had not been so close to the car in front of him, he would not have jammed on the brakes and the car behind might not have hit his car, or at least would not have hit it so hard. He thought a lot about the boy and about his dead friend. At one point, after finally falling asleep, he woke up in a cold sweat from dreaming of his son being killed in a car accident.

In the days that followed Bill became increasingly high strung. Walking down the street, he heard a car backfire. He jumped and was still shaking five minutes later, too afraid to get back into his car. He was irritable and jumpy, withdrew into himself, and ceased to enjoy doing things or being with his family. His concentration decreased, and falling asleep was a nightmare.

He started drinking in order to fall asleep. It didn't work very well. People noted he was consuming a lot more than usual and assumed his problem was primarily alcohol.

As the months went on, his work performance and relationships declined. He was placed on a performance improvement plan—probation. Meanwhile, his wife could no longer deal with his withdrawal and irritability, and she left him.

Treatment

Only a fraction of therapists have training in state-of-the-art trauma treatments. Currently, this consists of a combination of repeated retelling in a therapeutic setting of what happened in the disaster, an examination of any negative impacts on the individual's self-image and view of the world, and gradual re-exposure to activities that are being avoided. Repeated retelling of the story in a therapeutic environment is a crucial aspect of treatment. After a trauma incident, victims become phobic of the memories of the trauma. They fear being reminded lest they be flooded with anxiety. The process of retelling the story helps victims to desensitize to the memory and to no longer be flooded with anxiety whenever they come in contact with something that reminds them of what happened. It helps them change the memory from a traumatic memory that takes over and floods them with painful feelings to a normal, sad memory that they can stop thinking about when they wish. Exploring how the experience changed the person's self-image and worldview is very important. Exposure to traumatic events can lead people to feel that the world is much more dangerous than they had previously experienced it, to feel that people are untrustworthy, to feel that life is fragile and so they should not invest in the future, and to feel guilt for not having engaged in a heroic act during the disaster. Medication known as SSRIs (selective serotonin reuptake inhibitors) are often very helpful.

Dealing with Traumatized Colleagues

Whether you are dealing with a traumatized superior, peer, or subordinate, the most valuable thing you can do is encourage the person to seek help with a competent professional trained in the treatment of trauma. People are often not aware of how profoundly they have been affected by a traumatic event. They realize that they are not functioning well but may not realize the degree to which their problems are directly related to a trauma. In addition, because it is uncomfortable to speak about the traumatic incident, many people avoid therapy and even tell their friends and family that they are fine when they are not.

A superior, subordinate, or friend who can convince them to get appropriate help will be doing them and all who work with them and care about them an enormous service. Helping the individual to realize that help is available is one key step. It is also crucial to destigmatize their getting professional help so that they will be willing to go.

Conclusion

Eight percent of Americans develop PTSD at some time in their lives. Far more suffer from some painful and disruptive emotional reaction caused by an emotional trauma. PTSD can come from being in a situation that threatened injury, seeing someone else in such a situation, or even simply from hearing about a loved one having been in such a situation.

Those around the traumatized person see irritability and withdrawal. The victim suffers from these symptoms plus distress from frequently remembering the event, losing pleasure and interest in normal activities, and being easily startled and continually on edge. The symptoms can markedly impair the ability to work or have relationships.

Frequently, rather than appreciating that the person is suffering from reaction to a trauma, people assume that he or she simply has difficult personality traits, or is depressed, or is anxious and stressed by life in general. As a result, the victim does not get the necessary treatment and support.

The treatment of PTSD is best done by someone with special training in this area. Good treatment can have a remarkable impact on someone's ability to function within a matter of weeks.

Further Reading

Bessel Van Der Kolk. *Traumatic Stress*. Guilford Press, 1996.

Patricia A. Resick. *Stress and Trauma*. Psychology Press, 2001.

R. Lubit, C. Kellner, B. Ladds, & S. Eth. *Five-Minute Psychiatric Consult*. Lippincott Williams & Wilkins, in press.

CHAPTER 26

Burnout

Used Up

Burnout creates a high financial cost for companies as a result of impaired performance, reduced retention, disability claims, and increased medical costs. The financial cost to the individual is also substantial as a result of impaired performance with a negative impact on bonuses and promotions. The cost in terms of quality of life is more extensive, with a loss of pleasure in life, decreased ability to give to loved ones, and loss of a sense of fulfillment in one's work. Dealing with the problem entails some short-term costs but offers significant long-term gains. More often than not, however, the problem is ignored and left to take a heavy toll.

Burnout is the result of chronic high levels of stress. Burnout robs you of your enthusiasm and sense of accomplishment. It replaces them initially with apathy and frustration and eventually with resentment, irritability, and anger. Once you descend into detachment, cynicism, and despair, it can be very hard to find your way back to the excitement and sense of challenge and fulfillment that initially led you to throw yourself into your work. These painful feelings not only color your work hours but contaminate all aspects of life. Many turn to alcohol to deal with their distress. Physical complaints, withdrawal from friends, and depression are common.

Stress has important physical impacts on your body. The release of cortisol and catecholamines have a significant impact on your short-term and long-term health. They stress the cardiovascular system, can lead to brain changes, and affect the immune system. This is serious stuff.

Certain factors common in modern organizational design and functioning promote burnout. Awareness of the stress they cause allows us to find antidotes. Perhaps most important, many people face considerable role ambiguity. You may no longer report simply to one person. You may now be responsible to one or more project managers (each of whom feels you should be working full time for them), to the head of your unit, and in some cases to a functional leader. Negotiating between multiple masters and trying to keep them all happy is very difficult, particularly because they often want you to do things in different ways. Since they may not be clear on who has ultimate authority in different situations, and they do not want to talk together to work things out and give you a single, clear message, you are in a very precarious position.

Other types of ambiguity are also stressful. Some bosses do not give clear messages. Sometimes they are too busy. Sometimes they are not able to clearly express what they want. Further complicating matters, they generally do not realize they are being ambiguous. Although they could not find time to figure out and explain what they wanted, they will find the time to criticize you when they do not like what you provide them.

A lack of feedback also fosters burnout. We all need feedback and support to do our work. The harder we work, the more we need. We don't expect plants to grow well if we provide water but no sun or plant food. There are managers, however, who expect their subordinates to produce at top efficiency without giving them support, encouragement, and feedback.

Not being part of the decision-making process leads people to feel that things are being imposed on them, which leads to resentment, powerlessness, and alienation. Time pressure increases the sense that you are a pawn of outside forces who is being forced to work double time and sacrifice personal needs, sleep, and rest.

Burning Out

Jerry's energy, confidence, wit, and charm had impressed a number of companies. The company he chose did not offer the most money or the fewest hours. Rather, it offered a vision of helping people that the other companies could not match.

Jerry put in long hours. On his performance evaluation, he was told that his work was fine. He wondered what that meant.

Was it as positive as his manager ever spoke, or was it a veiled statement of disappointment? As time went on, some of the resources he was supposed to be able to call on were not available, and he began to wonder how important his work was to the company. Meanwhile, he was being pressed to handle more and more in less and less time. His hours skyrocketed, and he had little time for anything but work. His functional line leader and project coordinator started to give him different and conflicting directions, and Jerry could not figure out how to please both simultaneously. He asked them to speak directly to each other. They refused and said that it was his job to find a solution. Performance evaluations continued to say little more than that his work was fine.

His sense of doing a good job declined. He became increasingly apathetic and disenchanted with his work. Resentment and irritability grew. He started becoming cynical about his projects and his company. Meanwhile, he withdrew from friends and activities as well as work. He had neither the energy nor the interest to deal with friends and hobbies. After work and on weekends, he would crash in front of the TV and have a drink or two. In the past, he had never drunk alone. He was chronically irritable and no longer liked being around people. He simply wanted to be left alone. As his work quality deteriorated and friends became disgusted with him, he slid more and more deeply into depression.

An old friend came to visit from out of town. He did not want her to visit but felt he could not say no. She looked at him in shock. She asked what had happened, and he told her the story. She told him to get out of the company anyway he could, to just leave. He said no.

A few weeks later, after he lost his temper and screamed at a client, his boss insisted he see an EAP counselor. He was ordered to take a month vacation time or face suspension. He went to visit his friend. She talked with him about the things he used to care about. She refused to talk about work and careers. He began to regain his energy and his sense of humor. He asked for another month off and was given it.

When he returned, he was transferred to a new position. He was also given an executive coach and assigned a mentor. The company recognized his talents and abilities, and did not want to lose him or to destroy him. Meanwhile, the manager who had been over him was let go for failing to live up to company expectations in growing new managers by giving feedback, support, encouragement, and guidance.

Dealing with the Risk of Burnout

There are many things you can do to decrease the risk of burnout. The first is attitude management. Your expectations for yourself and for how people should treat you significantly affect how much you are drained by your job. For example, if you focus on doing your best and continuing to learn and develop skills, you have a great deal of control over achieving your goal. Your risk of burning out will be greatly reduced. Often, however, people set goals that are either largely outside of their control or very hard to reach. If you are competing with those around you rather than with yourself, there is a high likelihood of disappointment. When everyone wants to be above average, half of them will be disappointed. When everyone feels the need to be in the top 10 percent, almost everyone will be very unhappy. If you focus on competing with yourself, set reasonable goals, and keep an eye on others to make sure that you are in the ballpark of what is expected, not only will you have a much lower risk of burnout, but you will have less stress and will probably perform better.

Your tendency toward optimism or pessimism also affects your stress level and burnout risk. If you constantly fear disaster, you will be under tremendous pressure. In general, it is good to prepare yourself to be able to survive the worst, but if you think and live as if the worst were just around the corner, you will be quickly exhausted.

Remembering your values and what is important to you can help protect you from burnout. Is doing an outstanding job in this position the reason for life? What do you really care about? What do you want to see in your life as you look back at it after retirement? Many of us care most about being caring, warm people who are honest and who try to do good things for others. Nevertheless, on a day-to-day basis we tend to focus most of our attention on struggles at work and feel an overwhelming need to prevail, as if a basic value in our life were at stake. Giving each of these small work issues the power to make us highly stressed opens the path to burnout.

It is helpful to take a Zen approach and to focus on the process of what you are doing rather than on the ultimate goal. You should focus on the task at hand and not continually worry how it will affect your future or the ultimate project goal.

There are a number of concrete things you can do to lower your stress. Managing your time is crucial. You need to figure out how to be efficient, not how to work more hours. You can decrease your workload by avoiding micromanaging and by delegating more. Much of what people do is not seriously value-added. You need to assess what is value-added and what is not, and to focus on what really counts. You need to say no to excess demands for total work output or for perfection or for speed, whether the demands come from others or from yourself.

The general rules of stress management always apply. Eating well, sleeping well, having recreation time, and exercising are crucial in dealing with stress and avoiding burnout. Caffeine and alcohol cause problems and should be avoided or at least used in moderation. Relaxation exercises and meditation can help control stress. Finally, anxiety and depressive disorders should be treated.

Decreasing your anger can be helpful in lowering stress and the risk of burnout. Anger often comes from fear and hurt. Dealing with the fear and hurt will generally lessen your anger. When situations are frustrating, you can try to limit your exposure to them. You should also try to avoid ruminating about them. Instead, do the best you can and then let go. When others are irritating, rather than become angry, it is sometimes less upsetting to step aside from the struggle with them and try to empathize with their experience. Sometimes you can regain control of your anger by remembering the bad things that can happen if you let your anger control you. Sometimes it helps to remember that none of us is perfect and that some of your personality traits may be worse than the traits in the person you are furious with. Thinking of a time when you were able to control your anger and seeing if you can do similar things this time can be helpful. Try to not take others' comments personally. Try to remember that it is not the actual situation but what you say to yourself about the situation that makes you angry. For example, if you tell yourself that someone is not helping you more because she dislikes you or is inconsiderate, you will have a more painful reaction than if you say that she is not helping because she feels overwhelmed herself.

Find a Path Out of Burnout

We left Jerry burned out, taking a forced vacation, and transferring to a new position. The fresh start was helpful. He needed to learn new skills, however, to avoid a rapid recurrence of his burnout. His executive coach had a strong background in cognitive behavioral therapy (CBT) and was very helpful.

The therapist encouraged Jerry to think about what he really wanted to accomplish in his life. It would be nice to be a CEO, but to be a CEO without friends or family or to be a CEO over an economically successful company with unhappy, burned-out managers was not what he wanted on his epitaph. They also talked about the path to success, whether it lay with doing wind sprints or preparing for a marathon and pacing himself. Jerry was used to putting in extraordinarily long hours. In the end, however, it did not pay off, since his exhaustion led to a marked drop in efficiency.

Although uncomfortable in going to listen to music or going to sleep or exercising when there was work to be done, Jerry began to experiment with getting more rest and returning to the work the next day when he was more refreshed. He began to focus more on the total month's output and not on the number of hours he put in. By focusing on what was most value-added and learning to delegate more, he saw that he actually got everything done in much less time than he had spent before.

He spent a lot of time looking at his tendency to engage in black and white thinking and catastrophizing. When things were not perfect, he tended to think that they were unacceptable. When something was not going well, he feared disaster would strike. Jerry learned how to take a more balanced view of the situations and not panic.

Jerry also learned better ways to deal with irritating people and irritating situations. He learned how to avoid getting into power struggles and to let certain things be decided later, when people had cooled down. He also learned that it was often better to accept a compromise in which everyone was happy than to insist on what he felt was the best path after an exhausting struggle that burned up needed energy and damaged needed relationships.

The hardest issue to tackle was the tendency to be so invested in concrete results. Jerry learned to focus on the process of what he was doing, remaining calm, doing things the best he could, and not becoming overly invested in the outcome. He realized that winning the lottery and retiring a wealthy man would not provide a satisfying life. Being a good manager, helping some people, developing people under him, and taking care of a family would be much more satisfying, even if he never became a millionaire.

Conclusion

Burnout (Table 26–1) is a serious problem for both the individual who suffers from it and for the organization that wants to get the best out of its people. Burnout robs people of their enthusiasm and sense of accomplishment, and replaces them with apathy, despair, irritability, anger, detachment, and cynicism. The root causes are high levels of stress combined with inadequate support and encouragement.

There is a great deal that companies and individuals can do to avoid burnout. The most important is to remember that your career is a marathon, not a sprint. Pacing yourself will let you go much farther in the long run. Sprinting until you burn out is self-destructive. Taking care of yourself, delegating work rather than micromanaging, using stress management techniques, learning what is truly value-added and what is not, focusing on doing your best rather than on the outcome, and learning to deal with toxic managers and politics are key both to avoiding burnout and to long-term success.

Companies can also do a great deal to decrease burnout. Companies can work to decrease role ambiguity, select and train managers to be supportive and provide feedback, and as much as possible bring people into the decision-making process. Companies can also promote a culture supporting a work-life balance. Supporting flexibility in working arrangements is also helpful.

Table 26–1 Burnout

Symptoms	Causes	Treatment
Emotional detachment	Chronic high levels of stress	Improve your use of time through efficiency and better organization
Decreased enthusiasm and sense of accomplishment	Little feedback	Delegate
	Unclear lines of command and expectations	Don't micromanage
Irritability and anger		Push for support from boss
Resentment and apathy	Inadequate support	Focus on process and not endpoint
	Perfectionism	Know your limits
Alcohol abuse	Excess criticism	Take care of yourself
Exhaustion	Compulsive traits	Sleep
Despair	Black and white thinking	Relaxation
Cynicism		Exercise
Physical complaints	Catastrophizing	Avoid self-medication
Withdrawal from friends	History of anxiety or depression	Executive coaching and cognitive behavioral therapy to deal with
Depression		Stress
		Anger
		Compulsive traits
		Excess perfectionism
		Practice role playing and seek advice for dealing with difficult situations and people
		Treat anxiety or depressive disorders
		Avoid black and white thinking and catastrophizing
		Try to find humor in things
		Evaluate fit of person and job
		Take organizational steps to decrease pressure, including coaching for toxic superiors

Your Turn

- ◆ Do you know people who show signs of burnout?
- ◆ What are the signs?
- ◆ How is it affecting their work and life?
- ◆ What is the cost to the company?
- ◆ What about their personality and work/life style made them vulnerable?
- ◆ What factors in the company fostered burnout?
- ◆ What changes can they and the company make to help the individual?
- ◆ What can they and the company do to decrease the risk of burnout for others?
- ◆ Are you now, or have you ever been, in a state of burnout?
- ◆ What did it cost you?
- ◆ What could have been done to avoid it?
- ◆ If currently burned out, what can you do to get out of it? If in the past, what helped you get out of it?
- ◆ What can you do to decrease the chance your subordinates will burn out; what can you do to help them if they have burned out?

Further Readings

Christina Maslach & Michael Leiter. *The Truth About Burnout.* Jossey-Bass, 1997.

Hamlet provides a powerful example of someone in conflict and overwhelmed by stress.

CHAPTER 27

Bipolar Disorder

Invincible to Depressed and Back

There are high-level executives and professionals with bipolar disorder. Between episodes, they may function without impairment. Every few months or years, however, they may slip into either depression or mania and do tremendous damage to their company, career, family, life, and health if someone does not step in quickly to prevent them from making destructive decisions. Knowing the signs of depression and mania and taking steps to intervene when someone has impaired judgment as a result can avert irreversible damage.

People with bipolar disorder alternate between three states: normal moods, depression, and mania. Years may pass between episodes. When manic or hypomanic episodes occur, people can do tremendous damage to their lives, families, and businesses. Hypomanic people are either markedly irritable or have inflated self-esteem. Their thoughts are likely to race, and their speech may be rapid. They will have an overabundance of energy and need relatively little sleep. They may get a great deal of work done. During hypomanic episodes, people lose judgment and frequently engage in activities that are costly or risky. A hypomanic manager may make very risky investments, ignore laws and regulations, behave in a sexually inappropriate way with coworkers or clients, be irritable and insulting, speak incessantly, or ramble and brag about themselves. Feeling invulnerable, they may engage in reckless driving, spending sprees, and promiscuous sex. They may also become violent. Psychiatrists use the term manic rather than simply hypomanic when the individual becomes psychotic—loses touch with reality. Psychotic symptoms could include hearing voices talking about them or telling them what to do, seeing things only they can see, believing that they have special powers others do not have, or becoming paranoid and believing that there is a conspiracy to destroy them or someone is doing bizarre things to destroy them.

If the disorder is rapidly appreciated and the manager is relieved from work and treated, damage to the company and the manager's career can be prevented. If people wait, however, the manager will damage his or her relationships and reputation and will cost the company clients or money.

Symptoms of Bipolar Disorder

One or more weeks of persistent and abnormally elevated, expansive or irritable mood. And three or more of the following symptoms (four if the mood is irritable rather than elevated):

- Inflated self-esteem or grandiosity
- Decreased need for sleep (e.g., feels rested after three hours of sleep)
- More talkative than usual or pressured speech
- Flight of ideas or subjective experience that thoughts are racing
- Distractible
- Increase in goal directed activity (work/school/social/ sexual)
- Excessive involvement in pleasurable activities that have a high potential for painful consequences

When a normally conservative manager enters into a full-blown manic episode and reports that he has cosmic powers and has come to redeem mankind, there is usually little problem in recognizing that he is not fit for work and needs medical care. The problem is far more complex with a highly emotional, somewhat grandiose manager on an intense work assignment who is now speaking a little faster than usual, being a little more irritable than usual, working a bit harder than usual, being pushier than usual, and suggesting some risky actions. Superiors can say no to the risky actions. Subordinates, however, are in a very difficult position. To suggest that the normally flamboyant manager is now crazy would be difficult for a psychiatrist to do and impossible at this stage for a layperson to do. The damage done, however, when they pick up the phone and expend resources or behave inappropriately with a client can be immense.

Classic Bipolar Disorder

Dennis was a hard worker. A middle manager for a mid-sized company, he had a nice family and two young children. They all went to church each weekend but were not otherwise religious. He got together with friends periodically to play soccer or go fishing. He had no significant psychiatric history other than once being depressed and receiving antidepressants.

People were a little surprised when Dennis began to flirt with both his secretary and his boss's secretary. It was somewhat out of character, but not grossly inappropriate for the company. He also had three drinks rather than his usual one at Friday afternoon happy hour, and he became somewhat giddy. His unusual speed while driving a friend home was attributed to the alcohol. The combination of changes was noted, but no one thought anything of it other than that he was under extra pressure at work. He had in fact worked the last couple of nights with relatively little sleep. Colleagues suggested he get some sleep but he said he was fine; he wasn't tired.

Things began deteriorating. He became argumentative with clients and colleagues, and passed the line into sexual harassment with a summer intern. When confronted about these issues, Dennis apologized and made excuses about the amount of work pressure he was under. People were still puzzled but accepted his statement. Part of the problem was that no one saw the full picture, all of the problematic behaviors. As his speech became more pressured and he spoke forcefully about his considerable abilities and his deserving a raise, people became more concerned and thought that his narcissistic traits were finally coming out. People were surprised that he had been able to hide them for so long. Or, perhaps he was drinking too much. In fact he was. As he became increasingly boisterous and inappropriate, he was sent to his company's employee assistance program. From there he was sent to a hospital emergency room. His alcohol level was found to be low, while his markedly inappropriate behavior continued. The psychiatrist in the emergency room diagnosed bipolar disorder.

After starting Depakote, Dennis's symptoms quickly disappeared. He did not have his next manic episode until five years later. By then, he had changed jobs. He had also lost his wife as a result of the affairs he had had during his first hypomanic episode. When he started slipping into hypomanic symptoms again, no one knew what was happening, and the story replayed itself.

Some people with bipolar disorder cycle from irritable to euphoric within the course of a day. Nice one minute they are irritable and attacking the next.

Rapid Cycling Bipolar Disorder

Zahava was an enigma to those who worked with her. One minute she would be considerate and supportive, the next she could be publicly insulting your weight or intelligence. Some days she seemed almost grandiose in her level of confidence and some called her narcissistic. Other moments she seemed very insecure. It almost seemed as if she was two different people. People wondered a lot about her using drugs and in fact ordered a drug screen on her when she was acting particularly strange. It came back negative.

Zahava periodically entered a cycle of intense work in which she slept only a few hours a night, and was constantly on the go. Her energy was boundless; she talked fast, walked fast and actually got a lot done at the same time that she seriously upset many people. During these episodes she was often irritable, took unreasonable risks, and sometimes became inappropriately sexual with people.

After one of these episodes she seriously annoyed a key client. As a result, the head of the company finally insisted that she see a psychiatrist since he couldn't afford to lose any more good workers because of her abusiveness. The psychiatrist recognized the possibility that bipolar disorder could be a factor in her behavior and placed her on medications. Over time her behavior improved significantly. Freed from the intense internal pressure and turmoil she had experienced for so long she was now able to begin to learn new ways of dealing with people.

Dealing with Managers with Bipolar Disorder

Realizing that the problem may be bipolar disorder is the crucial first step. It alerts you that the person's judgment and condition may rapidly deteriorate. You do not want this person handling key accounts or controlling large sums of money while they are impaired.

This does not mean that you do not want them in your company. It only means that you need to monitor them more closely than you do the average manager and that there must be a way to constrain their decision-making power when they are sliding into poor functioning. Many people go years between episodes. Some people are highly productive during a hypomanic episode. Medication can decrease the frequency and severity of episodes.

One of the biggest problems in treating bipolar disorder is the tendency to deny the illness and not take medication. Another problem is that some people self-medicate with alcohol and make the problem much worse.

Conclusion

There are many highly successful people with bipolar disorder. People may go for years between episodes of depression or mania/hypomania. The key to doing well in life despite the presence of the disorder is to recognize when episodes are coming on, take time off from work before damage occurs, and get treatment to end the episode as quickly as possible. One of the biggest problems is that people often do not realize that an episode is coming on. People may think that the person is stressed or using drugs and may not insist that the person obtain psychiatric help. For unclear reasons, people with bipolar disorder have a marked tendency to deny having psychiatric problems until they have had several episodes. Friends and family can be very helpful in fighting the denial and insisting on treatment rather than sitting back and letting the person self-destruct.

Bipolar disorder is more common than generally appreciated. Roughly one percent of the population fulfills the diagnostic criteria. Five percent of people, however, have the basic problem although they do not adequately fulfill the criteria to be given the diagnosis. Nevertheless, their functioning can be seriously impaired. People generally go for years before the correct diagnosis is made and treatment is begun. Meanwhile, the individual does considerable damage to their career and personal lives.

Further Reading

R. Lubit, C. Kellner, B. Ladds, & S. Eth. *Five-Minute Psychiatric Consult.* Lippincott Williams & Wilkins, in press.

CHAPTER 28

Alcohol and Drug Abuse

Only the Bottle Takes Away My Stress

President Thomas Jefferson complained that

> The habit of using ardent spirits by men in public office has produced more injury to the public service, and more trouble to me, than any other circumstance that has occurred in the internal concerns of the country during my administration. And where I could commence my administration again, with the knowledge which from experience I have required, the first questions that I would ask with regard to every candidate for public office should be, Is he addicted to the use of ardent spirits?

Perhaps as many as 10 percent of all executives are impaired by alcohol or drugs. The yearly cost in terms of decreased productivity, absenteeism, increased disability costs, and increased healthcare costs has been estimated to be $80 billion to industry and $275 billion to the American economy as a whole. Alcohol abusing executives and managers are generally not very productive after drinking at lunch and are at greatly increased risk for inciting a sexual harassment claim against the company. The erratic behavior of managers using illegal substances can cost the company clients and workers. The toll from accidents related to substance abuse is tremendous. Alcohol is involved in roughly half of the 40,000 yearly vehicular fatalities. Ten times as many people are crippled on the roads from accidents. Substance abuse is also a factor in many work-related accidents.

Psychological functioning, judgment, and work performance are seriously impaired by substance abuse. Alcohol abuse chronically impairs sleep and concentration, and can lead to depression lasting months after the alcohol abuse ends. Many suicide attempts occur while intoxicated. When withdrawing, irritability and jitteriness occur. Sudden withdrawal can be fatal. After alcohol, the most common drugs of abuse by people in companies are marijuana, cocaine and opiate pain killers, "club drugs," and amphetamines. Cocaine and amphetamines (stimulants) initially bring euphoria but in time lead to irritability, depression, and sometimes paranoia. Mood swings, temper outbursts, difficulty sitting still, difficulty concentrating, and difficultly staying alert are common. In the short term, marijuana can impair concentration, memory, judgment, and coordination. In the long term, it may lead to depression, loss of energy, and loss of motivation. People initially receiving opiate narcotics for pain relief sometimes refuse to stop or cut back when their physicians tell them to and begin obtaining the medication illegally. When the medication is not available, withdrawal begins and the person experiences nervousness, nausea, vomiting, diarrhea, and muscle aches. Intoxication causes problems with concentration, sleepiness, judgment, and coordination. The symptoms of anti-anxiety medication abuse and withdrawal are very similar to those of alcohol.

Organizational Factors Affecting Substance Abuse

There are a variety of ways in which some work environments foster excess substance abuse. High-stress environments lead many to drink too much, particularly if the work culture supports it. Historically, business trips and some business functions have featured large amounts of alcohol. Many become drawn into the party atmosphere and consume far more alcohol than they would under other circumstances. Moreover, many work cultures are very tolerant of considerable alcohol use at happy hours. The combination of high stress, people around you drinking, and a culture tolerant of heavy use lead many down a dark path.

There are things that companies can do to limit the problem. First, bar alcohol during the workday and limit alcohol at parties—open bars are nice but are not really an entitlement. Second, have an employee assistance program (EAP) in place—EAPs have been estimated to save companies 5 to 15 times their cost. Third, be alert to the signs of substance abuse and quickly take steps to refer people who may be abusing alcohol or drugs to the EAP; do not make excuses for their behavior.

The general psychological warning signs for substance abuse are

- ◆ Erratic behavior
- ◆ Rapid mood swings
- ◆ Unexplained absences
- ◆ Unusual irritability
- ◆ Being sleepy or nodding off at work
- ◆ Decreased concentration
- ◆ Marked fluctuations in work quality
- ◆ Missing deadlines

Employee Assistance Programs (EAPs) can generally provide advice on how to deal with the manager who may be abusing alcohol even before he or she is formally referred to them. If you see a number of the signs listed above, it is generally a good idea to call your company's EAP for advice.

People who abuse alcohol generally deny how much they are drinking and the problems it is causing. Family, friends, and coworkers who accept the excuses for poor performance are supporting the person's denial, enabling their alcohol abuse, and doing them considerable harm. Similarly, making accommodations for the drinking manager's poor performance, bending rules, overlooking absences, and reducing workloads, without insisting on intensive treatment enable the alcohol abuse to continue.

Dealing with executives who abuse substances is particularly difficult. Their ability to control their own schedule and the reluctance of people to confront them enable them to hide their problem longer than most people can.

Primer on the Treatment of Alcohol and Drug Abuse

Alcohol treatment programs for executives often have more than a 90 percent success rate. Treatment entails:

- ◆ Detoxifying (if necessary)
- ◆ Attending Alcoholics Anonymous or Narcotics Anonymous
- ◆ Treating any concomitant psychological problems

- ◆ Developing a strategic plan for recovery
- ◆ Addressing character traits that impede recovery
- ◆ Stress management and lifestyle balance
- ◆ Modifying perfectionism and control
- ◆ Addressing excessive work and work addiction
- ◆ Finding and promoting attention to forgotten or new values, such as spirituality

The first step in alcohol and drug treatment is recognition that a problem exists. HR or a supervisor may refer the manager to the company's EAP program. Sometimes, this smoothly leads to treatment and the end of drinking. Many managers refuse, however, to recognize the problem until confronted by multiple relatives, friends, and colleagues. These confrontations can be very helpful and, if necessary, should be arranged.

Those who drink daily are likely to need detoxification, as are those using opiate narcotics. This can sometimes be done on an outpatient basis. Inpatient treatment is needed if there is a risk of withdrawal seizures, medical or psychiatric problems that limit the patient's ability to tolerate the stress of detoxification and treatment, or a nonsupportive home environment. If someone is drinking heavily and ceases alcohol abuse without being protected from withdrawal symptoms by appropriate medication, they are likely to become tremulous and possibly develop hallucinations and seizures and then die. Opiate withdrawal is generally not dangerous but is very uncomfortable.

It is crucial to deal with any underlying problems with anxiety, depression, trauma, or bipolar disorder that the individual may be self-medicating with alcohol. Some AA groups oppose any use of medication, including antidepressants. It is important to be careful which AA group one is referred to in order to avoid a conflict over the use of needed psychiatric medication.

Workplace stresses that foster substance abuse, whether relationship issues or overly burdensome responsibilities, can sometimes be dealt with by transfer. Recovering alcoholics are advised not to go on business trips until they are secure in their sobriety. Being away from familiar surroundings and constraints is risky. Being out of town both increases the desire to drink, since they are alone, and decreases inhibitions, since no one will know if they drink. Spending time away from your local AA or NA may also decrease your commitment to regular attendance.

Therapy often includes several components. Through psychoeducation, people learn more about alcoholism, the damage it does, the factors that encourage drinking, and how to deal with them. Psychosocial stabilization entails helping the person deal with stresses that make life so difficult that he or she runs to the bottle. Cognitive behavioral therapy helps people work on their stress and painful feelings that encourage drinking. It is also used to help character traits contributing to substance abuse, such as perfectionism, excessive desire for control, and avoidance of leisure activities. Relapse prevention teaches you how to be aware of the situations that are triggers for drinking and ways of avoiding them.

Medications are sometimes useful in the treatment of substance abuse. Antebuse helps people avoid drinking by making them very sick if they do. It is helpful for those who really want to stop but who face many social cues to drink and therefore need extra help. Businesspeople who are surrounded by parties and lunches with alcohol may fall into this group. Naltrexone can help people deal with cravings and avoid opiate abuse by blocking the high from opiates. SSRIs can be helpful in treating anxiety and depression that the individual might otherwise try to self-medicate with alcohol.

Periodic drug testing as a requirement for work can be a very powerful support for sobriety.

A Downward Spiral with Alcohol

Kyle was a hard-working, successful manager who rose through the ranks quickly. Generous with those he worked with, he was well liked. He often took on work from others who needed his help. His long hours, dedication, and perfectionism were appreciated and respected by those above and below him. His family was less enthralled. They appreciated how good a provider he was and that he was dedicated to his wife and children having whatever they wished. He was, however, a bit emotionally distant, a bit formal. He was comfortable slapping a friend on the back and laughing over drinks, but not in talking about feelings, especially his own feelings. He spent more and more time at work or with people from work, since his family was dissatisfied with his distance and his colleagues were happy with his backslapping. Being with colleagues meant going for drinks. Business meetings and trips also meant drinks. Two drinks at a time gave way to three and sometimes four. After work, drinks also increased from Thursdays and Fridays to almost each day.

Business trips became more common. He increasingly did work over three-martini lunches.

His concentration and sleep deteriorated. Productivity both on the road and after his three-martini lunches deteriorated even more. He then had to put in even longer hours and sometimes ask others for help. He paid people back by taking them out. One day, after drinking, he ran a company car off the road. With alcohol on his breath, he could have been in a great deal of trouble. A junior manager took responsibility. Kyle said he would do something about his alcohol consumption, but he did not. He began going in to work late at times, since he could not sleep well. Sometimes he simply didn't go in. At his level, however, no one challenged his schedule. His wife thought he was having an affair. He was, but it was with a bottle, not another woman.

One weekend, when he was with his family for the weekend and it was difficult to get a drink, he became very shaky as he began to withdraw. He spoke to his doctor. His doctor noted deterioration in his health. Kyle promised he would cut down on his drinking, but he didn't. He became unusually irritable. He was often late for family events and work. Family members and friends suggested he cut down. How much and how often he was drinking was impossible to miss. When confronted about his drinking, he became angry and denied that there was any problem.

After Kyle seriously upset a major client, the company finally stepped in. Kyle was referred to the company EAP, but refused. After consulting with the EAP, top management decided to speak with his family and to confront him en masse. Twenty people arrived at his house. Kyle wondered what the occasion was. One by one, colleagues, family, and friends took turns telling Kyle how they cared about him and that they would stick by him if he got help, but they had had enough of his drinking. He agreed to go into an inpatient detoxification program and then through intensive treatment as a prerequisite for staying in the company.

After detoxifying, he began looking at the triggers to his drinking. He began thinking about other things he could do with his time. He looked at his overly driven style and saw that it had driven him to drink and almost destroyed the success he had sought and achieved. With difficulty, he agreed to couple's therapy to try to find more pleasure in his marriage. He went to AA daily. Meanwhile, the company provided him with more assistance, a manager who had been through recovery. For a while, Kyle avoided business trips. When he did go on trips, he went with his assistant, who saw to his sobriety. He began to exercise and took up sailing again. He stayed sober.

Conclusion

Substance abuse is a very common problem for organizations. Both stress and a desire to be one of the gang and join in the partying can lead people to consume more and more. Meanwhile, a great deal of damage is done by substance abuse as it impedes performance, damages judgment, leads to erratic behavior and depression, and markedly increases the risk for accidents. People are often very slow to step in and forcefully tell someone that they need help. Doing so, however, is critical for the well-being of the person and the company.

Further Reading

Jeffrey Lynn Speller. *Executives in Crisis: Recognizing and Managing the Alcoholic, Drug-Addicted, or Mentally Ill Executive*, 1990.

PART VI

DEVELOPING
AND HARNESSING
EMOTIONAL
INTELLIGENCE

Low-Hanging Fruit

Enhancing your emotional intelligence and the emotional intelligence of your company can markedly enhance your success and productivity. Emotional intelligence improves the ability of people to communicate and work effectively together. It is the foundation of a company's social capital. Emotional intelligence also decreases the frequency and severity of toxic behavior and increases the ability of people to cope with whatever toxic behavior that does occur.

The return on the investment for your efforts to increase your own emotional intelligence and the emotional intelligence of your company will be substantial. It is one of the safest and most productive investments individual managers and companies can make.

Part VI Overview

The chapters in this section deal with different aspects of promoting emotional intelligence. Chapter 29 shows an individual how to enhance his or her emotional intelligence. Chapter 30 focuses on how to increase the level of emotional intelligence throughout an organization. The Addendum provides a template for decision-making when faced with toxic behavior.

- ◆ Chapter 29—Developing Your Emotional Intelligence
- ◆ Chapter 30—Using Emotional Intelligence to Develop Your
          Company
- ◆ Addendum

Further Reading

http://www.eiconsortium.org/

CHAPTER 29

Developing Your Emotional Intelligence

Surviving Toxic Behavior

Emotional intelligence—self-awareness, self-management, social awareness, and relationship management—is invaluable when dealing with toxic people. Moreover, without these skills almost any relationship can become toxic. Reasonable people can lock horns and become polarized on an issue, and may develop an enduring animosity if they do not understand each other's positions.

Enhancing your emotional intelligence is preventative medicine, a vaccine against the development of toxic relationships as well as a suit of armor limiting the damage that toxic managers can do to you. Emotional intelligence is key to understanding others' perspectives and needs, resolving conflicts, and wielding influence. It also helps you to know who is dangerous before problems begin, enabling you to take steps to decrease your vulnerability. Emotional intelligence helps you deal with the rigid, aggressive, grandiose, and unethical behavior you may be subjected to. Emotional intelligence also enables leadership to find, and then either coach or remove, managers who behave in ways that are toxic to others.

Components of Emotional Intelligence ▬▬▬▬

Personal Competence

Self-Awareness

- ◆ Aware of your emotions and their impact
- ◆ Aware of your strengths and weaknesses

Self-Management

- ◆ Emotional self-control
- ◆ Adaptability: flexibility in adapting to changing situations and obstacles
- ◆ Integrity, honesty, trustworthiness
- ◆ Drive to grow and achieve
  - • Achievement oriented
  - • Continuous learner
  - • Willing to take initiative
  - • Optimistic

Social Competence

Social Awareness

- ◆ Empathy and insight
  - • Understanding others' perspectives and feelings
  - • Appreciation of others' strengths and weaknesses
- ◆ Political awareness

Relationship Management

- ◆ Respect for others
- ◆ Conflict management skills
- ◆ Collaborative approach
- ◆ Sense of humor
- ◆ Persuasive: visionary, diplomatic
- ◆ Able to leverage diversity

People are born with varying levels of talent for understanding their own feelings and the feelings of others. Nevertheless, with conscious effort most people can make significant strides in improving their emotional intelligence.

The keys to developing your personal competence (self-awareness and self-management) are (1) paying attention to your emotional reactions to situations, (2) enhancing your understanding of why you react as you do, (3) thinking of alternate ways to interpret upsetting situations, and (4) finding constructive ways to deal with whatever emotional stress remains. The more time you invest in introspection and talking with confidants about how to understand your emotional reactions and behavior, the more your personal competence will grow. A good therapist can speed and deepen the process, as well as remove obstacles that prevent you from accurately understanding your feelings and reactions.

Social competence grows through a similar process: (1) paying attention to the emotions and behavior of others, (2) seeking to understand others' behavior through reflection and discussions with third parties, (3) thinking of various ways to deal with situations, and (4) observing the effects of your actions. You do not have to be directly involved in situations to learn from them. You can enhance your social competence by observing others, thinking about why people are behaving and reacting as they do, and seeing what behavior seems helpful in which situations.

Certain psychological issues can present an enormous barrier to developing emotional intelligence. Obstacles include a tendency to interpret situations in ways that lead to self-fulfilling prophecies, black and white thinking, having interpretations controlled by past painful memories, and holding attitudes that color your interpretation of experiences. These blinders can block learning. Psychotherapy can decrease the obstacles and enable learning to occur.

Controlling Our Interpretation of Events

Your emotional reactions to events are greatly affected by the meaning you give to them. For example, if you believe someone's rudeness is due to high levels of stress you will be less upset than if you see the rudeness as a sign of lack of respect for you. Similarly, if someone is late with an assignment you will probably be less upset if you attribute it to the person having ADHD or a personal tragedy, than if you believe it is due to lack of concern for the project and the people on the team. How we interpret events has a tremendous impact on our emotional reactions and subsequent behavior. Meanwhile, people often have biases in their interpretation of events that systematically affect the meanings the events have for them.

Rather than keeping an open mind people frequently jump to conclusions about the motivations of others. Moreover, people tend to jump to the conclusions that they fear the most. For example, people who are particularly sensitive to being devalued sometimes interpret others as devaluing them when it is not actually occurring. Similarly, many people observe annoyance on someone's face and assume it is aimed entirely at them. Some people will take an additional step and believe that the annoyance is a sign that they will soon be fired. This both leads to distress and can become a self-fulfilling prophecy. For example, believing that someone thinks poorly of you or is about to fire you is likely to upset you, damage your performance, and then lead the person to actually be upset with you.

Dealing with Your Own Feelings

Sometimes the most problematic aspect of someone being angry with you is your reaction. It can lead you to do things that are destructive to your own interests, such as creating open conflict in the office. Being aware of your feelings and not letting your distress interfere with your perception of what is happening or the way you choose to respond is the core of an emotional intelligence approach.

Facing someone's anger or opposition to the path we wish to take can trigger a "fight-or-flight" reaction. When our ancestors faced wild beasts thousands of years ago, this fight or flight reaction was critical to survival. It would have been very dangerous to stand and watch the animals approaching with their teeth barred, rather than running away or picking up a stone. However, in today's world, the fight-or-flight reaction can drive you to respond in ways that are self-destructive. In business, remaining calm and letting something roll off your back is often the best reaction. Doing this is often difficult, since it goes against biologically programmed instincts, but it can be very successful.

In addition to your instincts, childhood experiences programmed you with persistent sensitivities to various situations. For example, if you were subjected to a great deal of anger at home or school, you are likely to continue to be sensitive to expressions of anger at work and may therefore think that people are angrier than they actually are or fear that the anger will lead to dire consequences. Moreover, the ways you learned to deal with others' anger when you were young—withdrawing, standing firm, or attacking back—are likely to persist throughout your life unless you make diligent efforts to change your style. Similarly, if people were overly controlling of you, you are likely to be sensitive to controlling bosses and to have a stronger reaction to them than would someone whose parents and teachers were not invasive. The images that we have of the world, and the ways we interpret situations, change very slowly and often only with therapy.

Black and white thinking, seeing things in extremes, also interferes with our ability to interpret events in a balanced way. Some people see an obstacle, believe that disaster is just around the bend, and are filled with despair or anxiety. Others, however, in the same situation merely see a problem that needs to be overcome. Similarly, some people see a few drops of rain on a weekend filled with plans, assume there will be a downpour and fall into despair, feeling that their desperately needed rest is ruined and they may never have fun again. Others see the same raindrops and calmly reach for an umbrella. Learning to take a more balanced view both of problems and of opportunities is a major aspect of cognitive therapy.

Separating the Past from the Present

There are a handful of key steps to gaining control of your reaction to emotionally stressful situations. The first step is appreciating that you are having an emotional reaction.

Some people behave in an angry manner but deny feeling angry. Although their tone of voice, posture, and choice of words lets everyone else know that they are angry, they are unaware of it. Psychiatrists say that they are repressing the feeling. As a result, they are unable to get in control of the feeling or of their behavior.

Once you are aware that you are having an emotional reaction to a situation, the next step is to figure out what the situation is reminding you of from your past. If as a child you were bullied, or not listened to, or subject to a great deal of criticism, or had your life micromanaged, you are likely to have a strong reaction if someone treats you the same way today.

The final step now is to remember that you are no longer a child and that you have skills, power, and options that you did not have as a child. You can now weigh the costs and benefits of the different options for responding to difficult situations and practice the ways that will be most beneficial to you. This is the step that is healing. You need to go through this many, many times. You do not learn to ski like an Olympic medal winner in one afternoon, and you will not gain control of your emotions in one afternoon. The more you practice, the better you will become. If you think that doing this is a lot of work, just think how much work being upset is.

Many people say that there is no reason for them to work with a professional, since they are already aware of why they behave as they do. Professionals are helpful not only in getting in touch with your feelings but in helping people realize that they have other options now that they are adults, and that with practice they can learn new ways of dealing with painful situations.

It is also important to challenge any beliefs you have that are pressuring you to take actions that may be counterproductive. Sometimes people feel that failing to respond in kind to aggression leads it to get worse, or that failing to respond is a sign of weakness and is demeaning. I would argue that strength is demonstrated by feeling that the attack is so meaningless that one does not need to respond. It may also mean having the patience to select the time, place, and method of response that is optimal. Executive coaching and therapy can provide additional tools if we find that the inner pressure to react in non-optimal ways is too great.

Attitude Control

The attitude you have when dealing with people who upset you can either intensify the situation into a nightmare or shrink it into an unpleasant experience from which you can learn and grow. When an irritable manager is harassing you, you may prefer to escape rather than deal with it, learn, and grow. You would probably prefer to simply do your job. In reality, much of your job when you work in an organization, is to figure out a way to get along with and work with many people who are fairly difficult. You may not like this part of the job and wish that you did not have to do it, but you need to do it.

How things feel to you depends upon what you say to yourself about others' behavior. If a colleague walks past you on the street without saying anything, you may assume the person is angry with you, or that the person is preoccupied and upset, or that the person lacks manners. These three interpretations will lead to very different emotional experiences. In executive coaching with someone skilled in cognitive behavioral approaches, a person learns to keep an open mind and to not jump to painful conclusions.

Similarly, if you go on a trip expecting poor weather and thinking that it will be nice to be away from home even if you need to be inside much of the time, you won't be upset if it rains every other day. However, if you expect sunny skies every moment and it rains a couple of times, you may be markedly irritated. Similarly if you expect to be treated nicely at all times, you will become very irritable yourself. Then you, rather than your boss or colleague, will be the problem. In fact, this is probably what led your boss or colleague to become irritable.

The bottom line is that if you expect that there will be some anger pointed in your direction at times, and you avoid taking the anger personally, you will be much less stressed than if you expect that people you work with will always treat you respectfully.

A particularly self-destructive perspective is that being subject to someone's tirades lessens us. In general, this is the Western perspective. It is not, however, the only perspective. With practice, you can progressively ease your distress when subjected to others' anger by modifying your perspective. There is a Zen story of an old martial arts master who was challenged by an infamous young warrior who arrived at his village. The young warrior was powerful and had an uncanny ability to spot and exploit any weakness in an opponent. Against the advice of his concerned students, the old master accepted the young warrior's challenge. As the two squared off for battle, the young warrior began to hurl insults at the old master. He threw dirt and spit in his face. For hours, he verbally assaulted him with every curse and insult known to mankind. But the old warrior merely stood there, motionless and calm. Finally, the young warrior exhausted himself. Knowing he was defeated, he left feeling shamed. Somewhat disappointed that he did not fight the insolent youth, the students gathered around the old master and questioned him. "How could you endure such an indignity?" The master replied, "If someone comes to give you a gift and you do not receive it, to whom does the gift belong?"

Another valuable Eastern teaching is to see those who cause us distress as valued teachers who provide us with opportunities to grow.

Developing a perspective that helps you to weather irritable managers more easily takes time and practice and often coaching. The skill will be helpful to you in many situations for many years to come.

Conclusion

Developing your personal competence is crucial so that you can better weather the stress of working with toxic managers whom you will undoubtedly meet and so that you do not become a toxic manager to others.

The more you are aware of your feelings and the more you are in control of them, the better you will be able to interact with others in ways that foster cooperation, promote mutual respect, increase motivation, and avoid unnecessary escalation of disagreements and polarization. Personal competence is also a shield against burnout. Personal competence means that you are master of yourself rather than a slave to difficult situations and the painful feelings they evoke. Personal competence is power.

It is also the key to advancement. Research on emotional intelligence has shown that the area in which CEOs excel far beyond others is in having very high levels of self-control. This is the key to coming across as a professional, to gaining others' confidence, to developing a degree of charisma, and to avoiding self-sabotage.

We do not need to be passive in the face of toxic managers. There is a great deal that we can do to protect ourselves. The more we understand about their motivation, the more we learn about how to deal with the different types of toxic managers, and the more we develop our own emotional control, the better we will be able to limit their destructive impact.

Your Turn

- What type of toxic managers or managerial behavior (rigid, aggressive, arrogant) is most difficult for you to deal with?
- How do you generally respond to the various types of problematic managerial behavior?
  - What would be better ways to respond?
  - What gets in the way of responding more effectively?
  - What do you need to do to be able to respond more effectively?
- Have you ever had a self-fulfilling prophecy? What happened?
- Have you ever seen others involved in a self-fulfilling prophecy? What happened?
- Do you have any biases in how you interpret situations? Where do they come from? Do you actively try to counter them?
- Are there aspects of your past that color your experience of the present? What? Does this cause any problems for you? What can you do to limit the impact?

- ◆ Do you have any attitudes or expectations that get in the way of your understanding events or modulating your emotional reaction and response?
- ◆ Think of several events in which someone's behavior upset you?
  - How did you interpret the situations?
  - Could you have interpreted them another way?
  - Did the situations "push buttons" and remind you of painful past events?
  - What can you do to separate the present situation from the past?
  - Could a change in attitude have decreased your distress?
  - Think of times when persuading someone was difficult.
- ◆ Think of times when a conflict was difficult to resolve? What was tried? What was the effect? With twenty-twenty hindsight what would you have recommended people do?
- ◆ Think of times when persuading someone was difficult? What was tried? What was the effect? With twenty-twenty hindsight what would you have recommended people do?
- ◆ What are your strengths? How can you better utilize them to advance your career?
- ◆ What are your weaknesses? How can you protect yourself from them? How can you strengthen these areas?
- ◆ What can you do to foster your:
  - Insight into your emotions and their impact
  - Self-control
  - Adaptability
  - Integrity
  - Drive to grow and achieve
  - Awareness of your strengths and weaknesses

CHAPTER 30

Using Emotional Intelligence to Develop Your Company

Organizational Responses to Toxic Managers

Toxic managers undermine organizations by damaging morale, diverting people's energy from productive work, damaging cooperation and knowledge sharing, impairing hiring and retention of the best people, and making poor business decisions. Toxic managers are particularly destructive to a company's social capital, the trust and relationships within a company that enable people to work together effectively. Helping people to develop their emotional intelligence so that fewer managers behave in toxic ways and others are better able to deal with them will improve a company's social capital. Organizations that can screen out the most destructive toxic managers in the hiring and promotion processes and forge a culture that encourages the rest to constrain their behavior will create a significant competitive advantage for themselves. This is low-hanging fruit for companies that wish to foster productivity through developing their human capital.

Much of the money companies spend on managerial training does little good. People go to training sessions, learn a set of skills, use them for a few weeks, and then rapidly slide back into old behaviors. There are a number of reasons that the workshops fail to lead to enduring change. One

major reason is the failure to provide for the ongoing practice, encouragement, and supervision needed so that the skills continue to be reinforced
rather than slip away. Old habits die slowly and people readily slip back into
them until they have had extensive practice doing things in new ways.

Another problem is that many managers have not yet sufficiently developed their emotional intelligence to be able to effectively utilize the
skills taught in the workshops. Classic managerial skills include conflict resolution, problem recognition and solving, team building, motivating and
persuading, running meetings, delegating, supervising, hiring, promoting,
and developing people. Effectively exercising these skills is dependent on
emotional intelligence. To motivate and persuade people you need to know
what they want, what they fear, how they think about what you want them
to do and how they are likely to hear what you say. To effectively delegate
you need to understand people's strengths and weaknesses, know how
much supervision they need, and be able to constructively give directions.
To build and run productive teams you need to be able to know how people's styles of interacting, as well as their skill sets, will fit together on the
team. You also need to understand how group dynamics and politics can interfere with decision making and performance. Good conflict resolution
requires distinguishing between productive and unproductive conflict as
well as knowing how to resolve different types of conflict. You need to be
able to assess who is really high potential and who is narcissistic and glib,
who has traits that may be destructive to the organization, which difficult
managers are incorrigible and which can grow and learn. You also need to
learn more about how your own feelings and ways of interpreting events
may interfere with your understanding certain types of people and selecting the optimal way to deal with situations.

The ability to understand different types of people—what they want,
what they fear, how they perceive the world, and how they are likely to
perceive things you say and do—and accommodate your style to their needs
can make you a markedly better manager. Different techniques are needed for motivating, guiding, and communicating with people with different
personality styles. The hesitancy of many managers to pay attention to the
differences between people and to adjust their management style to the
specific person they are working with is puzzling. People understand that
cars need different types of gasoline, oil and tire pressures and accommodate to the cars' needs. If a manager put gasoline into every car in the company's fleet, when half of them required diesel, we would fire him. Yet if
a manager, used the same technique to motivate all of his people, ignoring
their different styles and needs, and half of the people performed poorly,
we would probably say that it was the fault of the people and not the

Table 30–1 Classic versus EI Based Management Development

Classic Managerial Skills	Contribution of EI Social Competency	Importance of Personal Competency
Decision-making skills	Understanding how group dynamics and politics can interfere with decision making and performance	Understand how your own feelings and experiences can interfere with understanding certain types of people and effectively managing them
Problem recognition and problem solving	Understanding why different types of people behave as they do	
Motivation and persuasion	Knowing how to motivate and persuade different types of people	
Conflict resolution	Knowing how to distinguish between productive and unproductive conflict, how to utilize productive conflict to innovate and forge better decisions, and how to resolve unproductive conflict without damaging morale and motivation Listening skills	Develop the self-control to minimize interference by your feelings in your work as a manager Develop the self-control to be able to deliver your message to people without undo influence of anger or nervousness
Team building	Understanding people's strengths and weaknesses and placing them in the right roles Making sure teams have the right mix of perceptual styles and skills	
Delegating and supervising	Knowing how to harness people's strengths and get around their weaknesses Providing the emotional support, guidance, and concrete resources people need to succeed	Understanding your own strengths and weaknesses and take steps to compensate for weaknesses Listening skills
Running meetings	Listening skills	
Hiring and promotion	Distinguishing between high potential managers and narcissistic, glib managers Assessing who is difficult and who is actually destructive Assess who can be trained and who is irremediable	
Developing people	Understanding why different types of people behave as they do, Giving constructive feedback Coaching Understanding strengths and weaknesses and when someone can stretch and grow	
Stress management		

manager since half of his people functioned well under him. In other words, to make effective use of management workshops, many managers first need to expand their understanding of how different types of people perceive the world, what motivates them and how they are likely to interpret and respond to things you might do to be helpful. Without these skills, the relationship with anyone you manage can become toxic.

Finally, manager training workshops often fail to yield expected results because the organization's toxic managers who are most in need of learning better management and leadership skills need something very different from what these leadership workshops offer. They need to learn how to control the feelings and ways of perceiving and responding to others that drive their destructive behavior. Unless these feelings and perceptions are intensively addressed, they will eventually win out over any new skills the managers are taught, and block enduring change.

The situation does not have to be bleak, however. There are effective ways in which organizations can successfully improve leadership and management skills. First, in the hiring process companies need to screen out those who are likely to be toxic managers. Second, they need to create a culture that strongly discourages toxic behavior. Third, if a company decides to keep a toxic manager in the hope that he or she will change, the company needs to provide more than a workshop on leadership. The manager needs coaching with someone capable of exploring and effecting change in personality traits that underlie toxic behavior. In conjunction with this, the manager should have an evaluation for any psychiatric conditions treatable with medication (anxiety, depression, ADHD, bipolar disorder) that might be driving the problems.

The Many Faces of Narcissism

The most toxic managers are the ones who have narcissistic personality traits: preoccupation with themselves, devaluation of others, entitlement to whatever they wish, and underlying fragile self-esteem that they desperately protect by stepping on others. Skilled, capable narcissistic managers (and even some who are not so capable) become grandiose. Highly ambitious managers with narcissistic traits become ruthless. Narcissistic managers under pressure to cut corners become unethical. If taking risks or hurting others is a thrill, they become antisocial or bullies. Compulsive managers with narcissistic issues become control freaks. Depressed, anxious narcissistic managers can become paranoid and potentially assaultive.

Many people, perhaps most of us, struggle at times with feelings of anger, anxiety, and despair, preferring to do things our own way and wanting things that are not ours to have. Most of us are able to keep these feelings under reasonable control almost all of the time. People with significant narcissistic traits, however, have unusually strong negative feelings as well as weak consciences that let them ignore the needs of others and the rules of society.

The most serious problem with narcissistic managers is that they are unlikely to change even with extensive coaching. Rather, they are likely to become more problematic as their power grows and they go on in years, rather than less problematic. If companies screen for narcissistic traits and think twice before hiring or promoting these managers, they can save themselves and their employees a great deal of grief.

How Do Toxic Managers Survive and Thrive?

Given how destructive they are to organizations, it is remarkable how common toxic managers are. Most people I speak to have had at least one toxic manager poison part of their career. One reason that toxic managers are so common is that the narcissistic personality traits that underlie a great deal of toxic managerial behavior help managers to be promoted. The narcissistic manager's high levels of expressed self-confidence, magnetic enthusiasm, and unrelenting drive to attain prestige and power enables them to climb the rungs of power and to be effective in some aspects of leadership.

High levels of expressed self-confidence can be useful in gaining the confidence of others. People often assume that self-confidence flows from competence, and they therefore trust those with great self-confidence. Driving ambition enables narcissistic managers to make the sacrifices necessary to rise in an organization and frees them from normal restraints on behavior. Ruthlessness enables managers to manipulate others to achieve their goals, steal credit for the work of others, and scapegoat others. Although lacking empathic concern for others, narcissistic people may have "street smarts" that enable them to assess whom they can manipulate and what levers to pull to manipulate them. They can feign interest in others and manipulate their bosses. Their intense ambition, lack of restraint, and ability to charm superiors, manipulate people, and forge quick, superficial relationships can make them masters of organizational politics.

Toxic managers are also able to survive in organizations because people often fail to speak out about their abuses. First, these managers usually direct their most inappropriate behavior at subordinates and not at the superiors who determine their fate. Subordinates are generally hesitant to complain about a manager because they fear that the complaint might reflect badly on them, that their manager will find out and take revenge, or that complaining will lower them to the manager's level. People also hesitate because they believe that eventually the information will come out and the manager will self-destruct without their sticking their necks out. Moreover, when people do speak up, there is a strong tendency to believe superiors over subordinates and to ignore complaints, especially if the manager is "making the numbers." As a result of these factors, the full scope of the problem never gets to those who have the power to do something about it.

Some organizational cultures and performance measurement/reward systems are tolerant of toxic behavior and others are not. Many organizations focus overwhelmingly on short-term profits and pay little or no attention to the human costs of how managers achieve financial results. If toxic managers achieve financial results, the organization's hierarchy may not notice or may not measure and consider their failure to develop subordinates, encourage teamwork, support morale, and treat others well. Many organizations either do not have 360-degree feedback or do not make significant use of it in promotion and compensation decisions. Rather, organizations may only reward those who make the numbers and have the political skill to claim credit for short-term profitability or sales.

The level of narcissism of the leaders will affect the level of narcissism present at the managerial level for three reasons. First, the organization's leaders serve as role models that managers emulate. Second, narcissistic leaders tolerate toxic managers who make the numbers but do not treat people well. Third, leaders are particularly tolerant of toxic managers who feed their own narcissism with flattery.

Flaws in organizational hiring and transfer practices permit toxic managers to attain jobs despite having had serious problems elsewhere. Leaders making hiring and promotion decisions often lean heavily on recommendations from people they know, or rely on their impressions from an interview, rather than adequately performing and using background checks. During interviews, narcissistic managers are likely to perform particularly well as a result of their outward confidence, willingness to distort their history, and ability to convincingly claim accomplishments they have not made. Many toxic managers survive and prosper because the influential contacts who supported their elevation to their present positions continue to support them despite evidence of problems. Some toxic managers survive by transferring from one position to another and burying their mistakes before their bad work catches up with them.

Even more surprising than the ability of toxic managers to survive and rise within a firm is the ability of CEOs who led companies to financial disaster to be hired by other companies.[1] Frank Lorenzo, after plunging two airlines into bankruptcy three times, convinced investors to give him millions of dollars to start a new airline. James Baughman, while superintendent of the San Jose Unified School District in California in 1992, admitted to lying about having earned a Ph.D. from Stanford University. He later spent several months in prison for stealing money from student body funds. Despite this record, he rose to the rank of director of recruiting at Lucent Technologies, where he served until he died of a heart attack in September 2000. Al Dunlap, after being fired from Max Philips and Son in 1973, was hired and later fired as president of Nitek Paper when the company's board accused him of overseeing a large accounting fraud. Nitek's chief executive stated that virtually all of the company's senior management threatened to resign if Dunlap remained at Nitek. Despite these serious difficulties, Dunlap was chosen to lead Scott Paper and then Sunbeam.

Weighing the Pros and Cons of Narcissistic Managers

Most of the time, prominent narcissistic traits in managers will eventually harm a company even though the traits may fuel the manager's rapid rise. How destructive a manager's narcissism is for a company depends upon the degree of narcissism, the particular aspects of narcissism that are most prominent (grandiosity, devaluation, recklessness, aggression), and the position the manager holds within the company. Self aggrandizement and overconfidence in one's abilities are not necessarily serious problems. However, high levels of aggression, devaluation of others, and a lack of moral inhibitions can rapidly lead to disaster. Narcissism supporting charisma in an executive tasked with providing the company with a guiding vision and clear strategy goals can be helpful. This is particularly the case in a turnaround situation in which a degree of ruthlessness may be necessary to survive. Narcissism, however, in an executive or manager who is needed to support people and forge compromises could be a disaster. If high turnover is a disaster, then narcissism in the leader will be a disaster. Some glibness in sales personnel can be helpful. But, willingness to say anything to make the sale will eventually damage the company's reputation. The aspects of narcissism most prominent in the manager are also crucial. Narcissism marked primarily by devaluation, entitlement, and a predisposition to berate workers is far more destructive than narcissism marked primarily by some self-aggrandizement and confidence in making decisions quickly.

Whether the positive aspects outweigh he negative ones depends on the needs of the organization at a particular point in time, the relative amounts of charisma versus mistreatment of others, how much the organization needs a charismatic leader, how much damage the organization suffers as a result of mistreatment of subordinates, and whether the leader is lucky enough to be making the right decisions.

Keeping the Barbarians Outside the Gates

There is a great deal that companies can do to avoid hiring and promoting narcissistic managers. There are three key elements: being aware of the warning signs, paying attention to them, and diligently looking into situations that present warning signs. We often ignore or make excuses when we see warning signs. We tend to believe bosses over subordinates even though it is subordinates who have firsthand information. We also often ignore the signs of narcissism because they remind us of some of our own behavior and because we often equate high confidence with capability rather than with grandiosity.

The easiest way to guard the walls from grandiose managers is by screening for them before they are hired. Behavioral event interviewing is a good way to begin the screening process. Ask applicants to talk about a time when things went well and a time when things did not go well. As the applicants speak about each of these events, pay attention to what they thought the key success and failure factors were. Do they keep all credit for themselves or share it with others? Do they go on and on about how extraordinary they were? Do they pride themselves on having manipulated or used others? Do they note mistakes they made, or do they blame others for all mistakes?

You can also ask applicants to describe situations in which they demonstrated the various skills that are crucial to the job for which you are considering them. For example, you can ask them to describe situations in which they demonstrated leadership and teamwork, developed others, and dealt with problems in subordinates' behavior. As they talk about these things, pay attention to whether they blame others for problems or take responsibility themselves. Do they look on others with respect or disrespect? Are they excessively self-congratulatory?

You can also ask candidates about what managers and leaders they admired and why; and what managers they did not like and why. Ask about tough and abusive managers they have observed, how they reacted, and what they did to cope. Ask about managers who pushed the boundaries of the rules (were unethical). Ask what they like and dislike about friends. Ask what they would do with their time if all employment paid the same or if they did not need money. Present ethical dilemmas and ask what they would do. Explore more deeply those answers that raise your concerns.

There are a number of other questions that can help you to spot problems with grandiosity. You can ask about their weaknesses, worst mistakes, what people have complained about in them, things they feel guilty about having done, and what they want to change about themselves. As they talk about life both at work and outside of work, look for signs of whether they value or devalue others, value or devalue honesty, show concern and respect for others or totally focus on their own needs and desire for glory, and are able to feel remorse and guilt.

These questions are fairly invasive. It is best for such questions to be asked by people other than those the potential hire will actually be working with and perhaps even by someone with whom the company subcontracts for interviewing. You can also do background checks and speak with people the applicant has worked with and people the applicant noted in discussions of work that went well and work that did not go well to see if others shared their perceptions of their behavior. You can check on military, legal, work, and school records as well. The extent of the investigation should be governed by the importance of the position and by the degree of concern that exists following the basic interviews.

The Minnesota Multiphasic Personality Inventory II (MMPI) and the California Psychiatric Inventory (CPI), paper and pencil tests, can present information about various psychological issues of importance to the workplace, including honesty and narcissism. The Hare Psychopathy Checklist provides a way of organizing interview material to look at antisocial behavior.

A final thing that we need to do is to contain the barbarian in ourselves. Most of us become inconsiderate, arrogant, rigid, and aggressive at times. It hurts the people above and below us and is bad for the organization as a whole. It not only hurts the target of our behavior but reinforces negative aspects of the organization's culture. It also diminishes us and makes it easier for us to do it again. Being aware of our own potential to behave in toxic ways, the cost to others and ourselves of doing so, and the underlying factors driving the behavior can help us to gain better control and become the managers we want to be.

Finally, we also need to be aware that we are vulnerable to letting ourselves fall into learned narcissistic behavior. Most of us could do so if given power, placed under great pressure, and denied feedback from subordinates. If we do not pay attention to this potential in ourselves, we may inadvertently behave in damaging ways. If we are vigilant about our own behavior, provide a good role model for others to follow, foster an organizational culture opposed to destructively narcissistic behavior, and respond appropriately to abuses that others commit, we can make major strides in improving the productivity and well-being of people in our organization.

Conclusion

Organizations can be severely damaged by a small number of toxic managers. A grandiose CEO can drive away the best people, divert people's energy, and make disastrous decisions. Toxic managers within the body of the organization can markedly damage the performance of their group. Criminal behavior and sexual harassment can lead to devastating lawsuits.

Organizations typically pay relatively little attention to toxic behavior. Rather than screening toxic managers out, organizations often mistake toxic traits for signs of great capabilities. People in organizations tend to equate confidence with competence, aggressiveness with being a go-getter, and antisocial glibness with true achievement. Missing crucial danger signs and mistaking them for predictors of high performance will lead an organization to be filled with potentially toxic managers.

Organizations can significantly decrease the prevalence of toxic behavior fairly quickly if they deal aggressively with the problem. Key steps in fostering this culture change include: ensuring that top leaders avoid aggressive, unethical, and rigid behavior; speaking out against it; obtaining 360-degree feedback on all managers and making use of it in performance evaluations and training; getting coaching for toxic managers; and avoiding hiring and promoting toxic managers; and removing the most serious offenders.

Actively working to better contain toxic behavior can have a tremendously beneficial impact for the productivity of companies as well as for the well-being and career success of those who work there. Organizations that do this may gain a significant competitive advantage. This is low-hanging fruit that remains to be picked. I wish you a good harvest.

Your Turn

- How does your organization respond to different types of toxic managers?
- Are various narcissistic traits seen as positive rather than as warning signs of bad things to come?
- How does the measurement and reward system impact the presence of various toxic behaviors?
- How does the culture affect the presence of various toxic behaviors?
- How does the hiring and promotion system affect the presence of various toxic behaviors?
- What procedures could your organization change in order to decrease the number of toxic managers?
- What would the obstacles be to fostering this change?

Endnote

1. A. Bennett & J. Lublin. Teflon Big Shots: Failure Doesn't Always Damage the Careers of Top Executives. *Wall Street Journal,* 31 March 1995. S. Romero, with R. Atlas. Lucent Investigates Record of Former High-Ranking Executive. *New York Times,* 21 February 2001, p. C1. F. Norris. An Executive's Missing Years: Papering Over Past Problems. *New York Times,* 16 July 2001. p. 1.

Addendum

First Steps Flow Chart

There is a lot to consider when facing a toxic manager. What are your options? What are the pros and cons of each option? Key issues to assess include:

Strategic Assessment for Dealing with Toxic Superiors

1. What is the cost of the situation?
   - Can I tolerate it?
   - What is it doing to my career?
   - What is it doing to my health and general well-being?
   - What is it costing my family?
2. What are my values?
   - Work/life balance?
   - Work success at all cost?

3. What are my options?

    - Can I improve my ability to tolerate the situation through changes in work style/schedule or through my own executive coaching/therapy?

        How costly is it to make these changes?

    - What are the likely outcomes of formal or informal complaints to superiors?

    - Are there other places I can go inside or outside of the company?

    - What is the market like for people with my skills?

    - How will these moves affect my career, family, health?

4. How likely is it that I can succeed in decreasing the toxic behavior?

    - What drives the person's behavior, and can I avoid irritating him or her?

    - What is his or her personality structure?

        How narcissistic is he?

        How angry a person is he?

        Does he have any empathy for others?

        Does he have a conscience?

        Does he or she have any capacity for insight?

    - Is stress a factor in the toxic behavior? Will the person's stress and toxic behavior decrease by themselves?

        Can I help change the situation?

    - Are anxiety and depression factors? Can I recommend he get treatment for them?

    - Can I avoid the person?

    - Am I somehow fostering the behavior I dislike? Can I approach the person differently?

    - Have I brought out such behavior in others? Do I need to change?

5. What are the potential outcomes of a complaint, including best-case and worst-case scenarios?

    - Who is the person?

    - What power does he or she have?

- Who is he or she supported by?
- What is the culture of the organization?
- What is the procedure for complaining in the company?
- What power do I have?

  What is my reputation?

  How long have I been there?

  What allies (peers and mentors) do I have?

6. What can I do so that my options are better in the future than they are now?

   - How can I build my power base?

     Develop allies

     Document inappropriate behavior

     Foster a relationship with a mentor

   - How can I build an escape route?

     Look for other options

     Develop contacts

     Develop skills

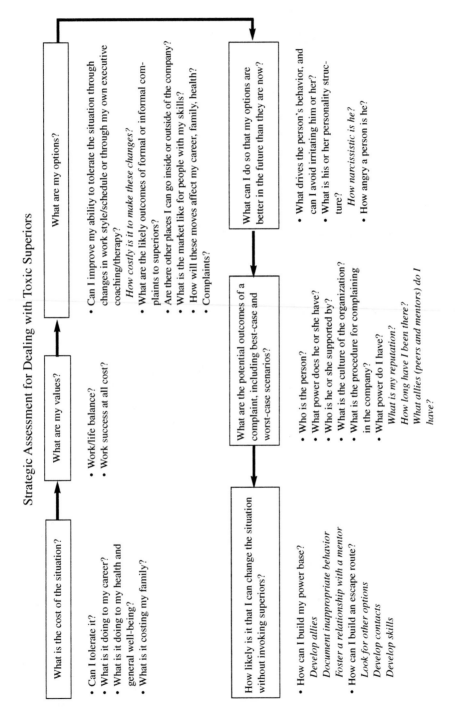

Strategic Assessment for Dealing with Toxic Superiors

What is the cost of the situation?

- Can I tolerate it?
- What is it doing to my career?
- What is it doing to my health and general well-being?
- What is it costing my family?

What are my values?

- Work/life balance?
- Work success at all cost?

What are my options?

- Can I improve my ability to tolerate the situation through changes in work style/schedule or through my own executive coaching/therapy?
  How costly is it to make these changes?
- What are the likely outcomes of formal or informal complaints to superiors?
- Are there other places I can go inside or outside of the company?
- What is the market like for people with my skills?
- How will these moves affect my career, family, health?
- Complaints?

How likely is it that I can change the situation without invoking superiors?

- How can I build my power base?
  Develop allies
  Document inappropriate behavior
  Foster a relationship with a mentor
- How can I build an escape route?
  Look for other options
  Develop contacts
  Develop skills

What are the potential outcomes of a complaint, including best-case and worst-case scenarios?

- Who is the person?
- What power does he or she have?
- Who is he or she supported by?
- What is the culture of the organization?
- What is the procedure for complaining in the company?
- What power do I have?
  What is my reputation?
  How long have I been there?
  What allies (peers and mentors) do I have?

What can I do so that my options are better in the future than they are now?

- What drives the person's behavior, and can I avoid irritating him or her?
- What is his or her personality structure?
  How narcissistic is he?
  - How angry a person is he?

Strategic Assessment for Dealing with Toxic Subordinates

1. What is the problem?
   - Grandiose narcissism
   - Unethical behavior
   - Rigid behavior
   - Aggressive behavior
2. How important are different factors in driving the problematic behavior?
   - Personality traits
   - Anxiety, depression, impulsivity
   - Stress
   - Organization's culture
   - Prior or current role models
3. What are the company's values?
   - Above all else make the numbers
   - High quality products
   - Good place for employees to work
4. What is the cost to the company and its people of the destructive behavior?
   - Reduced productivity; damage to strategy
   - Decreased innovation
   - Retention and recruiting problems
   - Potential lawsuits (How serious?)
   - Reputation problem
   - Damage to client relationships
   - Unhappiness
5. How likely is the person to perform acceptably if given coaching and therapy?
   - What is the cost to the company while waiting for change to occur?
6. What is the cost of removing the person?
   - How crucial are his or her skills?

- How crucial are his or her contacts?
- How replaceable is he or she?
- How likely is it that a new person will do better?
- How costly is the downtime in bringing a new person up to speed?

7. What must be done to remove the person?
   - Things to do to avoid a lawsuit

     a. Documentation and building the case for removal

     b. Attempt at executive coaching

     c. Probation
   - Prepare a successor

     a. Develop necessary knowledge and skills

     b. Develop client relationships

Strategic Assessment for Dealing with Toxic Subordinates

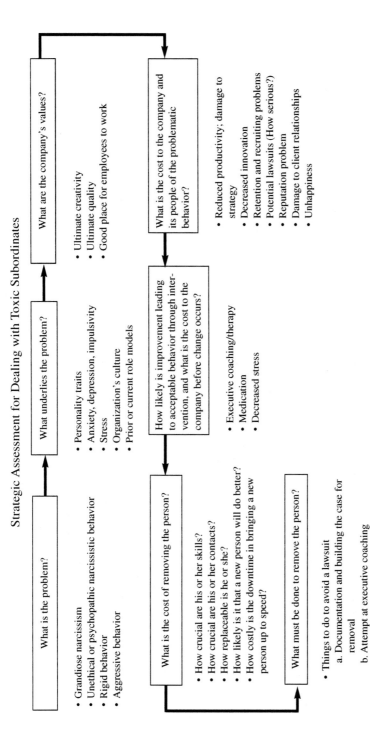

What is the problem?

- Grandiose narcissism
- Unethical or psychopathic narcissistic behavior
- Rigid behavior
- Aggressive behavior

What underlies the problem?

- Personality traits
- Anxiety, depression, impulsivity
- Stress
- Organization's culture
- Prior or current role models

What are the company's values?

- Ultimate creativity
- Ultimate quality
- Good place for employees to work

What is the cost to the company and its people of the problematic behavior?

- Reduced productivity; damage to strategy
- Decreased innovation
- Retention and recruiting problems
- Potential lawsuits (How serious?)
- Reputation problem
- Damage to client relationships
- Unhappiness

How likely is improvement leading to acceptable behavior through intervention, and what is the cost to the company before change occurs?

- Executive coaching/therapy
- Medication
- Decreased stress

What is the cost of removing the person?

- How crucial are his or her skills?
- How crucial are his or her contacts?
- How replaceable is he or she?
- How likely is it that a new person will do better?
- How costly is the downtime in bringing a new person up to speed?

What must be done to remove the person?

- Things to do to avoid a lawsuit
  a. Documentation and building the case for removal
  b. Attempt at executive coaching
  c. Probation
- Prepare a successor
  a. Develop necessary knowledge and skills
  b. Develop client relationships

Index

and culture, 265
dictatorial managers, 212, 241–246
and leadership behavior, 265
as obstacles to organizational
    learning/productivity, 263–264
oppositional managers, 211–212,
    247–251
organizational factors promoting rigidity,
    265
organizational impact of, 263–270
overview of (table), 268
passive-aggressive managers, 212,
    253–261
and recruitment/promotion practices, 265
rising within organizations, 264–265
types of, 210–212
and work processes, 265
Rigidity, 7
Role models, 8
Ruthless aggression, 203
Ruthless managers, 7, 19, 20, 99–108
    case studies:
        covert ruthlessness, 101–103
        overt ruthlessness, 100–101
    coping with, 106
    emotional intelligence approach to,
        103–105
    and Human Resources, 105
    impact of, 106
    narcissistic personality structure of, 99
    overview of (table), 106
    and powerful individuals, 104
    scapegoating, 99, 102–103, 162
    and senior management, 105, 106
    stealing credit of others' work, 99–100
    symptoms, 106
    and 360-degree feedback, 105
    underlying factors, 106
Ruthlessness, 9
    and aggression, 191
    and cold aggression, 95, 98

Scapegoating, 99, 102–103, 162
Schemata, 223
Selective serotonin reuptake inhibitors, 170,
    288–289
Self-esteem:
    of control freaks, 48
    of grandiose managers, 23
    and narcissism, 17–18
Seneca, 205
Senior management, 9
    and antisocial managers, 74–76
    and authoritarian managers, 236, 238
    and bullies, 115–116, 117
    and compulsive managers, 226

and control freaks, 48–49
and dictatorial managers, 244, 245
and frantic managers, 180–181
and grandiose managers, 33–36
and nonsexual harassment and discrimi-
    nation, 154–155
and oppositional coworkers, 249, 250
and paranoid managers, 60
and passive-aggressive managers, 258,
    260
and poor performance, 9
and ruthless managers, 105
and sexual harassment, 142–143
and toxic managers, 2–3
and unethical opportunists, 50, 87–88
and volatile managers, 169–170
Sexual harassment, 131–146
    and age, 136–137
    as aggression, 97–98
    and anger at women, 135–136
    case studies, 133–138
    Civil Rights Act (1964), Title VII, 131
    clueless offenders, 139
    company policy, 143
    cultural factors, 134
    current test for, 132
    dating and flirting at work, 143–144
    detecting, 132–138
    emotional intelligence approach to,
        138–143
    and Human Resources, 142–143
    lawsuits for, 140, 142–143
    of men, 137–138
    misogynists, 135–136, 139–140
    by a peer, 141–142
    and senior management, 142–143
    by a subordinate, 142
    by a superior, 138–140
Simple phobia, 285–286
    symptoms, 288
Social anxiety disorder, symptoms, 288
Social competence, 4–5, 332
    growing, 333
    relationship management, 5
    social awareness, 5
Social learning theory, 187
Social phobia, 283–284
Social skills training, 178
Stockholm syndrome, 110
Stress, 17, 161, 305–306
    and aggression, 191
Sublimation, 56
Subordinates:
    antisocial, 74
    authoritarian, 236
    compulsive, 225–226